the cinema of JOHN SAYLES

DIRECTORS' CUTS

Other titles in the Directors' Cuts series:

the cinema of EMIR KUSTURICA: *notes from the underground*
GORAN GOCIC

the cinema of KEN LOACH: *art in the service of the people*
JACOB LEIGH

the cinema of WIM WENDERS: *the celluloid highway*
ALEXANDER GRAF

the cinema of KATHRYN BIGELOW: *hollywood transgressor*
edited by DEBORAH JERMYN & SEAN REDMOND

the cinema of ROBERT LEPAGE: *the poetics of memory*
ALEKSANDAR DUNDJEROVIC

the cinema of GEORGE A. ROMERO: *knight of the living dead*
TONY WILLIAMS

the cinema of ANDRZEJ WAJDA: *the art of irony and defiance*
edited by JOHN ORR & ELZBIETA OSTROWSKA

the cinema of KRZYSZTOF KIEŚLOWSKI: *variations on destiny and chance*
MAREK HALTOF

the cinema of DAVID LYNCH: *american dreams, nightmare visions*
edited by ERICA SHEEN & ANNETTE DAVISON

the cinema of NANNI MORETTI: *dreams and diaries*
EWA MAZIERSKA & LAURA RASCAROLI

the cinema of MIKE LEIGH: *a sense of the real*
GARRY WATSON

the cinema of JOHN CARPENTER: *the technique of terror*
edited by IAN CONRICH & DAVID WOODS

the cinema of ROMAN POLANSKI: *dark spaces of the world*
edited by JOHN ORR & ELZBIETA OSTROWSKA

the cinema of TODD HAYNES: *all that heaven allows*
edited by JAMES MORRISON

the cinema of STEVEN SPIELBERG: *empire of light*
NIGEL MORRIS

the cinema of ANG LEE: *the other side of the screen*
WHITNEY CROTHERS DILLEY

the cinema of TERRENCE MALICK: *poetic visions of america (second edition)*
edited by HANNAH PATTERSON

the cinema of WERNER HERZOG: *aesthetic ecstasy and truth*
BRAD PRAGER

the cinema of LARS VON TRIER: *authenticity and artifice*
CAROLINE BAINBRIDGE

the cinema of NEIL JORDAN: *dark carnival*
CAROLE ZUCKER

the cinema of JAN ŠVANKMAJER: *dark alchemy*
edited by PETER HAMES

the cinema of DAVID CRONENBERG: *from baron of blood to cultural hero*
ERNEST MATHIJS

the cinema of SALLY POTTER: *a politics of love*
SOPHIE MAYER

the cinema of
JOHN SAYLES

lone star

mark bould

WALLFLOWER PRESS LONDON & NEW YORK

First published in Great Britain in 2009 by
Wallflower Press
6 Market Place, London W1W 8AF
www.wallflowerpress.co.uk

A catalogue record for this book is available from the British Library

ISBN 978-1-905674-27-5 (paperback)
      978-1-905674-28-2 (hardback)

Book design by Rob Bowden Design

Printed and bound in India by Imprint Digital

CONTENTS

Acknowledgements vii

1   Planting Seeds: Some Contexts 1

2   Part of the Machine: the *Piranha, Alligator, The Howling*
    and *The Lady in Red* Screenplays 30

3   Nothing to Lose But Chains: *Return of the Secaucus Seven, Lianna,*
    Baby It's You and *The Brother from Another Planet* 50

4   It's a Free Country: *Matewan, Eight Men Out, City of Hope*
    and *Passion Fish* 86

5   Telling Stories: *The Secret of Roan Inish, Lone Star, Men with Guns/*
    Hombres armados and *Limbo* 122

6   Living the Dream: *Sunshine State, Casa de los Babys* and *Silver City* 159

Notes 181
Filmography 190
Bibliography 195
Index 203

ACKNOWLEDGEMENTS

This book would not have happened if in 1996 Mike Sanders hadn't urged me to watch *Matewan*, or if sometime in the summer of 2000 Kathrina Glitre had not said of my subsequent enthusiasm for Sayles, why don't you do a book on him? Many, many people have helped out in all sorts of ways over the too-many years it took, including Susan Alexander, Yoram Allon, Caroline Bainbridge, Neil Campbell, Diane Carson, Carl Freedman, Raiford Guins, Heidi Kenaga, Jacob Leigh, Daniel Lindvall, Iris Luppa, China Miéville, David Seed, Greg Tuck, Mike Wayne and everyone in the Haematology unit at Wycombe General Hospital. Thanks also to the London Film Festival, Jacqueline Downs, Lisa Cullen (Axiom Films) and the Phoenix Cinema, East Finchley, for enabling me to see *Honeydripper* a couple of times before its general release. I owe more thanks than I can say to two people in particular: Kathrina Glitre, a patient listener and eagle-eyed reader, who has been there through every draft and every delay, watching and rewatching the films with me, helping me find out what they mean to me; and Sherryl Vint, who read and commented on every word written or rewritten in the final months of producing the penultimate draft, helped me to think through ideas new to me and express them more clearly, and then was way ahead of me on thinking about rewrites a year later. I could not wish for better friends, collaborators and critics. For all its faults, my work is better because of them. But as they will both understand, this book is for Billy, who stepped in and saved it.

Completion of this book was made possible by an AHRC Research Leave Award, matched by the University of the West of England. Parts of the introduction and my discussions of *The Brother from Another Planet* and *The Secret of Roan Inish* previously appeared in: 'The False Salvation of the Here and Now: Aliens, Images and the Commodification of Desire in *The Brother from Another Planet*', in Diane Carson and Heidi Kenaga (eds) (2006) *Sayles Talk: Essays on Independent Filmmaker John Sayles*, Detroit: Wayne State University Press, 79–102; 'Fantasising the Real: *The Secret of Roan Inish*', *Film International* 24 (2006), 28–38; and 'The Borderline Between Oneself and the Other: Aliens and Language in *AVP*, *Dark City*, *The Brother from Another Planet* and *Possible Worlds*', *The Yearbook of English Studies* 37.2 (2007), 234–54.

... but in his mother's words telling about Longago, in his father's telling about when I was a boy, in the kidding stories of uncles, in the lies the kids told at school, the hired man's yarns, the tall tales the doughboys told after taps;

it was the speech that clung to the ears, the link that tingled in the blood; U.S.A.

U.S.A. is the slice of a continent. U.S.A. is a group of holding companies, some aggregations of trade unions, a set of laws bound in calf, a radio network, a chain of moving picture theatres, a column of stockquotations rubbed out and written in by a Western Union boy on a blackboard, a publiclibrary full of old newspapers and dogeared historybooks with protests scrawled on the margins in pencil. U.S.A. is the world's greatest rivervalley fringed with mountains and hills. U.S.A. is a set of bigmouthed officials with too many bankaccounts. U.S.A. is a lot of men buried in their uniforms in Arlington Cemetery. U.S.A. is the letters at the end of an address when you are away from home. But mostly U.S.A. is the speech of the people.

John Dos Passos, *U.S.A.*

A river and the *drops* in this river. The position of *every* drop, its relation to the others; its connections with the others; the direction of its movement; its speed; the line of the movement – straight, curved, circular, etc. – upwards, downwards. The sum of the movement.

V. I. Lenin, *Philosophical Notebooks*

He uses his superpowers for good instead of evil, and that's very important today.

Billy Zane

CHAPTER ONE

Planting Seeds: Some Contexts

John Sayles is the pre-eminent American filmmaker of the last thirty years, at least in the sense that his films are *about* America, its peoples, landscapes, histories and languages. Considered by many the godfather of contemporary American independent cinema, he is a consistently and critically left-liberal filmmaker, a director, screenwriter, editor, actor, author, producer and sought-after script-doctor. Despite this, there remains relatively little critical writing on his work, with only an unauthorised biography (Molyneaux 2000), two interview collections (G. Smith 1998; Carson 1999), a monograph (Ryan 1998) and a collection of essays (Carson and Kenaga 2006) providing book-length treatments of his career, and only a few of his films have attracted much attention at shorter lengths. In this context, this volume is intended to perform two interrelated functions. Firstly, it will provide an up-to-date overview of Sayles' films, including a discussion of his first four screenplays-for-hire (*Piranha* (1978), *The Lady in Red* (1979), *Alligator* (1980), *The Howling* (1981)) in chapter two. Such work is a mainstay of his career – in addition to over a dozen films by other directors based on his scripts and script-doctoring work for which he does not always receive onscreen credit, Sayles has 'written fifty or more screenplays for hire (mostly unproduced, as is common in Hollywood)' (2004a: xi) – but I have elected to discuss these four examples because they not only provided his entrée into filmmaking but also demonstrated to him the limitations of independent exploitation filmmaking of the sort exemplified by Roger Corman. The following four chapters consider Sayles' 15 films as writer-director (*Honeydripper* (2007) is commented upon several times in lengthy footnotes but is not given here the detailed treatment it deserves). Although they all receive roughly the same amount of attention, my approach to each film will differ. For example, I focus on several scenes in *Return of the Secaucus Seven* (1980) to show that, despite the common complaint that Sayles lacks a visual style, from the outset he carefully constructed images so as to create specific meanings, while my discussion of *Passion Fish* (1992) articulates Sayles' construction of the subject as socially-determined and intersubjective through a mapping together of the narrative with G. W. F. Hegel's Master/Slave dialectic; *Lianna* (1983) is considered primarily in response to its reception in lesbian film theory and criticism, while *The Brother from Another Planet* (1985) is situated within the ways in which science fiction treats the alien; my examination of *City of Hope* (1991) depends upon a detailed explication of a complex narrative involving dozens of characters, while I consider *Lone Star* (1996) in terms of one key scene. These different approaches are essential to the second function of this book, the development of a critical perspective on Sayles' work, which remains a remarkable achievement in terms of its sustained critique of contemporary America but is nonetheless often problematic, not least because of its generic affiliations with the American naturalist tradition. The remainder of this chapter will establish the theoretical underpinnings of that perspective. The first, and more complex, part of it draws on a range of Marxist theorists so as to outline what is at stake in Sayles' development of American naturalism, and to draw attention in particular to questions of social totality, subjectivity and language. (Some of these theorists, such as Bertolt Brecht and Georg Lukács, profoundly disagreed with each other. However, in order to develop a more nuanced understanding of Sayles' films, I am less interested in adopting the approach of one specific theorist than with the possibilities provided by the community of voices within Marxist theory.) The second, shorter part considers two issues which inevitably arise in director-centred criticism: the notions of independence and authorship.

From Billy Zane to Brecht and Bakhtin, and back again

It might seem inappropriate – perverse even – to begin a book on John Sayles with Billy Zane, but he and Chandler Tyson, the character he plays in *Silver City* (2004), provide a key to much of what is fascinating about Sayles' films. Chandler is a political player, always for hire. A former tobacco lobbyist, he sells his services to property developer Mort Seymour (David Clennon) while simultaneously working for Colorado's state Development Agency *and* drafting the environmental regulations which Dicky Pilager (Chris Cooper) will introduce if elected as governor. Chandler is a minor character with just four scenes (and a slight presence in three others). Even so, he is woven into the narrative in several ways: he is engaged to Nora Allardyce (Maria Bello), the former girlfriend of Danny O'Brien (Danny Huston), the investigator who uncovers the much wider conspiracy to which Chandler's corruption is tangential; he works to lower soil standards regulations in collusion with Mort, who is also the husband of Danny's boss, Grace Seymour (Mary Kay Place); and he works with Pilager's campaign manager, Chuck Raven (Richard Dreyfuss), revealing to him Danny's past as an investigative journalist in order to get Danny fired. Additionally, Chandler is such an unrelenting prick that Nora eventually leaves him, opening up the possibility of a reconciliation with Danny.

As with minor characters throughout Sayles' films, Chandler's multiple points of connection to a multi-stranded narrative mean that he cannot be reduced to a mere plot function, as is typical of minor characters in Hollywood cinema, but instead appears to be the central character in a story whose edges we merely glimpse at those moments when it intersects with the film's narrative (which is itself, by and large, constructed from such intersections between the stories of numerous de-centred characters). Especially since *City of Hope*, Sayles' films are adept at creating this sense of a world much vaster and more complex than the narrative can contain. One way in which this is achieved is by ensuring that minor characters only ever seem minor in relation to the particular overarching narrative being constructed from the intersections of their stories. In Chandler's case, this implied fullness of being is accomplished by allowing him scenes other than those he shares with Nora and which link him to Danny, the film's most central character. Indeed, in Chandler's first scene we know nothing of these relationships and he thus exists in his own right, prowling around the model of the Silver City development, saying all the things he needs to say so that technically he never quite solicits a bribe. His lack of concern about corruption – it is just the way things are done – and his awareness of the need to nonetheless avoid the appearance of corruption is quickly sketched in as, patiently and with self-confident ease, he brings Mort to understand that, if he hopes to see the fractional reduction in soil standards necessary to obtain an 'economic initiative subsidy', it is essential he retain Chandler's services, which can be bought for 'a piece of the action'. This scene is not about tactful negotiations but about playing the game and maintaining plausible deniability. Chandler dominates the slow-thinking Mort, and takes a cool delight in leading him to this 'inevitable' conclusion, deriving pleasure not so much from the promise of a percentage but from having performed his role and exercised his relatively small amount of power with such competence. He is not a particularly subtle man (he warns Raven about Danny as much to do Danny ill as to aid Raven; and when at the Senator's party he sees Danny and Nora alone together, his summons – 'Nora, come on up. There's someone here I'd like you to meet' – is transparent); but, in the circles in which he moves, subtlety could easily be a handicap.

The importance of such fleshed-out minor characters, who appear so consistently in Sayles' films, is related to his attempts – rare in contemporary cinema, let alone Hollywood – to depict a social totality. Along with giving substance to minor characters, Sayles relatively decentralises the protagonist, both as a notion and as a specific character. Criticising Lukács' championing of Honoré de Balzac as a model for the contemporary realist novel, Brecht wrote:

> it is absolutely false ... it leads nowhere, it is not worth the writer's while, to simplify his problems so much that the immense, complicated, actual life-process of human beings in the age of the final struggle between the bourgeois and the proletarian class, is reduced to a 'plot', setting, or background for the creation of great individuals. Individuals should not occupy much more space

Honeydripper: relatively centralised

in books and above all not a different kind of space, than in reality ... For us, individuals emerge from a depiction of the processes of human co-existence. (1980b: 77–8)

Likewise, in Sayles' films, even when one can identify a character who is more central than others – this is easier to do, for example, in *Matewan* (1987), *Lone Star*, *Silver City* and *Honeydripper* than in *Eight Men Out* (1988), *City of Hope* and *Casa de los Babys* (2003) – there is still a very clear sense that the film as a whole is less centred on him or her than is typical in narrative cinema, and that part of this decentring of the protagonist occurs because of the dispersal of plot into the interactions of a host of rounded characters. This decentralisation of the protagonist is *relative*: while Sayles goes much further than such Hollywood examples of ensemble narrative as *Grand Hotel* (1932) or *The Towering Inferno* (1974), his concern with the interrelations of community, drawn out through the interweaving of narrative strands, means that he has never pushed it to the alienated extreme of, say, Richard Linklater's *Slacker* (1991) or Harmony Korine's *Gummo* (1997). Probably the closest comparison to be made is to the films of Robert Altman. However, Altman's large ensemble pieces, from *Nashville* (1975), which arguably provided a model for Sayles, to *Short Cuts* (1993), are, despite their interrelated narratives, more concerned with disconnection than interconnection, a preference also evident in other such comparable films as *Traffic* (2000) and *Crash* (2004). Furthermore, the privileging of the totality in Sayles' films – which is never complete but always in tension with the egocentric, individualistic tendencies which dominate narrative cinema – can be taken as a response to earlier Marxist critiques of mainstream filmmaking, which I will discuss below.

Sayles' films draw upon and develop the tradition of American naturalist fiction. Typically associated with writers such as Stephen Crane, Theodore Dreiser, Jack London and Frank Norris, naturalism has for many years been considered a peculiar offshoot of the realism of the preceding generation of William Dean Howells and Henry James. As recently as 1995, Donald Pizer could claim that such a view was 'generally accepted': 'whatever was being produced in [American] fiction during the 1870s and 1880s that was new and interesting, and roughly similar in a number of ways can be designated as *realism*, and that an equally new, interesting, and roughly similar body of writing produced at the turn of the century can be designated as *naturalism*' (1995: 5; emphasis in original). American naturalism has also typically been seen as being under the influence of the French naturalist writer Émile Zola,[1] who advocated (although arguably never achieved in his own fiction) a kind of experimental novel in which the author 'functioned like a scientist, observing nature and social data, rejecting supernatural and transhistorical explanations of the physical world, rejecting absolute standards of morality and free will, and depicting nature and human experience as a deterministic and mechanistic process' (Lehan 1995: 47). This determinism was largely derived from evolutionary science, and particularly its misapplication in Social Darwinism and theories of heredity and degeneracy, and as Louis Budd argues, writers such as Crane, Dreiser, London and Norris 'surpassed the realists [of the previous generation] qualitatively in exploring humankind's animal sides; their approach to psychology could let instinct overpower conscious will. Most distinctively, they pushed further toward determinism – economic or biological or cosmic – than American novelists had cared or dared to go before' (1995: 43). In the last two decades, much of this conventional wisdom about American naturalism has been challenged. It has been pushed back at least as far as Rebecca Harding Davis's 'Life in the Iron Mills' (1861) and Oliver Wendell Holmes' *Elsie Venner* (1861), and forward to the present, to include authors as varied as John Steinbeck, John Dos Passos, Upton Sinclair, William Faulkner, Ernest Hemingway, Nelson Algren, James Jones, James T. Farrell, Saul Bellow, William Styron, Norman Mailer, Robert Stone, Joyce Carol Oates, William Kennedy, Don DeLillo and William Gibson. The emphasis has shifted from a movement defined by four white male writers to a tradition which includes or contextualises the work of more women (for example, Charlotte Perkins Gilman, Kate Chopin, Mary E. Wilkins Freeman and, reassigned from the realist camp, Edith Wharton) as well as both male and female African-American writers (for example, James Weldon Johnson, Alice Dunbar Nelson, Angelina Weld Grimké, Nella Larsen, Jessie Fauset, Ann Petry, Richard Wright). The centrality of Zola's critical polemics and fictional examples has been challenged, determinism dethroned (or at least reconceptualised in terms of uncertainty, complexity and non-linear dynamics), and racialised and gendered biologism rejected. Naturalism has even been reconceptualised as a romance rather than realist form and as pro- rather than anti-capitalist.[2] And in the same essay in which he describes the 'generally accepted' view of naturalism as a phenomenon of the 1890s, Pizer goes on to discuss its 'enduring presence in twentieth-century American fiction':

> Nor has American naturalism been static or monolithic in theme and form … Indeed, one of the striking characteristics of the movement has been its adaptability to fresh currents of idea and expression in each generation

while maintaining a core of naturalistic preoccupations. The nature of this core is not easy to demonstrate, given the dynamic flexibility and amorphousness of naturalism as a whole in America, but it appears to rest on the relationship between a restrictive social and intellectual environment and the consequent impoverishment both of social opportunity and of the inner life. (1995: 13)

While these revisionist treatments rarely touch on other media, and thus overlook Sayles, there is no doubt that he has long been engaged in developing American naturalist filmmaking, as two major works of naturalist fiction will help to clarify.

Frank Norris structured his 'Epic of Wheat' trilogy around the production of wheat in Southern California (in *The Octopus* (1901)), its circulation in response to financial speculations in Chicago (in *The Pit* (1903)) and its consumption in Europe (in the novel he was researching when he died). This economic infrastructure is perceived through a persuasive, realistic superstructure in which the novels depict East coast, West coast and mid-Western life, ranging from ranch-hands and their bosses to different urban social classes. Dos Passos's *U.S.A.* trilogy (*The 42nd Parallel* (1930), *1919* (1932) and *The Big Money* (1936)) is an expansive account of the lives of numerous characters, with narration passing from protagonist to protagonist as the novels attempt to capture the vastness and complexity of American life in the first decades of the twentieth century. These multiple tales, through which characters interweave, are counterpointed by autobiographical sections called 'The Camera Eye' and selections of newspaper headlines called 'Newsreel', which situate the characters in broader contexts, as if to suggest a social totality far beyond the grasp of realism's typical concern with surface verisimilitude. Lukács argues that while 'the extensive totality of reality necessarily is beyond the possible scope of any artistic creation', the 'totality of the work of art is rather intensive: the circumscribed and self-contained ordering of those factors which objectively are of decisive significance for the portion of life depicted, its specific quality and its place in the total life process' (1978a: 38). Sayles' films, like the novels of Norris and Dos Passos, are engaged upon a mapping of American life, creating small-scale models which, through their social range and presentation of economic, social and cultural determinants, become intensive totalities which take on the appearance of the extensive totality of the real world. Events are always connected to each other through networks of social and economic relationships, or, more accurately, are part of the same socio-economic fabric.[3] Lukács insisted that 'only in the complicated intercatenation of varied acts and pleasures is it possible to determine what objects, institutions, etc., significantly influence men's lives and how and when this influence is effected' (1978b: 128). Mike Wayne argues that this requires 'grasping the social totality as a totality, in which practices, institutions and relationships exist not in isolation from one another, but in actual, dramatic, mutual and dynamic interaction' (2002: 225). Such is the quality of Sayles' individual films, while cumulatively they develop an even larger and more complex model of the US which makes the work of comparable near-contemporaries like Altman and Martin Scorsese seem, respectively, superficial and provincial.

In geographical terms, Sayles has provided finely-detailed depictions of a New Jersey city (*City of Hope*), the Louisiana bayou (*Passion Fish*), the Texas-Mexico border (*Lone Star*), a depressed Alaskan town (*Limbo* (1999)), the Florida Keys (*Sunshine State* (2002)), the Coloradan Rockies (*Silver City*) and a 'darktown' in 1950s rural Alabama (*Honeydripper*) – without producing the kind of regionalist fiction Raymond Williams defined in terms of its delinking of the specific locale from the much broader economy of which it is a part (see 1981a and 1981b) – while *Men with Guns/Hombres armados* (1997) and *Casa de los Babys* show an unnamed composite Central American country, tracing the influence of American political, military and economic interventions in and hegemony over Latin America.[4] To this catalogue can be added Sayles' novels *Union Dues* (1977) and *Los Gusanos* (1991), with their detailed depictions, respectively, of Boston and a Floridan community of Cuban exiles. Across all these differentiated territories, in all their environmental and socio-cultural specificities, can be traced the flows of capital, determining the lives of their inhabitants.

In this light, it is worth considering the emergence of Sayles as both a writer and a filmmaker in relation to the neo-regionalist 'dirty realism' identified by Bill Buford in 1983 which, in Fredric Jameson's words,

> follows and reflects [the] transformation of everyday life by the penetration of a corporate mass culture into its utmost recesses and crannies, with the consequent colonization and elimination of any of the residual enclaves that had hitherto remained exempt; those were enclaves of farming life just as fully as spaces of high culture, they were ghetto or community spaces fully as much as traditional village or classical urban forms of collective living. … Neoregionalism, like the neo-ethnic, is a specifically postmodern form of reterritorialization; it is a flight from the realities of late-capitalism, a compensatory ideology, in a situation in which regions (like ethnic groups) have been fundamentally wiped out – reduced, standardized, commodified, atomized, or rationalized. (1994: 147–8)

While Sayles' work is not prepared to cede difference and diversity or to presume the world of late-capital is as homogenous as Jameson here suggests, his films nonetheless repeatedly and increasingly turn to the tendency of capitalism to equivalise and homogenise. This tension is mediated by the licence naturalism grants to narrativise and emphasise the determinants of social life and intersubjective being in his films.

But naturalism is not without its problems. Jameson, perpetuating a Marxist (and deeply gendered) mistrust of the affective dimension upon which the political efficacy of Sayles' naturalist melodramas depends, argues that naturalism was historically concerned with disclosing 'the lower depths, the forbidden spaces of the new industrial city … to a horrified bourgeois readership', who could therefore derive 'the double bonus of sympathy and knowledge of the social totality on the one hand and of class reconfirmation and the satisfactions of the bourgeois order on the other' and thus assuage their 'fundamental petty-bourgeois terror of proletarianization' (1994: 150–1).[5] Lukács (for whom realism and naturalism were opposed ways of writing), criticised naturalism for presenting social problems as social facts, and this can be seen, for example, in Sayles' relatively uncritical depiction of hegemonic patriarchy and conservative gender roles (see Rieser 2006).[6] A similar critique was foundational in the development, during the 1960s and 1970s, of modern film theory, a central strand of which was concerned with the ways in which deeply ideological filmic representations normalised and naturalised dominant ideology while appearing merely to reproduce neutral images of reality. For example, in 1969 Jean-Luc Comolli and Jean Narboni, argued that '"reality" is nothing but an expression of dominant ideology' and called for filmmakers 'to show up cinema's so-called "depiction of reality"' so as to 'disrupt or possibly even sever the connection between the cinema and its ideological function' (1999: 752). Similar arguments can be found in the work of Jean-Louis Baudry (see 1985), Laura Mulvey (see 1975) and Peter Wollen (see 1985), for example, while the 1969 Third Cinema manifesto of Fernando Solanas and Octavio Getino argued, with admirable bluntness, that 'the 35mm camera, 24 frames per second, arc lights, and a commercial place of exhibition for audiences were conceived not to gratuitously transmit any ideology, but to satisfy, in the first place, the cultural and surplus-value needs *of a specific ideology, of a specific world-view: that of US financial capital*' (2000: 272; emphasis in original), and called for a guerrilla cinema which would decolonise minds and revolutionise consciousness. These new cinematic strategies were frequently articulated around ideas derived from Lukács' greatest critic, Brecht, who considered Lukács' championing of Leo Tolstoy and Balzac as providing *the* model of the novel to be nothing more than an attempt to establish bourgeois methods and techniques as an ahistorical norm (as if they did not derive from a specific historical conjuncture with its own particular array of class forces). For Brecht, realism was not a window on the world, but an argument about it, 'a major political, philosophical and practical issue' (1980a: 76).

This connection to Brecht is made explicit in Colin McCabe's 'Realism and Cinema: Notes on Some Brechtian Theses' (1974), in which he defined the classic realist text, including commercial film, 'as one in which there is a hierarchy amongst the discourses which compose the text and this hierarchy is defined in terms of an empirical notion of truth' (1985: 34). This hierarchy of discourses is organised at a metalinguistic level which denies its own status as an ideological discourse, as if it were recording rather than constructing the image of the world. Consequently, the classic realist text 'cannot deal with the real in its contradictions' and 'fixes the subject in a point of view from which everything becomes obvious' (1985: 44). This is not to say that such a text cannot be progressive. There is 'a level of contradiction into which the classic realist text can enter'; namely, that of the 'contradiction between the dominant discourse of the text and the dominant ideological discourses of the time' (ibid.). McCabe's example, of a text 'in which a strike is presented as a just struggle in which oppressed workers attempt to gain some of their rightful wealth' coming into contradiction with 'certain contemporary ideological discourses' (ibid.), has obvious resonances with *Matewan* and *Eight Men Out*, Sayle's Reagan-era films about workers, sixty years earlier, withdrawing their labour. However, McCabe contends that the critical and political utility of such texts is limited because they are either linked to a 'social democratic conception of progress – if we reveal injustices they will go away' or to 'certain ... tendencies which tend to see the working class, outside any dialectical movement, as the simple possessors of truth' (ibid.). To move beyond the limitations of mere progressivism, or the varieties of subversion offered by those moments which evade the metalanguage's incorporation into hierarchy, a revolutionary cinema must develop ways to articulate contradiction, to overcome the viewer's comfortable and comforting subordination to the text's normalised and naturalised representation of the world-as-it-supposedly-is.[7] McCabe cites as examples of films which have approached this condition *Kuhle Wampe* (1932), written by Brecht (who also dominated its production) and Jean-Luc Godard's *Tout va bien* (1972). He praises the latter in particular for replacing metalanguage with the need for the viewer 'to produce a meaning for the film', which in turn suggests 'not just ... a different representation for the subject but a different set of relations to both the fictional material and "reality"' (1985: 55).

The problems these various theorists and filmmakers identified with the classic realism of dominant cinema led to a strong tendency to regard experimental and avant-garde strategies – particularly versions of the Brechtian alienation device which shatters the filmic illusion of reality, revealing its artifice – as the essence of critical and revolutionary filmmaking, despite the ease with which such tactics were incorporated into dominant cinema, from *Blazing Saddles* (1974) to *Fight Club* (1999).[8] As Brecht himself warned, 'a vanguard can lead the way along a retreat or into an abyss. It can march so far ahead that the main army cannot follow it, because it is lost from sight and so on. Thus its unrealistic character can become evident' (1980a: 72). Moreover:

> For time flows on, and if it did not it would be a bad prospect for those who did not sit at golden tables. Methods become exhausted, stimuli no longer work. New problems appear and demand new methods. Reality changes: in order to represent it, modes of representation must also change. Nothing comes from nothing; the new comes from the old, but that is why it is new. (1980c: 82)

It is entirely possible that at that specific historical conjuncture (the late 1960s and early 1970s in parts of Western Europe and Latin America) Brechtian tactics – for example, Godard's 'development of the lateral tracking shot to establish a critical distance between viewer and the events on screen' (Walsh 1981: 130), or Solanas and Getino designing *Hora de los hornos: Notas y testimonios sobre el neocolonismo, la violencio y la liberación* (*The Hour of the Furnaces*, 1968) so that it could be stopped at various points to trigger debate, transforming the screening into an event in which the film was less significant than the collective political development of those watching it – could perform a revolutionary function. Certainly, in popular and filmic memory such an approach seems inextricably bound up with iconic moments like the 1968 Paris uprising, as in *The Dreamers* (2003), and anti-colonial struggle, as in *CQ* (2001), in which Billy Zane plays both the Che-like leader of a lunar revolution (in a film-within-the film) *and* the actor who plays him. However, it is a repetition of the error for which Brecht criticised

Lukács to assume that such 'Brechtian' tactics can or must always constitute the core of radical filmmaking at every historical moment. Sometimes, in darker days, merely keeping the possibility of critique and alternative conceptualisations of 'reality' alive is the most tenable radical cultural goal; and affective responses can play as important a role as intellectual ones.

Much of the revisionist work on naturalism has focused on the limitations of its critique of and the degree of its complicity in capitalism. Walter Benn Michaels, for example, argues that in *The Octopus*, Norris's mystical, at times ecstatic, identification of 'germination of the wheat with the emergence of a spiritual out of a natural body' effectively 'describes production itself as the transcendence of the material' (1987: 190). This replicates the 'abstraction of social products and practices from the laboring bodies that generate them' (McNally 2001: 1) upon which capital's operation depends, and produces 'a radical emptying of the category of production – the very category that the social-economic "protest" novel might be seen to embody requires' (Seltzer 1992: 26). Mohamed Zayani argues that Michaels' analysis of naturalism as validating capitalism is predicated on an abstract and monolothic model of capitalism which reduces it 'to a purely economic category' rather than recognising its existence as 'a totality that can be seen at work in the different spheres of social activities', and which fails to 'recognise the unevenness of social formations' (1999: 140). He calls instead for a 'conception of naturalism, and by extension of capitalism' which grasps 'not only the deep structure of the system, but also its unstable dynamics; not only the rivets of the system but also its rifts' and 'emergent impulses – that is, those elements that are operative within the system but not perfectly consonant with its logic' (1999: 141). A key figuration of the instability of capital's dynamics is that of utopian hope. For example, Christophe den Tandt argues that Theodore Dreiser's *Sister Carrie* (1900) expresses 'through its romance tropes the utopian yearnings that [its] documentary discourse cannot articulate' (1998: 19), while Amy Kaplan suggests that Dreiser, William Dean Howells and Edith Wharton 'share an impulse … to project into the narrative present a harmonic vision of community', typically focusing 'on class difference to forge the bonds of a public world that subsumes those differences': 'Where Howells imagines a community based on work and character, Wharton seeks community in the exchange of intimacy, and Dreiser posits a community of anonymous consumers and spectators with shared desires' (1988: 12). Sayles' films, for all their left-wing credentials, share similar problems to those identified by Michaels in Norris – in chapters five and six, I discuss in some detail their relationship to a flawed multiculturalism which functions as a variety of racism and colonialism – while also finding occasions for resistance, community and utopian hope in the uneven development of capitalism as a totalising world-system.[9]

Internationally, the last quarter of the twentieth century was dominated by the consolidation of the emergent world market, or 'globalisation', and the dissolution (with some exceptions) of so-called socialism, while on 'the American domestic front, a great many goals once seriously contemplated only by the hardest of the hard right have now either been attained or, at least, have been moved into the realm of respectable "mainstream" discussion', including the preference for balancing federal budgets over Keynesian adjustments designed to ameliorate the harshest social effects of capitalism; the partial repeal of the Social Security system ... and the partial privatization of its remainder; the explicit rhetorical repudiation of the New Deal in toto and the welfare state generally ... the partial defunding of what is arguably America's finest public policy achievement of all time, namely free public education; the dismantling of affirmative action and other measures designed to repair centuries of racial injustice; the promotion of free-trade agreements like NAFTA and GATT, which grant the unfettered international movement of capital priority over labor rights and environmental conservation; and, above all, the granting to the bond market (one of the most reactionary sectors of American financial capital) of a practically absolute veto over federal tax policy and public expenditures. (Freedman 2002: 33–4)

'What more,' Freedman asks, 'could the right want?' (2002: 34)

Despite all their 'successes' in the realms of economics and politics, the American right often appear 'shocked by the degree to which current American culture seems to them a creation of the left' (ibid.). Although this perception is grossly exaggerated, there has undoubtedly been a liberalisation in American culture (albeit opposed at every turn by a fierce conservatism, not least that of Christian fundamentalism). It is at least now the case that ideas of 'the intrinsic inferiority of nonwhites ... and the intrinsic inferiority of women ... are now increasingly on the defensive' (2002: 35). But to the extent that this liberalisation has occurred it is because 'In its relation to the economic infrastructure of capitalist society, culture is one of the most highly mediated forms of social production; and the degree of freedom (or better, perhaps, quasi-freedom) that this "distance" from the wage-relation and the extraction of surplus-value confers has indeed, in recent years, been used in ways much more progressive than could easily be guessed from the successive defeats that American progressives have suffered on the economic and specifically political fronts' (ibid.). Sayles' first film, *Return of the Secaucus Seven*, depicts various ways in which, under the emerging Reaganite dispensation, the countercultural left of a decade earlier carved out spaces within the fields of cultural production and reproduction (various characters are involved in theatre, music, political speech-writing and teaching); and just as history teacher Mike Donnelly (Bruce McDonald) teaches his students about the Boston police strike, filling in a part of their history others would rather see omitted, so Sayles in *Matewan* and *Eight Men Out* provides history lessons about forgotten labour struggles (the West Virginia Coalfield War, the Black Sox scandal). In response to the specific historical conjunctures in which he works, Sayles, like many other leftist and anti-colonialist filmmakers, from Ken Loach to Ousmane Sembène, has eschewed Brechtian/Godardian experimentation and persisted with forms of naturalism. In particular, as suggested above, he has focused on creating film worlds whose apparent complexity (*City of Hope*, for example, has 38 key characters and sixty speaking parts) prompts one to recognise the interconnectivity and multiple interpellations of social being and the variety and contradictions within the totality.

This sense of complex social being was largely absent from the subject as theorised by Comolli, Narboni, McCabe and their contemporaries, whose notions of determinism are redolent of a 'one-sided' Marxism. Michael A. Lebowitz (2003) offers a persuasive account of the ways in which the incompletion of Marx's project – of which the three volumes of *Capital*, themselves incomplete, were intended to form only one part – produced a deformed or 'one-sided' version of his analysis that has dominated subsequent Marxist thought. Most significantly, Marx did not write his intended volume on wage-labour, and thus while the methodology of *Capital* required Marx to treat people only as they existed as subjects-for-capital, his overall method also required consideration of capital's relation to subjects-for-themselves. In his preface to the first edition of the first volume of *Capital* (1867), Marx explicitly states that 'here individuals are dealt with only in so far as they are the personifications of economic categories, embodiments of particular class relations and class interests' (1976: 10). This clearly implies that his understanding of the subject as a whole being is much larger than the subject as conceptualised for his analysis of capital. While the lines of trudging workers in Fritz Lang's *Metropolis* (1926) offer a stark visual image of the subject-for-capital, it must be complemented and complicated by the more pleasing image of workers-for-themselves – goofing off, fishing, tramping, existing outside of the workplace and their relation to capital – that concludes René Clair's *À nous la liberté* (*Freedom for Us*, 1931). In 1844, Marx wrote of 'the *rich human being*' as being '*in need of* a totality of human manifestations of life' and as one 'in whom his own realisation exists as an inner necessity' (1975: 304; emphasis in original). In *The Communist Manifesto* (1848), Marx and Engels wrote that communism's goal was 'association, in which the free development of each is the condition for the free development of all' (1976b: 506). And Marx never abandoned this conceptualisation of the full subject, even imagining, in volume one of *Capital*, a situation 'contrary' to capitalism in which 'material wealth exist[s] to satisfy the needs of development on the part of the labourer' (1976: 616) and in which the worker would be capable of enjoying productive activity 'as something which gives play to his bodily and mental powers' (1976: 188).

Lebowitz rightly notes that one cannot predict what the missing volume on wage-labour would have said; but this does not mean that, pursuing Marx's dialectical method, one cannot trace the outlines of a 'two-sided' Marxism. Firstly, the 'Abstract Proletarian' – that personification of an economic category methodologically essential only for the part of Marx's analysis conducted in *Capital*, which Lebowitz describes as the 'productive worker for capital within the sphere of production ... and epitomized as the factory worker, that productive instrument' (2003: 138) – can no longer be substituted for real proletarians in all their fullness of being. No longer can Marxists insist that all other struggles for liberation, whether organised around race, gender or sexuality, are secondary to class struggle: rather, they are integral to it, just as those struggles are incomplete without also challenging both capital and these other categories of oppression, because 'every individual is an ensemble of the social relations in which she acts' (2003: 155) and 'the development of an individual is determined by the development of all others with whom he is directly or indirectly associated' (Marx & Engels 1976a: 438). As Lebowitz argues:

To move from consideration of the political struggle of workers insofar as they are wage-labourers to that of the working class in its other sides, accordingly, is a major leap only if we begin from a stereotyped conception of the worker and her needs in the first place. A strategy calling for 'alliances' between workers and new social actors takes as its starting point the theoretical reduction of workers to one-dimensional products of capital ... However, real workers have many determinations and exist simultaneously in many different social relations. Rather than an inherent opposition between 'new social movements' and the struggles of workers as a class against capital, the former should be seen as expressing those *other* needs of workers and as the development of *new* organizing centres of the working class, functioning in the broad interest of its *complete emancipation*. And, insofar as they are directed against capital's position as the owner of the products of social labour, such struggles have the potential of *unifying* (rather than maintaining the separation of) all those who have nothing to sell but their labour-power' (2003: 186; emphasis in original).

Regardless of whether or not Sayles can be regarded as a Marxist, his films do offer a strong sense of the subject of a 'two-sided' Marxism. While many 'one-sided' Marxists might disregard Sayles because he only occasionally places class struggle (in its 'one-sided' sense) at the centre of his narratives, his films do apprehend something of the fullness of the subject and the array of other social relations in which subjects are embedded – and they do so without ever losing sight of the economic determinants of being-under-capital. *Lianna*, for example, is primarily concerned with the eponymous protagonist's discovery and exploration of her lesbian sexuality and identity, but the struggles she faces in doing so are inseparably bound up in struggles around gender and class: when she leaves her husband, her years of supporting his career count for nothing, and she finds herself with little claim on the material rewards accruing from her labour as his wife (the reproduction of his labour power).[10] In the post-1970s rush to various identity politics which have taken a singular (and often swiftly reified) identity as the focus of their struggle, be it based on race, ethnicity, gender or sexuality, the interconnectedness of these categories in the subject's multiple determinations and simultaneous existence in many different social relations, in the subject's fullness of being, has often been lost.[11] And this is why Sayles' turn to naturalist depictions of social totality has been, and is, so fruitful, particularly as naturalism has developed away from such singular and transcendent forces of determinism as heredity and degeneration.

Discussion of totality, haunted by the spectres of 'totalisation' and 'totalitarianism', is deeply unfashionable, perhaps because, as Slavoj Žižek suggests, many prefer to silently abandon 'the analysis of capitalism as a global economic system' and accept 'capitalist economic relations as the unquestionable framework' (1997: 15–16). And those who do talk about 'capitalism as *universal* world system' often emphasise its 'basic homogeneity' (1997: 15; emphasis in original) as 'the most standardised and uniform social reality in history' (Jameson 1998: 72), treating 'the hybrid coexistence of diverse cultural life-worlds' (Žižek 1997: 15) within it as secondary, if not epiphe-nomenal. However, as derived from Hegel by Marx, 'totality' refers to 'the universal, all-sided, *vital* connection of everything with everything' (Lenin 1961: 146; emphasis in original) – it is not static and monolithic but dynamic and organic, full of diversi-ties and tensions and contradictions. It is the world in history, in process, in all its complexity. This is the extensive totality that the intensive totalities of Sayles' films map, and nowhere is this clearer than in their use of language.

Following Ferdinand de Saussure, twentieth century linguistics has been domi-nated by an idealist tendency which removes language from lived, material social being and imagines it as a non-material realm (*langue*) upon which we draw for individual speech-acts (*parole*). Mikhail Bakhtin countered this tendency, arguing that language is 'a social phenomenon – social throughout its entire range and in each and every of its factors' (1981: 259), and that it is only through communicative interaction with others that individuals come into being. Any 'single national language' is internally stratified 'into social dialects, characteristic group behaviour, professional jargons, generic languages, language of generations and age groups, tendentious languages, languages of the authorities, of various circles and passing fashions, languages that serve the specific socio-political purposes of the day, even of the hour' (1981: 262–3). Language is heteroglot, lively, unstable. Usage is determined by the tension between this centrifugal, anti-authoritarian dispersal and the centripetal forces concerned with centralising and unifying the language, with overcoming 'the realities of heteroglossia' (1981: 270), with limiting, rationalising and instrumentalising it, with crystallizing its variety into a unity. This dialectical process involves not merely a centripetal-centrif-ugal tension but also the operation of dialects and the other 'socio-ideological'(1981: 272) languages of various social groups in relation to each other: 'Actual social life and historical becoming create within an abstractly unitary national language a multi-tude of concrete worlds, a multitude of bounded verbal-ideological and social belief systems' (1981: 288), and these 'many worlds of language [are] all equal in their ability to conceptualise and be expressive' (1981: 286). Each and every word uttered repre-sents a dialogue between them, 'liv[ing], as it were, on the boundary between its own context and another, alien, context' (1981: 284). The 'living utterance having taken meaning and shape at a particular historical moment in a socially specific environ-ment, cannot fail to brush up against thousands of living dialogic threads, woven by socio-ideological consciousness' (1981: 276). A particularly sharp example of this occurs in Sayles' *The Secret of Roan Inish* (1994). Hugh Coneelly (Mick Lally) is telling his granddaughter Fiona (Jeni Courtney) about his great-grandfather, Sean Michael (Fergal McElherron). Forced to speak English at school, Sean Michael is punished for speaking his own language. Taunted beyond endurance by his classmates, he attacks the schoolmaster, shouting at him in his native tongue, 'I'm not your ox, you dirty foreigner, and you can shove this up your arse!'[12] The film cuts from a flashback to the present moment, in which Tess Coneelly (Eileen Colgan) chastises her husband for using such language in front of a child. Sean Michael's words pour out of him, an unstoppable expression, and play along the boundary of different linguistic contexts: his schoolmates and Hugh and Tess understand them; his schoolmaster, Fiona, who has 'no Irish', and the vast majority of viewers do not. Sean Michael's words brush up against dialogic threads, causing them to resonate among the colonised; but in the alien context of the coloniser they are meaningless – or, rather, meaningless in terms of what they specifically say, but meaningful in that they signal a deep-rooted and fierce resistance.

Bakhtin described the novel as being composed of 'heterogeneous stylistic unities', which combine together 'to form a structured artistic system', but noted that the unity of the text 'cannot be identified with any single one' of them (1981: 262). Rather, 'the style of a novel is to be found in the combination of its styles; the language of a novel is the system of its "languages"', and the novel 'can be defined as a diversity of social speech types (sometimes even diversity of languages) and a diversity of individual voices, artistically organised' (ibid.). As Sayles' films have often been wrongly described as lacking visual style (this criticism will be addressed more directly later), it is perhaps risky to utilise Bakhtin's work to think about them; but his argument, although explicitly about the novel, is primarily concerned with the construction and representation of social totalities. Moreover, there is no denying that Sayles is a literary artist, a short story writer, novelist and playwright as well as a screenwriter; and his fiction, especially *Union Dues* and *Los Gusanos*, is concerned, like his films, with the intensive mapping of an extensive social reality. Whether in novel or film, Sayles follows Bakhtin's injunction neither to 'strip away the intentions of others from the heteroglot language of his works' nor to 'violate those socio-ideological cultural horizons (big and little worlds) that open up behind heteroglot languages', but rather to welcome 'them into his work' and make 'use of words that are already populated with the social intentions of others' (1981: 299–300). This resonates strongly with the naturalist's negotiations between observer and participant, 'involvement and equanimity' (Dudley 2004: 95), as he or she 'assumes the role of disinterested intermediary between the concrete facts of experience and an audience separated from this experience by time, space, or – in many cases – race and class' (2004: 11–12) while nonetheless creating the work of fiction. When heteroglossia enters the text, Bakhtin argues,

> it becomes subject to an artistic reworking. The social and historical voices populating language, all its words and all its forms, which provide language with its particular concrete conceptualizations, are organised … into a structured stylistic system that expresses the differentiated socio-ideological position of the author amid the heteroglossia of his epoch … It is as if the author has no language of his own, but does possess his own style, his own organic and unitary law governing the way he plays with languages and the way his own real semantic and expressive intentions are refracted within them. (1981: 300, 311)

To make such claims for Sayles' films requires some evidence, which brings us back, at last, to Billy Zane.

Zane's acting is typified by a quasi-Brechtian distantiation in which one sees not merely performance but the performance of performance.[13] This is neither to claim that he is a cerebral actor, self-consciously and ironically distant from his roles (although he might be), nor to evoke either the manneredness retrospectively evident in 1950s Method acting or the endless quotation of trademark tics of subsequent Method actors (Robert De Niro's look back over the shoulder, Jack Nicholson's raised-eyebrow grin). Rather, it is to suggest something of the effect created by Zane's mannerisms and speech, his frequent distractedness and his hesitancies about gesture and dialogue – in short, Zane's style, which is fairly consistently that of an empty core, conjuring the semblance of a character, of humanity, out of a repertoire he has learned somewhere. In his first scene in *Silver City*, described above, Chandler comes across as a character who goes beyond mere cynical reason.[14] He does not make his crooked deal with Mort just because if he did not someone else would, but because such behaviour has become so normalised as to involve neither cynicism nor reason. Just as Chandler has no apparent beliefs or principles, so Zane creates the impression of a being without being, an emptiness which performs performance, who is utterly alien to the values of the film. The match between Zane's acting style, and a character whose job it is to speak the words of others, could not be closer. In this scene, Chandler's interjection into Mort's clearly rehearsed sales pitch – 'The lake is a nice attraction' – is delivered with a verbal emphasis (on 'is') as, nodding his head, raising his furrowed brow and slightly pursing his lips, Chandler looks from the model of the proposed Silver City development to Mort, but it is also delivered with a complete lack of affect. His subsequent mild exclamation – 'Live in the Rockies!' – ironically disparages the dream being sold by Mort and those who would buy into it, but again his delivery gives the impression of someone making the kind of comment one is expected to make in such a situation: even his ironies are quotations, borrowed from somewhere else. As Mort begins to solicit his aid, Chandler's comments on the unfairness of showing favouritism and the Development Agency's current emphasis on general legislation rather than individual cases are delivered as if by rote, without conviction, as lines the character (*not* the actor) must deliver before he can suggest that Mort retain his services. In this particular situation, Zane's performance of Chandler literalises Brecht's injunction that 'Just as the actor no longer has to persuade the audience that it is the author's character and not himself that is standing on the stage, so also he need not pretend that the events taking place on the stage have never been rehearsed, and are now happening for the first and only time' (1964: 194).

That the conversation has all along been heading to this juncture is evident in the alacrity with which Chandler says 'I could probably work on a commission basis' before Mort can even manage to finish protesting that his cash 'is tied up with the acquisition of the land'. When Mort replies, 'You mean like a piece of the action?', there is a curious and momentarily delayed change of expression on Chandler's face: he rapidly blinks six times and casts his gaze downwards as if struggling to process Mort's fall into a colloquial language. This appears to be something he had not anticipated or rehearsed, and for a fraction of a second he seems incapable of grasping Mort's meaning, before responding to this inappropriate bluntness by re-establishing the linguistic norms of such dealings. However, even as he refers to 'regulatory legislation', his own language becomes slightly less formal ('going to bat for' is quickly followed by 'suck up to'), as if Chandler is adjusting his performance in response to Mort's behaviour rather than rigidly adhering to his preconception of Mort.

Moments later, Chandler returns to using the language of others, explaining that 'There's no reason we couldn't raise the river and lower the bridge at the same time'. Chandler says this with such self-consciousness that he almost seems to be reading it from a cue-card. What is intriguing, though, is that he gets the expression, which is generally used to describe lateral thinking and innovative solutions, wrong. Chandler seems to mean that if Mort cannot raise the soil quality to the necessary level, then Chandler can lower the regulatory standards; but their collusion produces a confusion about the expression which now emphasises the convergence of their interests ('if you want the soil standards lowered, retain me on commission, which will give me a reason to work on lowering them') but conjures up an unintended image of disaster (if you raise the river *and* lower the bridge, you end up with a flooded bridge). Bakhtin argues that 'for the individual consciousness' language 'lies on the borderline between oneself and the other'; and that the word 'is half someone else's', becoming '"one's own" only when the speaker populates it with his own intention, his own accent, when he appropriates the word, adapting it to his own semantic and expressive intention' (1981: 293). The comedy of this moment lies in Chandler's limited success in populating the expression. He invokes it with an excessive, almost flirtatious, self-confidence, but what he actually says undercuts the meaning he wishes to produce (even Mort seems momentarily baffled before asking, rather more mundanely, 'How big a piece of the action would this be?').

Idealist linguistics would consider Chandler's speech-act (*parole*) as an instantiation of the potentialities inherent in language as an abstract system of differentiation (*langue*). Bakhtin, however, refutes the notion that prior to the speaker's moment of appropriation the word exists 'in a neutral and impersonal language (it is not, after all, out of a dictionary that the speaker gets his words!), but rather it exists in other people's mouths, in other people's contexts, serving other people's intentions: it is from there that one must take the word, and make it one's own' (1981: 293). Chandler continues to exemplify this process in each of his remaining scenes – for example, on handing his draft legislation for the 'Environmental Heritage Initiative' to Chuck Raven, he jokes that 'we thought it sounded better than "Developer's Bill of Rights"' – but it extends beyond his business life, defining his interactions with others. For example, when Nora introduces him to Danny, Chandler beams insincerely – once more blinking as he processes the information – and says 'Danny, ex, ex-boyfriend-from-hell Danny?' Whether derived from Nora's private description of Danny, or from Chandler's own limited understanding of the man Nora has described to him, Chandler uses this epithet in public – and to Danny's face – in order to establish his own sense of proprietorship over Nora, while implying that the description would not fit him and emphasising that it is he who now shares Nora's intimacy. Although it might sound like a mere faux pas, it is deeply territorial, not just establishing a distance between himself and Danny but also attempting to conform Nora to himself. Whatever anxiety it might betray on his behalf about Nora's fond regard for Danny, it is nonetheless an assertion of hierarchy and power.

There follows an awkward pause, until Danny comments on recognising Chandler from his television appearances as a tobacco lobbyist. Hitherto, the three have been arranged in medium shot: Chandler on the left of the screen and Danny on the right, with Nora midway between them. A brass curtain rail above Nora's head emphasises the eyeline between the two men. Chandler and Nora are linked by their stature relative to Danny who is slightly in the foreground and thus larger than them, and their relative proximity to each other, but there remains a clear space between them, emphasised by the strong vertical line of the restaurant's open curtain in the background. When Danny starts to challenge Chandler, there is a cut to a shot over Danny's shoulder, his head and back filling almost half the screen, with his foreground position again making him appear bigger than Chandler. Although the scene then cuts between each of the three characters, this particular set-up is repeated whenever Chandler is obviously, and uncomfortably, engaged in appropriating the language of others. When Danny recalls that Chandler said 'there was no scientific evidence that smoking can cause cancer', Chandler responds, 'I see myself as sort of a champion of the underdog', and as he says this he looks down, blinks repeatedly, looks offscreen towards Nora, tilts his head slightly and smiles a fraction, before turning back to face Danny. He continues, 'Every point of view, no matter how politically incorrect deserves an advocate in the court of public opinion.' It is as if he is trying out this reasoning for the first time, and despite the confidence suggested by his rich deep voice the words come out uncertainly, one at a time. He looks directly at Danny, then lowers his eyes, then looks directly at him again, before once more looking offscreen to Nora as he gets to the end of the line. Throughout, this exchange he is uncomfortable, knowing that Danny is never going to buy this bravura justification.

Bakhtin notes that:

> not all words for just anyone submit equally easily to this appropriation, to this seizure and transformation into private property: many words stubbornly resist, others remain alien, sound foreign in the mouth of the one who appropriated them and who now speaks them; they cannot be assimilated into his context and fall out of it; it is as if they put themselves in quotation marks against the will of the speaker. Language is not a neutral medium that passes freely and easily into the private property of the speaker's intention; it is populated – overpopulated – with the intentions of others. Expropriating it, forcing it to submit to one's own intentions and accents, is a difficult and complicated process. (1981: 293)[15]

This is precisely Chandler's problem. Calling the tobacco industry an 'underdog' is a dazzling attempt to expropriate the language of the oppressed and, moreover, a term which has specific resonances in American culture far beyond the overtly political; these resonances are complicated by his invocation of the bogeyman of 'political correctness', a reactionary term devised to perpetuate the marginalisation of certain groups of social 'underdogs', like women, non-whites, gays and lesbians and the impoverished (supporting the underdog is more commonly valorised when talking about sport than when addressing impoverishment and social marginalisation). Likewise, Chandler's glance towards Nora as he refers to 'public opinion' attempts to recruit her to his position by acknowledging her as a journalist and therefore a representative of 'public opinion'; but he does not recognise the extent to which her professional experience has taught her that this is not the case, that her frustration at the various measures which prevent her from doing her job 'properly' has made it clear to her that corporations and individuals do not have equal voices in the public sphere, that the language of politics, public relations and corporate lobbying is that of seizure and transformation, a centripetal, centralising force opposed to heteroglossia, to the language and expression of the people. The resistance of other people's words and contexts to Chandler's attempted expropriation is evident not just in his discomfort but also in the ease with which Danny, formerly a crusading journalist, is able to mock him, saying to Nora, 'I heard that you were with somebody new, but, hey, a champion of the underdog', sarcastically giving Chandler a thumbs-up and enjoining him to 'Keep up the good fight'.

Throughout this exchange between Danny and Chandler, the shots of Nora position her on the left-hand side of the screen, associating her more closely with Chandler, who is also positioned on the left, but she is never at ease with what he says. This contradiction – they are close, yet apart; a couple, but with a gulf between them – is opened up in the final scene they share. Nora is sitting on the front steps of her house one morning, in loose casual clothing, drinking coffee and doing the crossword, while Chandler, in tight-fitting cycling gear, prepares to go for a ride. The scene begins with them sharing the frame, but a wall provides a strong vertical line between them, separating them as clearly as do their clothes and her choice of cerebral, rather than his choice of physical, activity. And from the moment Chandler asks Nora about what she saw in Danny, the scene plays out in alternating shots of each of them, her on the left side of her shots, him on the right side of his, making manifest the distance between them that their dialogue reveals.[16] Nora recalls that when Danny was in the middle of investigating a story he would write names and facts on their apartment wall in magic marker and try to join them up. Chandler replies, 'So you had to live with it', his uncertain tone both indicating incomprehension and tentatively casting Nora as a victim – not so much reminding her that Danny was a boyfriend-from-hell as trying to expropriate the anecdote from a narrative about Danny and Nora into one about himself and Nora. She resists this recontextualisation by trying to explain that Danny's behaviour, however irritating it might have been, exemplified the intensity and political commitment she found so exciting in him; it was of far less consequence than his belief 'that journalists should change things … not just report'.[17] Chandler fails to recognise the extent to which Nora is talking about herself, and tries to recontextualise Danny as someone who 'wanted to be the referee and not just the scorekeeper'. He recalls that when he used to be a press liaison, he had a slogan on the wall that said 'You don't tell us how to stage the news and we won't tell you how to report it'. Chandler's sports metaphor emphasises once more how, to him, politics is merely a game (with clearly defined rules, although they might differ significantly from those espoused in public) and that ultimately there is no purpose to what he does beyond enabling the

Silver City: close, yet apart

extraction of surplus-value and ensuring that he gets a share of it. Danny, in contrast, still has the sense of purpose and principled belief that Nora has to suppress in herself in order to do her current job. Chandler's attempted assimilation of this narrative into his world, represented by an instrumentalism so normalised and naturalised that he is never at a loss for a cliché through which to express it, demonstrates for her the gulf separating the world she occupies with him from the one she shared with Danny.

The scene ends as Chandler, donning his cycle helmet, advises her, 'Power is a locomotive, babe. You either hop on board or it runs right over you.' With a smiling drawl signalling pleasure in his extension of the metaphor as well as a sense of his own superiority to Danny, he adds, 'Sounds like he laid down on the tracks'.[18] Nora looks at him with disbelief as he cycles off. The entire conversation has taken place on the border of two very different language-worlds, with Chandler not so much trying to understand Nora as colonise her language, making over its meaning so as to incorporate her into him, to bring her into the world in which he lives. The extent of his failure to do so is directly proportionate to the self-satisfaction he exudes as he exits the scene, certain of his victory. He does not hear Nora say of Danny, 'He was the love of my life.'

Bakhtin acknowledges that in the novel heteroglossia is generally 'personified, incarnated in individual human figures, with disagreements and oppositions individualised', but argues that 'such oppositions of individual wills and minds are submerged in *social* heteroglossia, they are reconceptualised through it. Oppositions between individuals are only surface upheavals of the untamed elements in social heteroglossia, surface manifestations of those elements that play on such individual oppositions' (1981: 326; emphasis in original). The subject positions occupied by Chandler, Mort, Danny and Nora vary enormously, sometimes converging, sometimes diverging. The lineaments of each position are suggested through the language each of them uses, the words that are activated along the borderlines of their different language-worlds, their attempted appropriations of each other's words, the narratives they construct as they seek to reposition their interlocutors and their resistances to such linguistic expropriations. Each character emerges in relation to the others with which he or she interacts, and what happens on this level happens across all levels of the film. Diverse social speech types and languages – heteroglossia – are welcomed into the film, and words already populated with social intentions interact within a filmic system which arranges them so that their contradictions are made apparent. This strategy is central to Sayles' films. In the case of *Silver City*, this thoroughgoing sense of language being embedded in the particular material and social circumstances of the speaker, and of the dialectical struggle over meaning when language-worlds touch each other, adds a critical dimension to its satire on the emptiness of mainstream political rhetoric by emphasising the instrumentalisation of language by those who would enclose meaning (and thus limit politics to a very narrow range of 'issues' and a repertoire of barely-distinguishable postures that leave the 'unquestionable' framework of capitalist economics intact), and by showing how intrinsic linguistic diversity and all it represents is to human social being.[19] The inspired casting of Billy Zane as Chandler Tyson reveals the hollowness we risk in conforming to the centripetal forces that would restrict heteroglossia and the rich fullness of a freely-developed humanity.

Independence and authorship

In the late 1960s, the desperate response of the major Hollywood studios to falling profits created the opportunity, so it is often claimed, for a revolution in American filmmaking, resulting in a 'period of relative experimentation … made possible by the economic insecurity of Hollywood, still casting around for forms of durable and predictable appeal after the massive postwar decline in audiences' (M. Smith 1998: 10). Jim Hillier teases out some of the implications of this supposed shift from inherently conservative 'production-line methods under the iron control of studio bosses and money men' to a regime which permitted directors greater 'artistic freedom and individuality' in their filmmaking (1993: 7), sceptically observing the alacrity with which Hollywood – and the burgeoning subject of Film Studies – seized upon the appealing fiction of the auteur as the guarantor of a film's meaning and meaningfulness. But as Hillier reminds us, 'the movie industry is, above all, an *industry*. It changes to preserve or increase profitability, not to produce better entertainment or art' (1993: 6; emphasis in original). This is perhaps most evident in the ascendancy of Steven Spielberg and George Lucas and the associated shift to big-budget, special effects-driven, cross-marketed blockbusters and event movies whose politics, economics and aesthetics have increasingly dominated Hollywood cinema. In this context, the ironies involved in Spielberg co-founding Dreamworks SKG and Lucas promoting the *Star Wars* prequel trilogy as the fulfilment of a personal vision require little elucidation. Despite the relative freedom from financial constraint enjoyed by these directors, they seem fated to keep on making more of the same. And even those of their contemporaries, such as Scorsese, who have made more convincing attempts to preserve something of the personal and independent approaches to filmmaking made possible by the innovations of the 1960s and early 1970s are only able to do so if they also make more conventional films in exchange; while the nature and degree of the independence of films by directors such as Spike Lee and Steven Soderbergh often seem to be determined by the relative box-office performances of their previous films.[20]

A major consequence for American filmmaking of this valorisation of spectacular cinema is the

> related reduction in narrative sophistication. Steven Spielberg's films …
> seemed frightened by the possibility that someone, somewhere, might miss
> the point (*any* point). Tropes of the classical Hollywood cinema, such as
> cross-cutting, subjective camera movement (now provided by the astonish-
> ingly ubiquitous Steadicam), or intensely emotive close-ups dominates today's
> film aesthetics with a vengeance. To me, this reduction, combined with the
> emphasis on effects-centred films, speaks to an anxiety about the very status of
> narrative as an explanatory system. Narrative implies history, depth, purpose.
> So, while Hollywood cinema continued to revel in the sensational, sensual
> realm of visual, auditory, and kinesthetic effects, the devaluation of narrative
> was hidden within a desperate overvaluation of overly explicit storytelling; a
> denial of its own undeniable supersession. (Bukatman 1998: 265)

This ousting of narrative and thinning of history recalls Fredric Jameson's suggestion that 'the cultural products of the postmodern era' replace feeling with 'intensities', a term which describes sensations that are 'free-floating and impersonal and tend to be dominated by a peculiar kind of euphoria' (1991: 16). He relates this 'waning of affect' to the 'waning of the great high modernist thematics of time and temporality, the elegiac mysteries of *durée* and memory' (ibid.). Sayles is no Marcel Proust, but his films do stand out from those of many of his contemporaries in their commitment to complex and implicit narrative as well as to the recovery of memory.[21] Their recon-struction and telling of suppressed and marginalised stories reinstate historicity and rebuke our often complicit amnesias.

The triumph of sensuous spectacle is not, of course, the complete story of New Hollywood, and the career decisions made by directors like Spielberg, Lucas and Scorsese represent only some of the possible routes through the negotiations of and compromises between business, entertainment and art required of those who would make films in America. The 1980s and 1990s also saw several flourishings of Amer-ican independent cinema, aided and abetted by the development of new distribution systems and technologies – from direct-to-video horror, crime, action, martial arts and pornographic films to New Queer Cinema and New Jack Cinema. However, as Justin Wyatt's counter-intuitive but not inaccurate description of *Teenage Mutant Ninja Turtles* (1990) as 'the most successful independent film ever made' (1998: 77) suggests, 'independent' is a vexed term used to describe a range of phenomena, from well-fi-nanced production companies locked into distribution deals with the major studios to self-funded guerrilla filmmakers maxing-out credit cards. While Greg Merritt's history of independent American film insists that the term can only be applied to 'motion picture[s] financed and produced completely autonomous of *all* studios, regardless of size' and which 'do not have a prior distribution arrangement (other than from a company owned by the filmmakers)' (2000: xii; emphasis in original), the actual currency of the term is such that it includes many of what Merritt would consider semi-indies and some Hollywood studio films. Geoff King, recognising the fluidities and ambiguities of his field of study, argues instead that independent film is always a relative designation operating in relation to 'formal/aesthetic strategies' and 'the broader social, cultural, political or ideological landscape', as well industrial contexts (2005: 2). While such debates might render the use of 'independent' to describe Sayles' films so in need of qualification as to be effectively meaningless, he has nonetheless for nearly thirty years charted a unique path through the institutions, economics, practices and possibilities of the New Hollywood, negotiating the kinds and degrees of relative autonomy with which he can operate from film to film.

Following his debut *Return of the Secaucus Seven*, Sayles has written and directed a further 15 films. With the exception of *Baby It's You* (1983), he has refused deals that do not give him control of casting and final cut, and has spent three decades struggling to finance a body of work committed to exploring the complexities of daily life in families and communities under capitalism. Driven by character, narrative and ideas rather than kinetic spectacle, his films stand in stark contrast to the values that have increasingly dominated American film production in this period. This can be exemplified by considering Sayles' films alongside those of James Cameron, both of whom worked on *Battle Beyond the Stars* (1980). Thanks to its costly special effects, this science fiction version of *Seven Samurai* (1954) and *The Magnificent Seven* (1960) was the most expensive film Roger Corman had produced to that date, costing an estimated $2 million. The division of labour between writer Sayles and Cameron (who receives credits for art direction, additional photography, miniature design and miniature construction) and their subsequent careers are indicative of the paths taken by American film production during the following decades. After further design and effects work for Corman, Cameron directed *Piranha Part II: The Spawning* (1981), an in-name-only sequel to Joe Dante's Sayles-scripted 1978 *Jaws* cash-in, and then made his mark with *The Terminator* (1984), the success of which saw him graduate to increasingly expensive pictures – *Aliens* (1986), *The Abyss* (1989), *Terminator 2: Judgment Day* (1991), *True Lies* (1994), *Titanic* (1997) – in which various combinations of star, production design, special effects and sheer sprawl dominated character, coherent narrative development and ideas. Cameron's films exemplify the tendency in American filmmaking in which originality and innovation have been relegated to the status of technical issues in the production of startling spectacle. In contrast, Sayles has produced a body of work in which character, dialogue and performance are central and special effects are as cheap as they are rare. In a period which has seen the average production cost of studio films rise from $10 million in 1980 (see Hillier 1993: 17) to $26.8 million in 1990 and $51.5 million in 1999 (see MPAA 1999),[22] only two of Sayles' films – *The Secret of Roan Inish* and *Limbo* – have had budgets in excess of $4 million. His budgets have not increased substantially since then, with *Casa de los Babys* costing only $1 million and *Silver City* $5 million, while the average production cost of a studio film rose to $65.8 million in 2006 (see MPAA 2006).[23] His work has proven consistently inventive in overcoming financial constraints through good writing, a strong commitment to his actors and, increasingly, intelligent and subtle cinematography, shot composition and editing.

The contrast with Cameron also recalls two of the critical commonplaces about Sayles, that he is a 'political' filmmaker (and, by implication, only a 'political' film-maker) and that his films lack visual style. The first complaint can be quickly disposed of with a quotation from Haskell Wexler, cinematographer on *Matewan*, *The Secret of Roan Inish*, *Limbo* and *Silver City*. Asked whether the films he himself directed would always be politically motivated, he replied:

> Well, I'd have to address myself to the phrase, 'politically motivated'. I mean suppose a guy says, 'I make films where I make the best bucks, I make films where they pay me most, I'm interested in entertainment and screw all this ideology stuff.' Now you couldn't find a stronger political statement than that, yet no one says that's a political statement. Whereas if I say, 'I make films that I feel are positive human statements that enlighten or enlarge man's view of life and of the earth and of one another', well that becomes a polit-ical statement. Now that's because our culture has adapted itself to accept consumerism, to accept the profit motive, to accept the personal selfish atti-tude as 'nonpolitical' … I maintain that every act that a person takes as a social human being is a political act. (In Schaefer and Salvato 1984: 251)

In a similar vein, Sayles prefaced his response to a request from progressive magazine *Mother Jones* to give 'his take on the 20 best political films of the past two decades' thus: 'I could do a list titled "The Empire Strikes Back" of pictures from *Rambo* to *Adventures in Babysitting* that have, whatever their entertainment quality, served only to maintain the status quo, strengthen stereotyping, and push people apart [but they] get enough airtime' (Sayles 1996).

Criticisms of Sayles' visual style typically founder on the failure to distinguish between style and stylishness or visual prominence. Andrew Klevan argues that '"having a style" is not simply possessing an individual, distinctive or original manner, but reflects the ability of the filmmakers, and not only the director, to provide salience to the multitude of visual information provided, precisely to put in place the patterns which will guide the viewer's attention through the significant elements of a work' (2000: 63). In this respect at least, Sayles has always had style, however unadorned it might sometimes appear.[24]

If the frequency with which the term auteur is bandied about in Peter Biskind's *Easy Riders, Raging Bulls: How the Sex'n'Drugs'n'Rock'n'Roll Generation Saved Hollywood* (1998) is at all indicative of a self-conscious New Hollywood film culture, it is also the case that from the early 1970s the studios were prepared to promote some notion of the director as author or star. Audiences, along with much journalism and popular writing on film, have proven susceptible to the glamour of this idea. However, after a fairly lengthy investment in elaborating the concept of the auteur in response to its many and obvious shortcomings (its romanticism, ahistoricism, and its simplification of the production process; its tendency to reduce social, economic and political deter-minants to the 'bogeyman' image of interfering and philistine studios), Film Studies more or less rejected it. The subsequent adaptation of theoretical frameworks from semiotics and structuralism, Marxism, feminism and psychoanalysis, however instrumental it has been in the development of Film Studies as an academic discipline, however fruitful it has been in extending and enhancing our understanding of film, has also frequently resulted in the loss of any notion of creativity.

The auteurism of Andrew Sarris, and of Peter Wollen (who attempted to translate it into structuralist terms), was primarily concerned with repetition, focusing on recurrent structures, themes and types and pointing to such continuities and coherences as evidence of a particular director's authorship. But, as Victor Perkins has observed:

> What a director does well is at least as important as what he does often. That is a matter of skill, certainly, but one that goes beyond skill to embrace such values as eloquence, subtlety, vividness and intensity. Adequately to describe a director's authorship involves an exposition of these and other qualities. (1990b: 59)

Auteurism also tends to regard any collaboration as a source of interference. This romanticised notion of director-as-author achieves its apotheosis in Wollen's contention that the director, conceptualised as a structure within the text, should not be confused with the material being who actually directed the film; in effect, he or she is just another obstruction. Clearly, this denial of materiality makes a nonsense of auteurism as a theory of authorship, as Perkins suggests: 'instead of confronting the problem of intention raised by the relationship between the "auteur structure" and a director's choices and designs, Wollen fell back on an immaterial force with all the explanatory power of an ectoplasm' (1990b: 62).

Material conditions always pertain, and in constructing a director-centred criticism it is imperative to conceptualise them as being by no means *necessarily* a constraint.[25] Perkins rightly insists on the importance of recognising that 'one of the prime requirements for a filmmaker is flexibility to improvise, and to adjust his conceptions to the ideas and abilities of his co-workers, to the pressures of circumstance, and the concrete nature of the objects photographed' (1990a: 160). He argues the following:

> The director's authorship can not be produced by eliminating the results of collaboration ... An authorship theory must find room for processes which may enable the director to take responsibility for discoveries, incorporating them into the film's intention. It must allow for the possibility that a movie may be enriched, rather than impaired, by changes from an original concept ... It must allow for the fact that many directors establish their authorship by seeking enrichment and fostering change. (1990b: 61–2)

He expands upon this with a discussion of the final shot of *My Darling Clementine* (1946), concluding that:

> In deciding to print *those* takes and use *this* one, Ford was authorising the effects and meanings of the images ... The film director is, like all creators,

his work's first audience. He can try it out on himself and take it through a long series of adjustments and refinements to get as close as he can to a work that satisfies him, that does what he wants it to do. One way of understanding the director's role is to see him checking and adjusting the elements of the film as each of them is taken to its point of registration so as to satisfy himself of the ways in which in their developing context they respond to an active reading … The logic that acknowledges powers of invention and construction in the reader can not withhold them from the author. (1990b: 64; emphasis in original)

The importance of this passage lies in its recognition of authorship not just as being subject to material conditions but also as a process extended over time, and this is particularly relevant to any consideration of Sayles' authorship. A period of years sometimes separates writing a screenplay from filming it, and other projects often intervene. For example, having shot *Return of the Secaucus Seven*, Sayles had to go to work as a writer-for-hire in order to finance editing it; *The Brother from Another Planet* was written and shot very quickly because of delays in putting together the financing for *Matewan*; *Eight Men Out* was the first screenplay he wrote but, because of the legal entanglements surrounding Eliot Asinof's source book, it was the sixth film he directed; *Men with Guns* was delayed, and *Lone Star* shot instead, when the Zapatista uprising prevented location filming in Mexico.

Robin Wood offers some useful insights into how a theory of authorship must negotiate between the director as a material being and an understanding of the products of his or her authorship, the films themselves. Firstly, because it is impossible to recover with absolute certainty the director's intentions, there is often a tendency in rejecting the intentionalist fallacy – 'the notion that an artist's *expressed* intentions have a definitive authority in interpreting his or her work; the complementary notion that the author's intentions are what the critic is supposed to interpret and evaluate' (1991: 20; emphasis in original) – to deny the director the slightest degree of intentionality. However, it is obvious that on some levels, directors do do things deliberately and with design, and their own subsequent commentary is therefore not without value. Moreover, intentionality itself is a rather more fluid concept than it might seem, as Stanley Cavell's Babe Ruth analogy suggests: 'Obviously he may not be aware that he [bends his knees slightly before swinging], but does it follow that it is not done intentionally? If there is reason to believe that bending his knees is an essential part of what makes him good at batting – an explanation of how he does it – I find I want to say he does it intentionally; he means to' (1976: 235). Secondly, while knowledge of the director's life might be interesting, its usefulness must be restricted to 'confirm[ing] or consolidat[ing] a reading arrived at from a careful analysis of the film itself' (Wood 1991: 21). It is tempting to look for the source of Sayles' recurrent valorisation of productive labour – exemplified by his treatment of the striking miners in *Matewan* and David Strathairn's characters in *Passion Fish* and *Limbo* – in his own experience as a manual labourer or, as his films often contain problematic father figures, in the example of his father, who not only put himself through college in the evenings and on weekends but is also reputed to have built his own house, learning how to do so as he did it; or to trace Sayles' refusal to reduce the cops in *Union Dues*, *Matewan*, *City of Hope*, *Lone Star* and *Silver City* to stereotypes, to the fact that his maternal great-grandfather, both grandfathers and three great-uncles were all policemen; or to argue that his sympathy for the unemployed and the marginalised arises from his own relationship with Hollywood. However, as Wood argues, to reduce films in this way is a mechanism for avoiding their more profound implications.

Next, Wood urges recognition of the ideological construction of the director, and the potential of his or her work to expose dominant ideological structures either through conscious intention, unconscious impulse or some level in between. Sayles' work achieves its effects through both intention, as complexly defined, and accident, and one of the most interesting consequences thus to arise within his films is the tension between their critique of American capitalism and their less intentional (although not necessarily unintentional) exposure of the shortcomings of American left-liberal politics. Wood also notes the ideologically-constructed and determinant narrative patterns, genre conventions and connotative signifiers with which directors must work. This is important for an understanding of Sayles' films as their meanings are often heavily dependent upon the use, adaptation and mixing of generic codes. An important part of *Matewan*, for example, is the way in which it works with and against the western and the melodrama; and *Lone Star* adds a detective narrative to a similar blend. This returns us to the notion of intentional authorship. As Wood observes, 'it is but a short step from conceding [the director's] ability to underline and effectively suppress meanings to arguing that he is also able, out of his materials, effectively to construct them' (1991: 25).

I have tremendous sympathy with the efforts made by Perkins and Wood to retain a director-centred criticism, not least of all in the counterweight they offer to the tendency to overvalue the active role played by the audience in the construction of meaning, particularly in the recent efflorescence of audience research. However, the approach I have sketched out above is not without its own difficulties. Although the critic cannot reasonably deny the director those powers of invention and construction to which Perkins refers, he or she must be aware of the trap into which Cavell's Babe Ruth analogy falls; namely, that of sliding between 'intention' in the phenomenological sense and 'intention' in the psychological sense. Babe Ruth's knee-dip was indeed the product of human consciousness but probably only in the former sense. To clarify this, consider whether Cavell would be justified in saying that when Babe Ruth (who held records both for home runs and for striking out) failed to dip his knees it was because he did not intend to hit the ball. Surely even the most reductive psychology would hesitate to suggest this; and therefore Cavell's contention must be regarded with equal scepticism. Consequently, the kinds of confirmation or consolidation that knowledge of the director's life can give to a reading of a film must be questioned, because although, as Wood argues, it is logically a short step to arguing for a director's ability to construct meaning, it is a very big leap to argue from one's perception of meaning to the director's very specific intentions. The meaning one perceives is the product of human consciousness – people did make the film – but to attribute it directly to the director's intentions is to slip from the phenomenological to the psychological, and from a complex to an untenable linear model of causality.

An example of this problem can be drawn from Jack Ryan's discussion of the character of Hickey (Kevin Tighe), one of the union-busting Baldwin-Felts agents in *Matewan*. In a harrowing scene, Hickey tells Danny (Will Oldham) how he won a medal:

> I was sittin' alone in a ditch in France and this Kraut jumps in right next to me and I took my bayonet and I stuck him, right in the face. And then another jumps in and I stick him too, and another and another. And another, they just kept coming, one at a time, all night long. And in a little a bit I got to worried that they weren't all dead so I stuck 'em all again a couple of times just to make sure. And in the morning, they said that I was a war hero.

Ryan says of this that 'Hickey understands the bloody irony in being honored by his country for killing people' (1998: 131), and supports his argument by quoting Sayles' comments on Hickey's character, the full version of which is given here:

> In *Matewan*, I try to give even the most negative of characters something else to play besides evil. At one point we learn that Hickey, one of the Baldwin agents sent to town to stir up trouble, is a war hero with a traumatic past in the trenches. This information is meant not as an excuse or a Freudian explanation for his actions but to give him some room to breathe, to remind us that the man's life is not contained by this one incident in it, as well as to establish him as a guy familiar with killing. (Sayles 1987a: 22)

Despite having watched *Matewan* numerous times, it was not until I read Ryan that it occurred to me that anyone might think Hickey is telling Danny the truth. This scepticism stemmed not from squeamishness, but from a resistance to the way the story, taken at face value, seemed to represent a clumsy reduction of Hickey to a one-dimensional character. In my understanding of him, Hickey would relish inventing – or at the very least embellishing – such a story just to terrorise Danny. Sayles' character description of Hickey (1987a: 94) – from which Ryan's line about irony is taken almost word-for-word – is even more ambiguous than his retrospective account quoted above. Consequently, neither Ryan's interpretation nor my own contradicts Sayles, but because of this ambiguity it is impossible for either of us to claim that our understanding of Hickey coincides with Sayles' (or that of Kevin Tighe or any of the other personnel involved in the construction of the character). Therefore, while Hickey is an intentional product of human consciousness, any attempt to fix his meaning in Sayles' intentions is as bogus as trying to explain all of Hickey in terms of one night in the trenches, regardless of whether or not it "happened"; and what applies to a character applies to the film as a whole.

Tom Gunning's model of the system of film narration is helpful in thinking about ways to discuss films made by the same director without falling back into auteurism

Matewan: war hero

or romanticism. He identifies several levels of filmic discourse: the profilmic ('every-thing placed in front of the camera to be filmed'), the enframed image ('at this level … the profilmic is transformed from pre-existent events and objects into images on celluloid'), and editing ('the cutting and selection of shots as well as their assembly into syntagmas') (1994: 19–20). He continues:

> Each of these levels integrates the one before, transforming it as it does so. Their effect on a spectator is generally due to their interrelation, and I separate them for analysis. These three aspects of filmic discourse … almost always work in concert and represent the mediation between story and spectator in film. They are how films 'tell' stories. Taken together, they constitute the filmic narrator. (1994: 21)

Although the filmic narrator resembles, as Gunning acknowledges, Wayne Booth's notion of the implied author (see 1961) – both are functions of the text's discourse – it is a different discursive construct to the one proposed by Wollen in that it is not reducible to recurrent structures, themes and types. It allows for continuities across a director's work, but does not regard discontinuities as deviations, disruptions, fail-ures or evidence of some reprehensible external intervention. The narrator is not the director, but is complexly related to him or her, just as it is to the levels of discourse from which it emerges. Consequently, I will refer to Sayles only when talking about the biographical subject, and in exploring his films I will ascribe any necessary agency to the filmic narrator (who, for ease of expression, will share the name of the particular film) rather than the director. However, such distinctions can never be clear-cut and absolute, and this strategy is intended not as a solution to the problems outlined above but as an ongoing restatement of them.

CHAPTER TWO

Part of the Machine: the *Piranha*, *Alligator*, *The Howling* and *The Lady in Red* Screenplays

This chapter will consider four of Sayles' early screenplays for other directors. In the case of *Piranha*, *Alligator* and *The Howling*, he was hired to rewrite an existing screenplay by a company already committed to making the film (each time, he discarded everything but the title and started from scratch) but with *The Lady in Red* he had *carte blanche* to develop a screenplay from Roger Corman's sketchy notion of 'a female *Godfather* story about the woman who was with John Dillinger when he was shot' (G. Smith 1998: 34). These films offer useful insights into the countercultural and New Left paradigm which shapes Sayles' work, most obviously in the first half of his career. Moreover, *The Lady in Red* demonstrates several of the difficulties involved in developing a naturalist cinema, not least in terms of the economic and other determinants of the kinds of film produced and distributed. Additionally, it represents an intriguing moment in the development of the kind of filmmaking Sayles would subsequently pursue, as he devoted considerable energy to researching the background for his story (in a manner akin to Zola, who Lukács condemned) but then centred the story on a character who embodied the contradictions of the period in which she lived (in a manner akin to Sir Walter Scott or Balzac, who Lukács admired).

The opening shots of *Piranha* exemplify the difficulty of writing about a screenwriter from the evidence of the finished film. For example, Sayles' 'shooting script' for *Piranha*, dated March 1st 1978, opens with a young couple hiking through moonlit woods. After an inconsequential exchange, they move off out of shot and the camera tracks in on 'an overgrown sign along the side of the path' which reads 'U.S. ARMY TEST SITE – AUTHORIZED PERSONNEL ONLY'; there is then a cut to a wire fence, 'looming in the moonlight, underbrush grown up to its base' (Sayles 1978a: 1). However, the film itself reverses this sequence of events, opening with a shot of the night sky, the camera slowly craning down to reveal barbed wire, then the wire mesh fence and then the sign, which now also warns against trespassing. There is a cut to the woods, a location of almost fairy-tale gothic, into which the young couple intrude.

It is impossible to establish the provenance of these changes, but if they can be conditionally attributed to director Joe Dante, then the following observations may be made. Sayles and Dante are confident in their use of formulaic material. Both versions of the opening shot are clichés, unequivocal statements of genre. Sayles starts with characters and the mildly suspenseful suggestion that they are about to wander into danger, whereas Dante begins the movie with a clear sense of the forbidden and consequently the promise of transgression and reprisal. Dante's bolder approach – neither is subtle – is probably the more effective, in part because it is self-consciously an opening shot, one that echoes *Rebecca* (1940) and *Citizen Kane* (1941) as well as *Jaws* (1975). In addition to its relatively minimal narrative function, this shot addresses the audience's relationship to the film with the tongue-in-cheek reflexivity of the self-promoting exploitation movie, suggesting Dante's surer sense both of the visual and of his audience, which can be traced through further differences between the screenplay and the film. For example, later in Sayles' pre-title sequence one of the characters makes explicit mention of *The Creature from the Black Lagoon* (1954) and *Attack of the Crab Monsters* (1957). Dante, however, prefers visual to verbal intertextuality, including just the former reference, but casting science fiction and horror veterans like Kevin McCarthy, Dick Miller and Barbara Steele and interpolating a diegetically-motivated clip from *The Monster That Challenged the World* (1957). However, this preference can also betray him. The second shot of *Piranha*, in which mist coils above a brook in the forest, unnecessarily and perhaps counterproductively establishes the woodland setting as a gothic one more appropriate to Dante's subsequent Sayles-scripted film, *The Howling*. In pursuing the image for its own sake, Dante confuses, if only fleetingly, the generic markers which open the film.

There are, of course, problems with this analysis. Not only does it depend on comparisons between *Piranha* and a non-existent alternative version, but it also excludes the possibility of further collaboration between Sayles and Dante in developing the film, despite the fact that Sayles went on location with Dante for final rewrites. How then can a screenwriter's work be discussed with any confidence? As the example of *Piranha* suggests, it can neither be reduced to the published scripts nor expanded to the finished film. Some middle ground must be found. Although it is a far from satisfactory solution, some approximate sense of Sayles' contribution as screenwriter-for-hire can be gained by concentrating on the verbal and narrative elements of the movie rather than those visual and aural components (shot construction, *mise-en-scène*, editing, casting, performance, soundtrack) with which his relationship is more tenuous or indeterminate. This is not unproblematic. For example, *The Howling* again demonstrates Dante's preference for visual over verbal allusions. The cast once more features actors familiar from the horror and science fiction genres in film and television (John Carradine, Dennis Dugan, Patrick Macnee, Kevin McCarthy, Dick Miller,

Slim Pickens, Kenneth Tobey and Dee Williams) and there are a number of other visual gags, including diegetic and non-diegetic clips from *The Wolf Man* (1941), a photograph of Lon Chaney, Jr and wordless cameos from Roger Corman and Forrest J. Ackerman. Despite the film's knowing script, the principal verbal intertextual gag – the naming of characters after directors of previous werewolf films (Charles Barton, Terence Fisher, Freddie Francis, Erle Kenton, Lew Landers, Jacinto Molina, Roy William Neill, Sam Newfield, George Waggner and Jerry Warren) – is largely suppressed, only becoming clear during the end-credits. Here, the main problem with attributing verbal elements to the screenwriter and visual elements to the director is that it assumes Sayles is responsible for this in-joke about character names although it seems much more typical of Dante's fannish sense of humour.[26] Therefore, if one cannot even be certain that the writer got to name his characters, it is clear one must proceed with caution when considering his contribution to the finished film.

The Howling (Joe Dante, 1981)

If the 1970s was 'the Golden Age of the American horror film', the 1980s represented 'its decline – worse, the hideous perversion of its essential meaning' (Wood 2003: 63). The three horror films made from early scripts by Sayles are on the cusp of this transition. The last of them, *The Howling*, offers an interesting variation on Robin Wood's basic model of the horror movie. Freely adapted from Gary Brandner's novel, it retains only a few character relations, basic situations and isolated moments.[27] Having been contacted by serial killer Eddie Quist (Robert Picardo), television news reporter Karen White (Dee Wallace) agrees to help the police trap him. She meets him in a film booth at the back of a sex shop. He is in the middle of turning into a werewolf when the police arrive and shoot him. Apparently dead, he regains human form. His body later disappears from the morgue. Traumatised, Karen can remember nothing of what happened. Dr George Waggner (Patrick Macnee) recommends she spend some time at the Colony, an isolated therapeutic community he runs. Once there, her husband Bill Neill (Christopher Stone) is soon bitten and seduced by Marsha (Elisabeth Brooks). Scared by nocturnal noises, and convinced Bill is acting oddly because he is having an affair, Karen summons her best friend, Terry Fisher (Belinda Balaski), for support. Alone one day, Terry recognises a view of the coastline from a picture drawn by Quist and discovers his cabin in the woods. She is attacked by Marsha's brother T.C. (Don McLeod) in his werewolf form, but escapes and makes her way to Waggner's office, where she finds out that Quist is Marsha's other brother and contacts her boyfriend, Chris (Dennis Dugan). Werewolf Quist appears from nowhere and attacks her. As Chris, equipped with silver bullets, races to the rescue, Karen finds Terry's corpse and evades Quist by throwing acid in his face mid-transformation; but she is captured and taken to a barn, where it becomes clear that everyone in the Colony, possibly including Waggner, is a werewolf. Chris kills Quist, rescues Karen, traps the werewolves in the barn and torches it, but as they make good their escape, she is bitten by werewolf Bill. When Karen returns to her job, she departs from the autocue – and transforms into a werewolf – during a live news broadcast to warn her viewers of the monsters

The Howling: the beast from within

among them. By prearrangement, Chris then shoots her. Among the sceptical audience watching the news, is Marsha, sitting in a bar with some admiring men, one of whom orders her a hamburger, rare.

Wood, drawing on Herbert Marcuse's grafting of Freudian elements onto Marxist theory, describes the horror movie in terms of basic and surplus repression. The former is essential to our development as a species and as individuals in society. It is the mechanism by which we learn to postpone the gratification of desire in order to achieve less immediate goals. The latter is culture-specific and describes the processes by which the subject is urged to embrace socially-defined goals and roles. As Wood notes, '*basic* repression makes us distinctively human, capable of directing our own lives and co-existing with others; *surplus* repression makes us into monogamous heterosexual bourgeois patriarchal capitalists … – that is, *if* it works. If it doesn't, the result is either a neurotic or a revolutionary (or both), and if revolutionaries account for a very small proportion of the population, neurotics account for a very large one' (2003: 64; emphasis in original). Consequently, Wood described the basic pattern of the horror film as 'normality is threatened by the Monster' (2003: 71). The Monster signifies Otherness, a concept whose 'psychoanalytic significance resides in the fact that it functions not simply as something external to the culture or to the self, but also as what is repressed (though never destroyed) in the self and projected outward in order to be hated and disowned' (2003: 66). Although this figure of Otherness represents the re-emergence 'of all that our civilisation represses or oppresses' (2003: 68), Wood, like many other writers on horror, places a particular emphasis on sex: 'in a society built on monogamy and family there will be an enormous surplus of repressed sexual energy, and that what is repressed must always strive to return' (2003: 72).[28]

As if aware of Wood's argument, *The Howling* opens with Waggner, in a television interview, opining:

> Repression is the father of neurosis, of self-hatred. Now, stress results when we fight against our impulses. We've all heard people talk about animal magnetism, the natural man, the noble savage – as if we'd lost something valuable in our long evolution into civilised human beings. Now, there's a

good reason for this. Man is a combination of the learned and the instinctual, of the sophisticated and the primitive. We should never try to deny the beast, the animal, within us.

Brandner's novel draws a crude equation between lycanthropy and 'a savage, abandoned kind of sex, a kind he had never known' in which 'desire for the woman overpowered his every civilized thought' (1978: 97). Although the film lacks the novel's explicitness, it does maintain a similar connection: in the sex shop, Quist, while he transforms, forces Karen to watch violent pornography in which a woman is tied to a bed, gagged and raped by two men. Later, the fragmentary recollection of this rape scene overlays her inability to remember what happened in the booth, rendering Bill's attempted intimacies too traumatic to pursue (and Bill himself becomes a werewolf because of wounds received during sex with the purportedly nymphomaniac Marsha).

In his discussion of *The Texas Chain Saw Massacre* (1974), Wood notes an interesting inversion of genre norms: 'normality is clearly represented by the quasi-liberated, permissive young' and 'the monster is the family' (2003: 80; see also Bould 2003). In *The Howling*, the main source of the horror is the family – the Quist siblings – and the Colony of which they are a part and, despite Waggner's words quoted above, it is clear that he created this community by encouraging repression, by convincing its members to abandon the old ways so that they can pass unnoticed in human society.[29] *The Howling* also shares something of *The Texas Chain Saw Massacre*'s apocalyptic sensibility. There is talk of an increasingly violent society, and the police who patrol the red light district sense a growing tide of human 'flotsam and jetsam'. Waggner describes Quist's murders in terms of right-brain dominance, linking the non-rational and the creative in the human brain, and Karen's final words link the werewolves to the 'struggle between what is kind and peaceful in our natures and what is cruel and violent'. Such moments suggest a universalisation of the beast within, that the Colony is not an anomaly but a microcosm, and although the principal action is resolved with Karen's death, Marsha, her *doppelgänger*, remains at large. Representing all that Karen has repressed but which, in Wood's words, 'can never be annihilated' (2003: 78), she will surely return. This is reinforced by the clip from *The Wolf Man* that follows the end credits. Although it is shown on a television screen, it occupies an extra-diegetic space and, tongue-in-cheek, directly addresses the audience as within it the old gypsy woman Maleva (Maria Ouspenskaya) dismisses Larry Talbot (Lon Chaney, Jr), recently bitten by a werewolf, with the words, 'Go now and heaven help you'.

Piranha (Joe Dante, 1978) *and Alligator* (Lewis Teague, 1980)

Of the 'five recurrent motifs' that Wood claims 'have dominated the horror films since the '60s', he notes that it is in the revenge-of-nature film that the 'connection' between the family and the Monster 'is most tenuous and intermittent' (2003: 75), and this is reflected to a certain degree in *Piranha* and *Alligator*. Far more significant, however, is their success in uncovering a repeated slippage in Wood's work between repression and oppression, and their related treatment, albeit awkward, of Sayles' concern with the ways in which material determinants are experienced by individuals. Wood suggests that:

> One might perhaps define repression as fully internalized oppression (while reminding ourselves that all the groundwork of repression is laid in infancy), thereby suggesting both the difference and the connection. A specific example may make this clearer: our social structure demands the repression of the bisexuality that psychoanalysis shows to be the natural heritage of every human individual and the oppression of homosexuals: obviously the two phenomena are not identical, but equally obviously they are closely connected. What escapes repression has to be dealt with by oppression. (2003: 64)

In this passage, Wood first suggests that repression is internalised oppression, and then that it is a mechanism for mopping up those socially undesirable tendencies which have not been successfully repressed. His focus on repression leads him to marginalise questions of oppression, even though his first formulation attributes primacy to oppression and considers repression merely as a special case of oppression.

It is worth recalling at this point some of the critical, theoretical and political preoccupations of the historical moment in the second half of the 1970s when Wood wrote his seminal essay. Central to the counterculture of the late 1960s and early 1970s and, to a lesser degree the New Left, was the desire to develop a critique of consumer capitalism without necessarily rejecting the pleasures it offered. In the work of Marcuse and others, unrestrained sexuality came to signify the pleasure and freedom of which the commodity was a mere shadow form. The period also witnessed a growing concern that Marxism did not really possess a theory of the subject. This was exemplified by the turn against structuralist-Marxism, and in particular against Louis Althusser's model of ideology. Althusser (1971) argues that the subject is always-already hailed or interpellated by ideology; that is, the subject is a linguistic, discursive and ideological construct. Because of the simple version of causality which dominated the understanding of this model, it seemed to offer a crudely mechanistic notion of the subject as nothing more than a position, or series of positions, within ideology (see Bould 2002). Consequently, Althusser was by and large rejected in favour of Antonio Gramsci (whose work influenced Althusser, but was translated into English later), whose concept of hegemony implies a more fluid causality and the possibility of a social subjectivity able to negotiate with and resist ideology's attempts to position it, and Marxism turned increasingly to psychoanalytic theory for a model of the subject. In short, and as Wood's work implies, cultural criticism became more interested in the subject than the apparatus (whether state or cinematic), in repression rather than oppression.

Waggner's commentary at the start of *The Howling* betrays a similar slippage to that found in Wood's discussion of the horror film. He refers to that which has been lost 'in our long evolution into civilised human beings', a problematic phrase, redolent of Social Darwinism, which blends the cultural (civilised) into the biological (evolution into human beings). By normalising repression in this way – locating the source of social ills in the beast that lurks within us all, and emphasising internalised management of the self as the means of combating the ever-impending apocalypse – Waggner conceals its actual source in oppression. This is reinforced by *The Howling*'s portrayal of lycanthropy, the signifier of that which is repressed, as a less than desirable condition, and by its generally negative, even contemptuous, treatment of those who fail to heed Karen's warning. *Piranha* and *Alligator* deal with such matters in a markedly different way.

Noting Hollywood's tendency since the 1970s to make its 'own exploitation movies', but with sufficiently high budgets 'that they tend not to *look* like exploitation movies', Jim Hillier quotes 'an anonymous Universal executive' as saying 'What was *Jaws*, but an old Corman monster-from-the-deep flick – plus about $12 million for production and advertising?' (1993: 47; emphasis in original).[30] It is only appropriate, then, that New World should produce *Piranha*, probably the best of the many *Jaws* rip-offs, and one which, like *Alligator*, sustained a left-liberal social satire, the critical element typical of Corman pictures usually erased in Hollywood's big-budget co-optations of his exploitation aesthetic.

Jaws – a cross between *The Birds* (1963) and *Rio Bravo* (1959) – is clearly a Watergate-era film. It indicts the mayor of Amity and those who collude with him for downplaying and covering-up the shark attacks, regardless of the cost in human lives, in order to keep the beaches open and the tourist dollars flooding in; but it transposes the 'real' threat to society onto something from outside of society (the shark), and suggests, as in *All the President's Men* (1976), that there is nothing wrong with the existing social order, that it can be redeemed, just as long as good men – and for much of *Jaws* women do not seem to exist – play their part. *Piranha* is not the straightforward revenge-of-nature movie exemplified by *The Birds* or *Jaws*. In both of those films, no material explanation is provided for the upheavals in the natural world, and, in the absence of a clear cause, a reactionary motivation is found in active female sexuality. *The Birds* suggests that the avian assaults are connected to the sexual desire of Melanie Daniels (Tippi Hedren), symbolised by the lovebirds – and the disruption – she brings to a mother-dominated household. *Jaws* is more ambiguous, although the first shark attack is again occasioned by female desire and the shark cannot be defeated until the men remove themselves from the company of women and form a homosocial bond. In both films, as one supposedly natural order is upset so is another. In contrast, *Piranha*, which filters 1950s monster and giant insect films as well as the revenge-of-nature movie through a countercultural distrust of the state, suggests a more complex, not to say reasonable, notion of causation and, ultimately, responsibility.

Piranha does open with sexual horseplay, in which Barbara (Jane Squire) is more dominant than David (Roger Richman). This leads to the first attack, in which David and then Barbara are killed by a school of genetically-engineered piranhas. While searching for the missing teenagers, it is Maggie (Heather Menzies) who releases the piranhas into the river (in the shooting script, it is Paul (Bradford Dillman) who does so); and later on it is hinted that Dr Hoak (Kevin McCarthy) continued his experiments after Operation Razorteeth was officially closed down either because of the failure of his relationship with Dr Menger (Barbara Steele), or her manipulation of him, or his jealousy of her greater professional success. To this extent, then, *Piranha* follows the revenge-of-nature pattern, blaming women for their usurpation of the active role, whether sexual or professional. However, it distinguishes itself from its more illustrious precursors by not only failing to punish Maggie for her presumption and permitting her an active role in destroying the piranhas, but also by refusing the misogynistic metaphysics and ideological obfuscations which tend to underpin the revenge-of-nature universe.

In *The Beast from 20,000 Fathoms* (1953) a nuclear blast awakens a rhedosaurus and in *Them!* (1954) the radiation from atomic tests mutates ants to gigantic proportions. In such films, the military tend to be doubly exonerated: these monsters are unintended side effects, and thus the military are not held responsible for their revival or creation, and it is the military who ultimately dispose of the threat. *Piranha* has no time for the fiction of the side effect. On their way downriver to warn people of the piranhas' presence, Hoak reveals all:

> Of course [the government] paid. Whether it's germ warfare, the bomb, chemical warfare, there's plenty of money. Special agencies. They pay. They pay a lot better than they do in private research ... To destroy the river systems of the North Vietnamese. Our goal was to develop a strain of this killer fish that could survive in cold water and then breed at an accelerated rate. We had everything. Blank cheque. And then – the war ended ... They poisoned the water. After all that work, they poisoned the water ... We developed a lot of mutants and a few of them were able to resist the poison. They ate their own, their own dead, and then began to breed like some wild species. Suddenly there were hundreds, maybe thousands ... Well, that's science in the service of the defence effort ... I never killed anybody. If you want to talk about killing, you talk to your politicians, the military people. No, no, I'm a scientist ... It was pure research. No scrounging for grant money, no academic politics. You don't know what that means to a scientist ... I continued the experiment. There was so much more I could do with the species. So much further I could take them. You're not holding me responsible? I think you are. You pulled the plug, and you're holding me responsible. Incredible. You're blaming me.

In this extended exposition, efficiently blending back-story and characterisation, *Piranha* demonstrates an awareness of the overdetermination of events and the complexity of responsibility. Hoak is responsible for the piranhas' attacks to the extent of his complicity with the military project, but that complicity is itself the complex product of a desire to undertake scientific research in an environment which has largely subjugated such activity to military or commercial objectives, the notion of 'pure research' being as much a fantasy as the 'side effect'. When he finally recognises that this does not free him from responsibility, he sacrifices himself to save a child, but *Piranha* circumscribes the effectiveness of this intervention by one good man. Beyond saving the life for which he clumsily (and perhaps unnecessarily) exchanges his own, this action has no consequences. Whereas *Jaws* reaffirms the social order through such

Piranha: the piranhas … they're eating the guests

interventions, it is only after Hoak's death that *Piranha*'s cynical critique of the social order commences in earnest.

While neither profound nor especially radical, this critique dismisses *Jaws*' displacement of responsibility for the nature of the social order onto an anomaly arising from outside. Like the killer mutant babies of *It's Alive* (1974) and its sequels, the piranhas are the product of the social order, here represented by a secretive military in cahoots with a corrupt real-estate/entertainment business which is busy repackaging shoddy secondhand attractions for a quick profit while the piranhas eat the guests. This satirical vision looks forward to postmodernist formulations of America as the desert of the real – effectively captured in *Sunshine State* – while retaining a counter-cultural sensibility which limits the success of Paul and Maggie's heroic interventions. Menger has already let slip that this might not be the first time the piranhas have escaped, and, having previously made it clear that the security of her position is 'more important than a few people's lives', the movie closes with her continued collusion with the military. Despite certain knowledge that the piranhas can survive in both fresh and salt water, she reassures a reporter that sea water will kill them. Although in a proximate sense, the actions of Paul and Maggie, like Hoak's sacrifice, have meaning, it is made clear that the social order they restore is deeply compromised and possibly beyond redemption.

A similar pattern can be found in *Alligator*. In the opening sequence, an alligator-wrestling bout goes wrong. Despite witnessing the savage attack, in which the wres-tler's leg is torn apart, young Marisa (Leslie Brown) buys a baby alligator. Her parents are less than thrilled, and one day when she is at school her father flushes her pet down the toilet. Twelve years later, an alligator – possibly the same one – is found living in the sewers. Feeding on the remains of puppies which have been the subject of illegal growth hormone experiments, it has grown to giant size and started eating people. Marisa (Robin Riker), now a leading herpetologist, teams up with a disaffected cop, David (Robert Forster), to track it down.

Marisa, like Maggie, is self-assured and sexually confident (although she still lives with her mother). A psychoanalytic reading of the movie might suggest that her focus on her career is derived from seeing the alligator's assault on phallic masculinity and from her father's early death from overwork. This would also explain her attraction to the older David since his male pattern baldness, the subject of a running joke, represents a similarly compromised masculinity: he is uncomfortable with aspects of his job and other cops do not want to work with him because some years earlier he surrendered his gun to a criminal who then shot his partner with it. The alligator could, then, be seen as symbolic of a repressed aspect of Marisa's sexuality which must emerge and wreak havoc before she can successfully transfer her desire from her absent father to David. In this respect, and following Barbara Creed's (1993) analysis of *Alien* (1979), much could also be made of the movie's extended use of sewer tunnels. However, the sewers do not so much resemble the female interiors of *Alien* – or even *Them!*, in which the giant ants nest in a storm drain – but *The Third Man* (1949), in which Harry Lime (Orson Welles) emerges as a monster not from outside of the authoritarian social order but as a product of it, prepared to rationalise his profiteering and dismiss its human costs. As such, he is a model capitalist, and the sewers, in which he freely comes and goes between the different sectors of postwar Vienna, suggest the less savoury interconnections of a social order which elsewhere – in the casual collusion between the various armies of occupation – is officially sanctioned. Similarly, *Alligator* devotes considerable attention to the systematically corrupt interweaving of big business and city government. When David's investigation gets too close to the endemic malpractice of Slade Pharmaceutical, which includes illegal research and dumping failed experiments into the sewer system, Slade (Dean Jagger) merely phones the mayor, who has David sacked. In the screenplay this interconnection is even closer as the story is set in Slade City.[31]

But like all good monsters, the alligator returns to destroy its creators. At the start of the film, as Marisa's father heads upstairs to flush her pet alligator down the toilet, in the background, clearly audible, is a television report on the 1968 Chicago police riot, in which Mayor Daley ordered the brutal suppression of those gathered to protest and demonstrate outside the Democratic National Convention. This was no anomaly, particularly not in 1968:

> During the riot following the assassination of Martin Luther King, [Daley] ordered his police to 'shoot to kill any arsonist' and 'shoot to maim or cripple anyone looting a store in our city'. Police wounded 48 and killed four blacks. When students marched against the war in April, Daley dispatched his police, who attacked the peaceful crowd. The mayor's spokesman declared that 'these people have no right to demonstrate or express their views'. (Anderson 1995: 216)

It is unsurprising, then, that twelve years later the alligator should emerge from its hiding place into the ghetto, but then quickly move upmarket, first to the suburbs and then to Slade's rather more exclusive estate, where his daughter (Margie Platt) is about to marry Helms (James Ingersoll), Slade Pharmaceutical's chief scientist. Although the movie does not quite fulfil Sayles' 'original idea … that the alligator eats its way through the whole socio-economic system' (Hillier 1993: 47), it does succeed

Alligator: moving upmarket

in reaching and killing both Slade and the mayor. Clearly, then, despite the alligator's interruption of the wedding, a union which suggests the perpetuation of a corrupt dynasty, the alligator symbolises something more than sexual repression.

After the alligator breaks out from the sewers, the city hires a big game hunter, Colonel Brock (Henry Silva), to track and kill it. Supremely self-confident, he is macho, racist, sexually predatory, hard-drinking and heavily-armed. In the screenplay, he hires four members of a street gang called the Zombies (the implications are clear) whose own names – Hector, Mick, Chi Chi and Tyrone – suggest an ethnically-diverse group among whom a Ramon (the name the young Marisa gave her pet alligator) would not be out of place. Although this connection is muted in the film – an earlier scene with the gang was dropped, the four become three young African-American men – it does retain Brock's scenes with the gang. Outside a liquor store, he offers them ten dollars per day to act as his expedition's 'bearers, its native guides'; when one of them holds outs for twenty dollars, Brock agrees, dubbing him 'the local chieftain'. Later, when they track the alligator to an alleyway, he insists that 'the bearers follow the hunter into the lair, they back him up', but in a neat refutation of the stereotyping of African men in countless jungle films, they are neither overcome by terror nor reduced to creature-fodder, as the leader of the trio responds, 'Not in this jungle, mister'. These interchanges are an early instance of the developing concern, which can be traced through Sayles' films, with language, the ideological interpellation of the subject and the processes of hegemony. Significantly, the gang members tolerate Brock's racist descriptions of them, but do so knowingly in order to get paid. Although they respond to his (ideological) hailing of them, they do not accept, internalise or validate his terminology or the ideological positioning it implies; his words mark out the borderline separating their worlds, a demarcation already suggested by his character, which belongs on a different continent in an earlier era and an entirely different genre. Following the turn to Gramsci described above, this quiet refusal and ironisation of Brock's attempted positioning of them might be described as a form of resistance; but a more careful reading of Gramsci is necessary to grasp the dynamic operating in these brief scenes and to understand their relationship to the film as a whole.

Gramsci argues that the dominant social group 'leads kindred and allied groups' through 'intellectual and moral leadership' but 'dominates antagonistic groups' through the exercise of force, including armed subjugation if necessary (1971: 57). This combination of consent and coercion represents the '"normal" exercise of hegemony' in a 'parliamentary régime'; and when the state resorts to violence 'the attempt is always made to ensure that force will appear to be based on the consent of the majority, expressed by the so-called organs of public opinion' (1971: 80). This description of class domination provides a compelling interpretation of the 1968 Chicago police riot and all that it can be taken to represent in terms of the suppression and dispersal of the countercultural movement. However, Gramsci's admittedly fragmented account of hegemony demonstrates a greater concern with the mechanisms and functions of consent, arguing that coercion is in itself an inadequate means of maintaining the dominant class position:

> Undoubtedly the fact of hegemony presupposes that account be taken of the interests and the tendencies of the groups over which hegemony is to be exercised, and that a certain compromise equilibrium should be formed – in other words, that the leading group should make sacrifices of an economic-corporate kind. But there is also no doubt that such sacrifices and such a compromise cannot touch the essential; for though hegemony is ethical-political, it must also be economic, must necessarily be based on the decisive function exercised by the leading group in the decisive nucleus of economic activity. (1971: 161)

In adapting Gramsci's model of hegemony to the study of cultural texts during the last three decades, many critics have overemphasised the voice and power of the groups subjected to and by the exercise of hegemony, and frequently constructed the subject as an entity who reads against the grain or poaches texts and thus resists subordination to the dominant social class (this reached an absurd extreme in John Fiske's equation of 'two secretaries spending their lunch hour browsing through stores with no intention to buy' with the Vietnamese freedom fighters US troops found indistinguishable from 'innocent villagers' (1989: 39)). However, as the above passage indicates, because the compromise between the dominant and subordinated classes 'cannot touch the essential', such actions are not a form of resistance but a means of maintaining some self-esteem while negotiating one's own subordination. In *Alligator*, although the Zombies' mockery and manipulation of Brock is admirable – they are very clearly not what he imagines them to be and, unlike him, they do not get eaten – their 'resistance' does nothing to affect the class and race privilege he represents. They survive merely to survive another day, whereas the alligator – and in this context it is worth remembering that 'alligator' has been used as a racial slur – attacks the members of the power structure which keeps them subordinated. His return is the return of the oppressed.

Gramsci's work offers a further insight into the destruction of the alligator. He argues that before a subordinated class can gain power it 'can (and must) "lead"'; and 'when it is in power it becomes dominant but continues to "lead" as well'. Not

only must there 'be a "political hegemony" even before the attainment of govern-
mental power' but once in government the previously subordinated class 'should not
count solely on the power and material force which such a position gives in order to
exercise political leadership or hegemony' (1971: 57). In contrast to such conscious
revolt, the alligator represents a spontaneous eruption of rage. That this is a no more
effective means of resistance to domination than that demonstrated by the Zombies
is confirmed by the fact that he can only attack functionaries rather than the power
structure itself. Enjoyable as it is to witness his rampage, it is nonetheless the case that
the film sets out to win the audience's consent to his defeat through the construction
of David and Marisa as likeable individuals and an unlikely couple and other narrative conventions. Any twinge of conscience or regret is assuaged by the postscript in
which we see a new flushed-away baby alligator arrive in the sewers. The oppressed
will return again.

The Lady in Red (Lewis Teague, 1979)

Wood's description of the horror film – 'normality is threatened by the Monster' – is
followed by a vital caveat: the term 'normality' is used 'in a strictly non-evaluative sense,
to mean simply "conformity to the dominant social norms"; one must firmly resist the
tendency to treat the word as if it were more or less synonymous with "health"' (2003:
71). Both *Piranha* and *Alligator* share this perspective, demonstrating that it is not
their eponymous creatures but 'normality' that is the real monster. Sayles' screenplay
for *The Lady in Red* constitutes his first significant attempt to produce a cinematic
analysis of that monster.

While the initial idea for this film was Roger Corman's, who had already found
success with gangster films both as director (*Machine Gun Kelly* (1958), *The St Valen-
tines Day Massacre* (1967), *Bloody Mama* (1970)) and as producer (*Boxcar Bertha*
(1972), *Big Bad Mama* (1974)), this time Sayles had neither previous drafts nor a
source text to adapt. At some point, the assignment became, in Sayles' own words, 'a
very personal movie' and he 'seduced New World Pictures into making a movie that
was much classier than they really needed to make or wanted to make' (in Molyneaux
2000: 90). Extensive archival research into life in 1930s Chicago led to a screenplay
which interwove the exploitation thrills required by Corman (as indicated by the film's
alternative titles, *Dillinger's Mistress* and *Guns, Sin and Bathtub Gin*) with a strong
sense of the material determinants of Polly Franklin's (Pamela Sue Martin) seemingly
inevitable trajectory – not unlike that of the protagonist of Stephen Crane's *Maggie:
A Girl of the Streets* (1893) – into a life of prostitution, doomed romance, violence
and crime. Anticipating his later historical epics *Matewan* and *Eight Men Out*, it was
135 pages long with seventy speaking parts and a period setting. When the budget on
Lewis Teague's directorial debut was suddenly reduced to $800,000, Sayles worked
with him to cut the screenplay to about 100 pages. Further pruning left a movie of
just ninety minutes, in which, according to Sayles, 'all the scenes where the people
machine-gun other people are left in ... and the ones that explain why the people are
machine-gunning other people are gone' (in Schlesinger 1999: 22).[32] However, even as

this compromised version shows that Cormanesque exploitation tends to close down the possibility of political filmmaking (except the type to which Haskell Wexler refers, which is not normally considered political), a number of concerns which recur in Sayles' own films do emerge: the recovery of lost voices and histories; the living-out of material determinants; the disastrous impact of capitalism on ordinary lives; the role of the media in the usurpation of the real by the simulacral. Consequently, *The Lady in Red* is important to an understanding of Sayles' films, not least in terms of their depiction of capitalist modernity.

Carl Freedman argues that 'modernism' and 'postmodernism' are not to be understood in relation to formal or stylistic distinctions: 'any properly *aesthetic* distinction … between [them] must come to grief' (2000: 183; emphasis in original) on the proliferating qualifications, exceptions and special cases which inevitably follows the erection of such schemes. The response to this problem is not to abandon the terminology of the postmodern and 'declare that there is simply *modernism*' but 'to *historicize* the terms of the comparison radically' (2000: 184; emphasis in original): 'What now needs to be stressed about the modernist era is that … modernism sprang from a socio-economic matrix in which the power of essentially *pre*modern survivals was still considerable and in many ways even dominant, and in which the struggle between the modern and the premodern was especially intense … Modernism was produced by a modernity that still had many of its decisive battles yet to win against the forces of aristocracy, agrarianism, royalism, and religious reaction' (2000: 186–7; emphasis in original). The peculiar historical moment of modernism accounts not only for the stylistic and formal diversity of the modernists, but also their political variance from the extreme right to the far left. Moreover, because America was the nation 'in which the process of social modernization was most advanced and premodern survivals the weakest' (2000: 187), it was there that modernity was most readily embraced. World War Two, widely accepted as a convenient chronological marker of the shift from the modern to the postmodern, was also

> the epoch-making social upheaval that radically redrew the balance of forces between archaic survival and deepening modernization, overwhelmingly to the advantage of the latter. The new era inaugurated in 1945 – characterized by the increasing multinationalization of monopoly capital and by the growing pre-eminence of nuclear, electronic, and computer technologies – is thus one in which modernity has to an unprecedented degree come into its own: so that modernity is no longer so elaborately defined by a vital agon with its premodern other. This, the era of postmodernity, might therefore more usefully be called the era of *pure* modernity – which means, particularly within the metropolitan nations of what used to be called the First World, an era in which capital itself is now more untrammeled than at any previous point in history. Postmodernity, we might say, is the era in which capitalist modernization is so thoroughly triumphant that, owing to the lack of contrast on which visibility depends, it becomes somewhat difficult to see. (2000: 187–8; emphasis in original)

Freedman quotes Jameson's depiction of the postmodern condition as the situation 'in which late-capitalism has all but succeeded in eliminating the final loopholes of nature and the Unconscious, of subversion and the aesthetic, of individual and collective praxis alike, and, with a final filip, in eliminating any memory trace of what thereby no longer existed in the henceforth postmodern landscape' (see Jameson 1990: 5). However, Freedman qualifies this position by emphasising 'the importance of the "all but" in *all but succeeded*' (2000: 188; emphasis in original), insisting that 'we must leave open the possibility not only of authentic subversion (which may well be nearly impossible to imagine concretely today) but also, and more ominously, the possibility of a yet more postmodern – that is, a more completely modernized and commodified – age than our own' (2000: 188–9).

Within this framework, one can apprehend the ways in which Sayles' films are riddled with traces of the conflict between premodern and modern forms. For example, in *Eight Men Out*, 'Shoeless' Joe Jackson (D. B. Sweeney) stands for an idealised vision of baseball rooted in a rural past, and Eddie Cicotte (David Strathairn) represents values like decency, honesty and fair play which the forces of modernity, embodied in club owner Charles Comiskey (Clifton James) and gambler Arnold Rothstein (Michael Lerner), discard in their pursuit of profit. In different ways, Buck Weaver (John Cusack) and the journalists Ring Lardner (John Sayles) and Hugh Fullerton (Studs Terkel) negotiate between these premodern and modern positions. In *Passion Fish* and *The Secret of Roan Inish*, the protagonists retreat from the urban into premodern rural settings in order to construct alternative worlds; this movement recurs in darker tones in *Limbo*, where the wilderness contrasts with the postmodern thematisation of nature, but is not permitted to become a bucolic idyll.

The Lady in Red can be described almost entirely in terms of this conflict. The film opens with Polly finding some slight relief from farm chores by singing and dancing to herself in the barn while she collects the hens' eggs to take to town. Ruth Levitas argues that 'We learn a lot about the experience of living under any set of conditions by reflecting upon the desires which those conditions generate and yet leave unfulfilled. For that is the space which utopia occupies' (1990: 8). Under capital, that utopian space is often represented by entertainment, which, as Richard Dyer explains, 'offers the image of "something better" to escape into, or something we want deeply that our day-to-day lives don't provide. Alternatives, hopes, wishes – these are the stuff of utopia, the sense that things could be better, that something other than what is can be imagined and maybe realised' (1985: 222). This is not to say that entertainment 'presents models of utopian worlds' but that its 'utopianism is contained in the feelings it embodies' (ibid.).[33] The pathetic spectacle of Polly's rendition of '42nd Street' captures some sense of this hope and desire for a modern world free from deprivation and the tedium of daily labour, but it is heavily counterweighted by her surroundings and the inertial drag of the premodern, represented by her father, a brutal and fanatically religious man who rejects the modern as inherently iniquitous. For once, putting on a show in the barn does not offer symbolic resolution to scarcity, exhaustion, dreariness and fragmentation, but instead begins to open up the gulf between the social tensions, inadequacies and absences identified by Dyer and solutions which are merely symbolic. (The viewer is constantly reminded of this gulf by the soundtrack's ironic repetitions of a distinctive passage from '42nd Street'.) Deprived of the imagined utopian modernity, Polly steals the publicity photos for *42nd Street* (1933) from her local cinema's display window, an act which signifies her marginalisation from the processes of modernisation: she can get no closer than these stolen reified fragments of a commercialised fantasy of the utopian sensation for which she yearns.

This theft is witnessed by a woman in a red dress which Polly openly admires. Their brief exchange is interrupted by a gang of robbers bursting out of the bank opposite. The woman, their lookout, takes Polly as a hostage, forcing her to ride on the running-board of the getaway car. For a few brief minutes, Polly is swept up in a very modern world of automobiles, guns and a high-speed chase, but as soon as the police are eluded she is dumped by the roadside. The police station at which she is questioned swarms with newspaper reporters insisting that it must have been the Dillinger gang and determined to find any uncertainty or ambiguity in her account which will enable them to make such claims. (As Polly will later discover, newspapers are more concerned with providing thrilling entertainment for their readers than in anything as mundane as veracity: a press subordinated to profit-making is not a free press.) After the police finish with Polly, she is picked up by Jake Lingle (Robert Hogan), a reporter who offers to replace her torn and dirty dress. He takes her to his hotel room, ostensibly to photograph her in her new red dress. Instead, although she is a virgin and scared of her father, she is persuaded to sleep with him; afterwards, he kicks her out. When she returns home, her father beats her.

This opening section introduces the techniques and themes of the more substantial story to follow. Rejecting the fantastic mode of other early screenplay assignments, *The Lady in Red* does not resort to fantastic imaginary beings to represent the impact of capitalist modernity on individuals and communities. Rather than relying on the symbolic capacity of the monster, the movie delineates an individual – Polly – in such a way as to make her extraordinary story a representative one. In doing so, Sayles attempts a reconciliation of naturalism of the kind Lukács dismissed with the kind of realism he praised. In his 1936 essay 'Narrate or Describe?', Lukács quotes at length Zola's account of his method so as to deride it as capable of only producing description:

> A naturalistic novelist wants to write a novel about the world of the theatre. He starts out with this general idea *without possessing a single fact or character*. His first task will be to take notes on what he can learn about the world he wants to describe. He has known this actor, attended that performance ... will speak with the people who are best informed about his material, he will collect anecdotes, character portraits ... read documents. *Finally* he will visit the locale itself ... spend *some days* in a theatre to become familiar with the minutest details ... his evenings in the dressing room of an actress and will absorb the atmosphere as much as possible. And once this documentation is complete, the novel will write itself ... *Interest is no longer concentrated on originality of plot; on the contrary, the more* banal and general it is, the more typical it becomes. (1978b: 120; emphasis in original)

The Lady in Red: the underworld meets the elite

When Sayles began work on the screenplay, he had no central character beyond knowing that on one specific night she must leave a cinema with Dillinger. David Chute notes the 'extensive research' Sayles undertook to produce a script 'rich in social observation' (1999: 10). Gerry Molyneaux writes that, to 'avoid past script formula treatment', Sayles 'turned to the Chicago Historical Society records, especially to its documents about the working people' and wrote 'a screenplay supported with sociological insights' into the period (2000: 90); and he reports Pamela Sue Martin's recollection that the original script 'had all sorts of political innuendoes and things about unions, all of which were butchered out' (2000: 92). The film itself, with its curious pacing and obvious gaps, produces not only a sense of too much going on for its short running time but also of it having been intended as a detailed account of a particular social environment. Despite the media's creation of the Lady in Red as some kind of femme fatale, to which the film draws specific attention, Polly is just an ordinary young woman, a typical character. There is a correspondingly attenuated sense of her interiority. Lukács criticises Dos Passos for his development of this approach, noting of *Manhattan Transfer* (1925) 'that the characters either fall into no relationships at all or at best transient and superficial relationships, that they appear suddenly and just as suddenly disappear, and that they take no active part in a plot but merely promenade with varying attitudes through the externalised objective world described in the novel' (1978: 135). What Lukács seems particularly to deplore in this naturalism is that it 'levels' rather than establishing proportions, that it does not lend itself to the creation of 'a central figure in whose life all the important extremes in the world of the novel converge and around whom a complete world with all its vital contradictions can be organised' (1978: 142). Such a character, he contends, renders the events depicted as 'inherently significant' (1978: 116) because his or her direct involvement in them functions as an organising principle through which proportion can be established. The Hollywood narrative tradition which Sayles had to attempt to reconcile with his Zolaesque researches itself favours a form of centration on a protagonist, whose path through the world/narrative of the film organises it for the viewer, albeit in a form consistent with the commercial operations of the star system. Consequently, Polly is a character in whom the extremes of the film's world converge, a figure in whom, like the 42nd Street of the song, 'the underworld can meet the elite', but one who never rises above her typicality. Longing for the utopian modernity represented by the glamour and excitement of films, red dresses and car chases, she is soon caught in the alienated and alienating machinery of that world, represented by Lingle, who has no qualms about making her into a sexual commodity to be bought with a cheap red dress. But for Polly, the dress signifies something important and, despite Lingle's lesson in the ways of capitalist modernity, she finds she cannot stay on her father's farm and runs away to Chicago.

She goes to work in a sweatshop, a job which should provide her with the necessary schooling in the process of commodity fetishism but does not quite. There, she is attacked by a co-worker, Mae (Terri Taylor), who is sleeping with the sleazy boss Patek (Dick Miller), for the marginally better hourly rate and job security it provides, and who feels threatened by the passing attention Patek pays to Polly. The fight is broken up by another lady in red, the socialist Rose Shimkus (Laurie Heineman), who befriends Polly, gives her a home and shows her the ropes, offering such ambiguous advice as 'You've got to become part of the machine' and 'You don't put out more than that, he'll can you', and noting, more ironically, 'Six, seven bucks a week, you've got the world by the balls'.

When Mae miscarries at work, Patek, who denies the child is his, takes the opportunity to set thugs from the Industrial Squad on to Rose. As she is dragged away, Polly leads a workplace rebellion. She stands up to Patek, but he fires her and tells the other women to get back to work. In an inspired borrowing from *Spartacus* (1960), someone yells 'Fuck you, Patek', and when he demands to know who said it, someone who clearly did not say it takes responsibility; and then another, and then another. Experiencing a rudimentary class-consciousness, the women rise up and bombard Patek with garments and scraps of material. Prominent among the items thrown is, of course, a red dress, and this is a significant pointer in the film's analysis of the modern capitalist social order: although Polly's plight is articulated quite strongly around the experience of working-class women and gendered oppression, there remains an irreducible element of her story which is about the class oppression fundamental to capitalism. This potential to be representative of all workers, not just female workers, offers an important parallel to the processes whereby a class-consciousness which is sensitive to the particular circumstances of individuals can emerge: antagonistic to neither the subject nor identity politics, it is fundamentally a politics of identification.

In *The Condition of the Working-Class in England* (1845), Friedrich Engels noted that 'as a matter of course ... factory servitude, like any other ... confers the *jus primae noctis* upon the master ... The threat of discharge suffices to overcome all resistance in nine cases out of ten, if not in ninety-nine out of a hundred, in girls who, in any case, have no strong inducements to chastity' (1975: 442; emphasis in original). Later, he describes this as just one of many respects in which 'the operative is his employer's slave' (1975: 470), and records a witness report of 'girls who had good work, and who had worked overtime, who, nevertheless, betook themselves to a life of prostitution rather than submit to [the] tyranny' (1975: 469) of the factory owner's power to arbitrarily extend the working day. A similar regime is found in Patek's sweatshop, and although Polly's departure is forced upon her – after the rebellion, the film cuts to her looking for work – she soon finds herself compelled by poverty into prostitution. With growing disillusionment – at the unemployment office she identifies herself ironically as Ruby Keeler – she takes a job at a dance hall, but the other girls convince her that the five cents she is paid per dance (her first night's work nets her 95 cents) is no way to make a living. On her first attempt at soliciting, she is arrested by an undercover vice cop.

In jail, she is reunited with Rose, who has contracted tuberculosis, a condition made worse by a spell in solitary for standing up to the brutal warden Tiny Alice (Nancy Anne Parsons). When Polly is also threatened with solitary for defending Rose from Tiny Alice, she agrees to participate in 'the furlough scheme': in exchange for paying Alice $15 per week (plus $5 so that Rose can complete her sentence in the infirmary), Polly is unofficially released and sent to work in a brothel run by Anna Sage (Louise Fletcher). Of her new salary, fifty per cent goes to Anna to cover over-heads, including doctor's bills and a large police bribe. A further 25 per cent goes to the mobster Luciano. Tiny Alice's cut is deducted from what is left. Ironically, despite the nature and illegality of her work and the substantial surplus-value being extracted from her labour, Polly is better off financially than she has ever been. However, the cost to Polly is also high, as she becomes hardened to the life into which she has been forced (Lingle is one of her customers, another makes her pretend he is her daddy). Turk (Robert Forster), the one customer who treats her with some decency, turns out to be a hitman, and when she refuses to identify him to Elliot Ness (Phillip R. Allen) as the murderer of the deputy mayor, it is unclear whether she is motivated by fear or gratitude. She certainly has no reason to trust the police.

Polly's alienation is manifested in the way in which she clings to her dream of becoming a star. That she recognises the discrepancy between this and her actual life is evident in the lies she tells Rose about having a respectable job as a dancer; and that these lies are desirable ones must account for Rose's credulity. When Tiny Alice boasts about making Polly a prostitute, Rose attacks her but is stabbed to death. In an echo of the sweatshop rebellion, the other prisoners turn on Tiny Alice and kill her as a rudimentary consciousness of their shared position bursts out in rage. Although Polly cannot know that her friend's death is among the costs of her job, the loss of her other best friend, Satin (Chip Fields), is attributable to a risk all the prostitutes face: she is butchered by Frognose (Christopher Lloyd), a psychotic mobster whose presence is tolerated because he works for Luciano.

When Anna is forced to close down the brothel, she tries to turn legitimate, opening a diner with the help of Polly, Pinetop (Rod Gist), Pops Geissler (Peter Hobbs) and Eddie (Glenn Withrow); and Polly begins to dream again of escape. She falls in love with Jimmy Lawrence (Robert Conrad), a regular customer who, unknown to her, is really Dillinger, and together they plan to move to California. Significantly, in the montage which establishes their romance he teaches her how to play baseball in the tall grass of an idealised country setting; and they speak of California as being a freer, less regulated place where they can leave their lives and identities behind. This premodern fantasy contrasts sharply with the film's predominantly urban and interior settings.

Anna, meanwhile, has invested in a more modern world, seeing her new business as the next stage of her trajectory away from the harrowing form of prostitution into which she was forced when she first arrived in the US, and from her criminal past. But she is not allowed to escape. Immigration officials pressurise her into informing on her underworld connections, and with the help of Lingle and the corrupt cop Hennessey (Buck Young) she betrays Dillinger. When Dillinger is shot down outside the Biograph Theatre, Lingle is on hand to finally photograph Polly in a red dress and ensure that she is portrayed as Dillinger's betrayer and an informer, putting her life in danger. She kills the hitmen Frognose sends after her, and Pinetop kills Frognose but Lingle escapes (only to be killed later by Turk, repaying his debt to Polly). With Pinetop, Pops and Eddie, she robs the Mob's own bank, but it goes wrong. Only Polly survives, escaping with the money, yet any pleasure the viewer can take in this is compromised by two incidents in the final moments of the film. Fleeing on foot across country, Polly finds a girl not unlike her younger self toiling on an isolated farm and demands that she give her her dress. This reworking of parts of the opening sequence – a farmgirl meets a glamorous female criminal; a dress is exchanged – suggests that what befell Polly can and will happen all over again to other women and other workers. There is no escape, and this is underlined when the truck driver from whom Polly hitches a lift to California asks her if she has ever been 'all the way'. For a moment, this seems like a sexual advance, but he is only enquiring whether she has been to the ocean before. Anna could not escape into the modern, and Dillinger could not escape into the premodern, and although Polly seems optimistic about the future, this wordplay implies that she too might not be able to leave her old life behind, casting a darker shadow over her future.

The screenplay for *The Lady in Red* is an important precursor to Sayles' own films, establishing the dialectical conflict between the premodern and the modern which increasingly underpins his understanding of both historical and contemporary settings. Polly also represents Sayles' first portrait of a modern subject 'impelled', as Mohamed Zayani notes of naturalist protagonists of the 1890s, 'by the compulsion to repeat that is at the core of capitalism' (1999: 112). Jennifer L. Fleissner argues that the typical naturalist plot concerning the modern young woman 'is marked by neither the steep arc of decline nor that of triumph, but rather by an ongoing, nonlinear, repetitive motion – back and forth, around and around, on and on – that has the distinctive effect of seeming also like a stuckness in place' (2004: 9). This not only describes Polly – compelled to repeat the same actions, whether those of a seamstress, waitress or prostitute, without ever really getting anywhere – but also many of Sayles' other female characters, including *Lone Star*'s 'tightly-wound' Bunny (Frances McDormand), *Limbo*'s self-harming Noelle (Vanessa Martinez) and each of the six would-be mothers in *Casa de los Babys*, all of whom I discuss in some detail below. However, perhaps the most important aspect of *The Lady in Red* to note in considering Sayles' career is that although he has continued to write and rewrite screenplays for other people he has, on the evidence of the finished films, never again invested so much energy and hope in projects he would not himself direct.

CHAPTER THREE

Nothing to Lose But Chains: *Return of the Secaucus Seven*, *Lianna*, *Baby It's You and The Brother from Another Planet*

This chapter begins by engaging with some of the early criticism of Sayles' films. It addresses the still fairly commonplace complaint that he is not a particularly visual director, analysing sequences from *Return of the Secaucus Seven* to demonstrate how careful shot construction is central to the creation of meaning even in his first film. It then responds to the widespread criticism *Lianna* drew from lesbian audiences and critics by focusing on two aspects of the film: firstly, Sayles' developing visual style; secondly, the commitment of his films to depicting multiple determinants of 'two-sided' social being and the various relational webs we inhabit. *Baby It's You* carefully establishes this social totality, taking a high-school romance past graduation and into a world in which barriers of class and ethnicity, both internal and external, operate ambivalently, while also demonstrating the power of the commodity-image in American life – a critique developed still further in *The Brother from Another Planet*. This chapter closes by reintroducing the question of language, which will be further developed in later chapters.

Return of the Secaucus Seven (1980)

Sayles' debut film as director builds on his earlier fiction, echoing 'At the Anarchists' Convention' (1979b) in its return in later life to those whose radicalism has been lost or marginalised while, like *Pride of the Bimbos* (1975), detailing the inescapability of personal and social history through a narrative decentred across an ensemble. Its characters are the people the 1960s radicals of *Union Dues* might have become, and like that novel it charts the contrast between working-class, geographically-located communities and dispersed middle-class friendship groups and social networks, emphasising the ways in which shared histories, geographies and narratives make communities. It explores the shifting, permeable boundaries of social classes; the tensions between lived and overly-mediated experience; the displacement of 'truth' by image; the limitations of political structures which reduce opposition to tactical manoeuvrings within a dominant strategic system; and the impossibility, and powerful pull, of the American Dream, represented most strongly by J.T. (Adam Lefevre), the first of Sayles' hopeful singers probably doomed never to escape their constrained circumstances.

The set-up is simplicity itself, even if the plot it generates becomes rather complex. Every year, Mike Donnelly (Bruce McDonald) and Katie Cipriano (Maggie Renzi) rent a house in Washington Valley, where Mike grew up, and a group of their ex-college friends visit for a weekend. Frances (Maggie Cousineau), who has strong feelings for J.T., decides that this is the year to make her move. Irene Rosenblum (Jean Passanante) brings her new boyfriend, Chip Hollister (Gordon Clapp). Maura Tolliver (Karen Trott) and Jeff (Mark Arnott) cannot come because of his parents' wedding anniversary celebrations. Lacey Summers (Amy Schewel), who is in the summer stock company playing in town, invites them to the Friday night perform-ance. Maura arrives unexpectedly with the news that she and Jeff have split up. After the play, she walks home with J.T. and they sleep together. Frances, who is in the same room, pretends to be asleep. Next day, Jeff appears unannounced. J.T. tells him about sleeping with Maura. Jeff seems to take it in his stride, but during a pick-up basketball match with two of Mike's old high school friends, Ron Desjar-dines (David Strathairn) and Howie (John Sayles), things get out of hand and J.T. is injured. Meanwhile, the women play Cluedo™ and discuss their lives since they last met up. That afternoon, they all mess around in a swimming hole with Ron and Howie; that evening, they have a barbecue and go to a bar. Mike, Howie and Ron reminisce; Jeff and J.T. chat up a couple of women, but decide not to pursue it; Howie leaves to work the nightshift at the hotel; J.T. sings some of his songs; Ron and Frances hit it off, and get a room in the hotel; Katie gets very drunk; Maura and Jeff argue noisily but briefly. The seven who drive home together find a dead deer in the middle of the road. They are questioned by the police but released when a friendly drunk, who used to referee Mike's basketball games, admits to killing the deer. That night, while listening to Katie vomiting, Jeff and J.T. tentatively reaf-firm their friendship. On Sunday morning, Irene offers to invest in J.T.'s recording career, but he will not take her money. Jeff and Maura speak calmly, considerately, while acknowledging that their relationship is over. Chip and Irene set off for home. Frances gives Maura and J.T. a lift to the bus stop – he is broke so Maura insists on paying his fare. Jeff sneaks off, leaving an apologetic goodbye note. Frances falls asleep on the sofa. Mike takes down the volleyball net. Katie wonders what to do with all the eggs they did not use.

Sayles claims writing a script he could direct – and finance – himself, rather than writing-for hire, involved having 'to stop thinking in pictures … and start thinking in budget' (1987a: 5); he further underplays the visual element in his storytelling:

> I concentrated on telling the story through the words of the characters … and the images were more about establishing a certain cultural setting and grouping certain people together than about telling the story in pictures. There are a few mostly visual sequences, most notably the basketball game in which two of the characters vent their sexual jealousy on the court, but this was something we could shoot in a semidocumentary style in a very short time. [The film] was … a story that couldn't be told only in visual terms, no matter how much time, money or experience we had. It is a story about the complex relationships of human beings, and … human beings do most of their communicating verbally. (1987a: 6)

This defence of an unadorned visual style signals the 'often arduous and contradictory efforts' to which the naturalist will go in order 'to eradicate the spectatorial privilege of authorship' (Dudley 2004: 177), simultaneously acknowledging and denying the importance of his organisation of the visual field so as to create meaning, while stripping the basketball game of its complexity. Chip wants to fit in, despite preferring tennis or squash, ill-fitting borrowed shoes and an obvious lack of talent; something of him is caught in his single-minded efforts to score rather than pass the ball. Mike's professed indifference to Ron quickly disappears as he join forces with his old high-school buddies against his less physical college friends, suggesting that they *do* still have something in common (or that for Mike they represent something he has lost). The conflict between J.T. and Jeff only emerges as the game becomes increasingly vigorous, and it seems to be not so much about sexual jealousy as about some reawakened competitiveness between them. Even such a cursory consideration shows the visual element communicating considerably more of the complexity of human relationships than Sayles allows.

Echoing Sayles' own assessment of the greater relative importance of the verbal in *Return of the Secaucus Seven*, Jack Ryan suggests that financial restrictions resulted in a 'pragmatic, realistic cinematic approach, marked by economical camera work that is subservient to the story, the play of his characters' (1998: 53); lacking 'memorable, elaborate imagery', it 'appeals to the ear rather than the eye – speech governs image' (1998: 55). As with much criticism of Sayles' films, he attributes its success entirely to its 'literary elements, story and characters' (ibid.) and thus profoundly underestimates the importance of Sayles' understated visual style. André Bazin argues that 'every realism in art was first profoundly aesthetic' and that the 'flesh and blood of reality are no easier to capture in the net of literature or cinema than are gratuitous flights of the imagination' (1972: 25).[34] While Sayles' visual aesthetic might be sometimes rudimentary in his earliest films, to suggest that it is completely subordinated 'to the story, the play of his characters' is erroneous. Consider, for example, the sequence in the bar when Howie tells Mike about his kids:

Return of the Secaucus Seven: talking (next) to each other

Howie:	You know what it's like? It's like … remember that guy Ace. Ace…
Mike:	Ace Campana.
Howie:	Ace Campana. 11th Grade he buys that old T-Bird…
Ron:	With the lightning bolt painted on the side…
Howie:	…Right, right, and every day after school he's down at the Texaco station pumping gas to pay for the insurance. Every minute of every weekend he's under the fucking thing. He's got grease under his fingernails, grease in the cracks between his teeth…
Ron:	He had a name for it, didn't he?
Howie:	Spitfire, like the fighter plane. He had to do more work to support that fucking car…
Ron:	Yeah, but when he bombed down Main Street…
Howie:	That's my point. That's my point. He felt like a king. That car was like his girlfriend, like his baby, right? Only he didn't have time for anything else. You thought of Ace, you thought of that old T-Bird, like one of those Greek things, the horse ones…
Mike:	Centaurs.
Howie:	Centaurs. Half-man and half-T-Bird. Anyhow, that's what it's like having these kids.
Mike:	It can't be all that bad.
Howie:	It's not that it's bad. It's all the work, all the time you got to put in.

After cutaways to other parts of the bar, the film returns to Howie saying:

And sometimes I'll go out with Carol, and we've got all three of them with us, and none of them is screaming and they're being good, and they're my kids, and I want everybody to look. Stacy, Stacy is, she's a little person, she's got little arms and little legs that work, and she talks now, and she's a person. And she didn't used to be there before. Except for Carol and me, she wouldn't exist. I feel like Ace Campana must've, bombing down Main Street.

Howie struggles to express feelings without sacrificing masculinity, to put something that moves him greatly into words the other men can understand, while Ron and Mike's interjections reveal characters keen to keep discussion more superficial, albeit in different ways. However admirable the quality of the writing, though, it is essential to recognise the role of the visual in generating these meanings. The first half of this sequence is shot with a static camera, showing Ron, Howie and Mike side by side in mid-shot, Ron in profile with Mike and Howie square-on. Their lower bodies are hidden by a partition; behind them is the bustle of a fairly busy bar. The top few buttons of Howie's shirt are undone, and most of the time he is talking he does not look at either of his companions. Throughout, Ron fidgets, sometimes paying attention to a conversation which seems to leave him a little uncomfortable, sometimes turning away. He exchanges a greeting with a man who passes by, fiddles with his drink, raises his hat and wiggles his tongue suggestively at someone out of shot to the right, looks away. Mike's attention is on Howie, but the way he says 'Ace Campana' suggests he would rather reminisce than get caught up in the point Howie is trying to make. His later one-word contribution – 'Centaurs' – reinforces this sense of maintaining distance. When we return to this group, Howie occupies the entire (slightly closer) medium shot, lending weight to his words but also isolating him from Ron and Mike. He is no longer making conversation but working something out for himself. This reverie is abruptly ended after 'bombing down Main Street' as the film cuts back to the wider shot of the three men as Ron asks when Howie must go back to work.

Although this exchange consists of just three shots from two static camera positions, the visual elements work in conjunction with, rather than subordinate to, the dialogue. Central to this is the exaggerated sense of frontality. Initially, the three men sit in a line, unable to look directly at each other, making Howie's slightly drunken sentimentality more plausible. He can share this feeling without compromising his masculinity because he does not have to look at Ron or Mike. Although he does look at them, they are seated so that he is looking away from them and thus chooses when to make eye contact. This sense of isolation is reinforced by the shot of Howie alone. Despite occasionally looking out of shot at Mike, he is caught up in his own thoughts, the edges of the frame protecting him from revealing too much. The cut to the wider shot snaps him back into the world of constant work. There is nothing overtly stylised about this sequence, but its meanings are generated by the interaction of dialogue and *mise-en-scène* (including the positioning of the three men in relation to each other and the camera), the framing and the editing. This is by no means an isolated example.

Throughout the film, careful attention is paid to framing and blocking. Compare, for example, the pair of shots in which Maura 'seduces' J.T. and in which J.T. and Jeff reaffirm their friendship. The first starts with Maura, lying on the sofa, propped up on her left arm, looking down out of the shot from the top right quadrant of the screen. She whispers, 'J.T.', and he sits up into the left half of the frame so that their eyes are on the same level. This single shot is held for over four minutes while they talk, kiss, decide to make love. In the second shot, an hour further into the film, Jeff is lying in his sleeping bag across the bottom of the screen, with his head in the lower left quadrant. J.T., propped up on his left arm, is facing in the other direction and looks down

Return of the Secaucus Seven: left alone

at the reclining Jeff as they talk. Their conversation is conducted in soft, almost post-coital tones. In the first shot, Maura seems the more powerful figure, looking *down* at J.T., and briefly appears a seductress until the more-than-willing J.T. raises himself up to her eye level. In the second shot, J.T. is positioned similarly to Maura, but because Jeff is in the shot from the start, J.T. does not possess a position of seemingly greater power. J.T. cannot seduce Jeff into forgiving him, and the shot does not end with an embrace. Such differences within the similarities between these two shots are instrumental in creating their meanings.

The film's small budget restricted the number of occasions on which the use of a mobile camera was possible, but when the camera does move it is directly involved in creating a more complex set of meanings than a static set-up might allow. Again, it is worth considering two shots. When everyone leaves the theatre after Lacey's dreadful play, the camera tracks back slowly as Katie denigrates Lacey (to Mike, who is out of shot to the right). Katie, moving more quickly than the camera, proceeds from medium close-up to close-up before exiting the right of the frame. The camera, which stopped moving as Katie approached, picks up Irene and Chip and tracks back, keeping them in medium close-up; the camera stops, and they too exit the right of the frame. The camera then picks up Maura and J.T., while Frances, just visible in long shot, steps onto the porch behind Maura's head, and tracks back as they move into medium close-up. The camera stops as they stop and face each other. From offscreen, Katie shouts, 'You guys coming with us?' Frances becomes more clearly visible behind Maura's head as J.T. replies, 'No, we're gonna walk, okay?' Maura and J.T. move off as Katie calls, 'Frances?' In long shot, Frances steps down off the porch, replies that she is coming. Alone, and wrapped tightly in her shawl, she moves to the centre of the screen, still in long shot.

By commencing with Katie talking to an offscreen Mike, and then tracking back with each subsequent couple before Frances is captured alone in long shot, the film suggests a potentially infinite number of couples heading out of shot together, emphasising Frances's isolation. By tracking back with each couple, keeping them in midshot, the camera ends up far enough away from the theatre that Frances is diminished not only by being alone but also by being in long shot. This distance contrasts sharply with Maura's proximity to J.T., positioned so that her face obscures Frances, over-turning expectations about who will sleep with him. Denying Frances a medium shot or close-up encourages an imaginative investment in what she must be feeling.

The second shot comes when J.T. and Maura quietly make love on the floor. The camera, pointing diagonally downwards, tracks back across the room, following the shadows on the carpet, and up and over Frances's body – she has her back to J.T. and Maura – and down on to her face. She is wide awake, her face devoid of expression. Although she has finally got her close-up, she reveals nothing, perpetuating our imaginative involvement in her situation. Again, the camera movement is essential, empha-sising not just the continuity of physical space and connectivity of human relation-ships but also Frances's isolation. This strong and paradoxical sense of both proximity and distance could not have been achieved by cutting from J.T. and Maura to Frances lying awake – it is created not by the script but by camera movement.

The complex intertwining of human social relationships is captured initially by Mike's coaching of Chip in the group's shared histories:

Mike: Okay. Let me try to get it right the first time through. Katie and
           Maura went to college together. They were roommates with Lacey
           for a while. And I met Katie when I was going with Lacey, but we
           didn't get interested until much later. J.T. and Jeff went to Cornell
           together until Jeff dropped out to go into VISTA[35] and Jeff just
           dropped out. Jeff and Maura met in VISTA, and they were living
           together when I was in VISTA working in Kentucky.
Chip: Was Katie in VISTA?
Mike: No, but she and Maura stayed good friends, and that's when I got
           to know her.
Katie: Frances and Irene…
Chip: Were at Rochester together.
Mike: Right, and they lived downstairs from Katie and me in Boston for
           a while, which is when she met J.T.…
Chip: I know about Irene and J.T.
Mike: …who was visiting me, 'cos we met through Jeff in Kentucky. That
           was a long time ago, J.T. and Irene. Think you got its straight?
Chip: Yeah, I think so. Only who's Jeff?

The effectiveness of this dialogue does not lie in the specifics of the story it tells but in the mere fact of its complexity, a shared fabric of being demonstrated by the accom-panying footage of the volleyball game in which so many of the people Mike names are shown co-operating and competing, shifting position in relation to each other. The volleyball game is not just one of the film's more active sequences. More than a meta-phor, it is the lived being of these friends' complex interrelationships.

Such evidence of a visual style could be considered examples of merely competent filmmaking were it not for the fact that Sayles' films, even at their most 'realistic', are conscious of their own artifice. The title sequence of *Return of the Secaucus Seven* consists of grainy black-and-white mugshots of the seven, over which is heard Spanish guitar music, suggesting, like the title, a western (even as it recalls the iconic Chicago Seven radicals). These generic cues are promptly undercut by the opening shot of Mike plunging a blocked toilet, a deliberate contrast which announces the film's artful construction. Elsewhere, scene transitions are carried by dialogue. For example, when Jeff meets Frances outside the theatre he asks what Chip is like; she replies, a 'little straight'. Cut to the house, and Katie asks her, 'What do you mean, "straight"?' Similarly, when Chip asks Mike 'who's Jeff?', there is a cut to Jeff's arrival in town. Sayles describes this process as 'a way of tumbling into the next scene' (in G. Smith 1998: 55), of providing transitional momentum in place of camera movement; but it is a technique which also announces itself, drawing attention to the artifice of Sayles' naturalist aesthetic.

Consider, too, the sequence of J.T. hitchhiking. In the first shot, J.T. stands by the roadside, in the centre of the frame, guitar case resting upright against his leg, thumb out. Extra-diegetic music starts as a car approaches. The car goes past and the music abruptly stops. Cut to a medium shot of J.T. The music starts up again as another car approaches and he sticks his thumb out. This car, too, goes by, and the music stops again. And it does not start up again because a third car pulls in, and Frances leaps out and rushes to embrace J.T. She says, 'You look like an album cover out there, with your guitar on the side of the road.' These are early, minor examples of Sayles' occasional metalepsis, that is, his breaking of the boundaries between narrative levels, firstly between the diegesis and the extra-diegetic soundtrack as they seem to interact too knowingly, and secondly through Frances's recognition of a visual cliché within the diegesis, implying that she has seen the same image as the viewer and thus somehow occupies a position outside the text. The film also announces consciousness of its own artifice during the preparations for the barbecue in which the sound of Jeff making hamburger patties serves as a percussion-break for the extra-diegetic music, and less overtly by the relationship between extra-diegetic music and the visuals during the basketball game and the waterhole interlude.

A further element of self-conscious artifice can be found in the film's various depictions of role-playing. Lacey's play is a broad Restoration comedy about a woman who disguises herself as a man so that she can follow her soldier lover to war, and through deceit confirm his love for her. The overt artifice of the narrative and the acting style contrasts with the covert artifice of the film – most obviously in the difference between the play's narrative arc and that of Jeff and Maura – and historicises aesthetic conventions. The group also pretend to be students in Mike's history class; Mike and Katie ironically exchange greetings from *Leave it to Beaver* (1957–63); Jeff and J.T. play at being characters from *The Hustler* (1961); Katie, Maura and Irene play at being the imprisoned women from *Salt of the Earth* (1954); and Jeff mocks the pretensions of prog rock-loving music journalist, Lee (Nancy Mette), saying:

My problem [with country music] is the repetitiveness. Women, wine, white line fever, over and over. Whereas progressive [rock] is existential. You've got these chromatic melodies, right? To use for like a springboard into all kinds of experiments. Even the backbeat is full of nuances. You know that there's a central rhythmic idea going on but you're never quite sure when it's gonna pop up. Now you … you … put your … er … your … your … counterpoint on top of that, your passing tones, your arpeggios, your polyrhythms, your parallel scales, your vocal harmonies, and it's uncertain, right? It's exploratory. It's like life.

This self-consciousness plays an important role in the distinctions the film makes between lived and overly-mediated experience, between the image and the 'truth' it displaces, and this in turn has important implications for the vision of politics the film evokes.

Marshall Berman writes of the experience of modernity:

To be modern is to live a life of paradox and contradiction. It is to be over-powered by the immense bureaucratic organisations that have the power to control and often to destroy all communities, values, lives; and yet to be undeterred in our determination to face these forces, to fight to change their world and make it our own. It is to be both revolutionary and conservative: alive to new possibilities for experience and adventure, frightened by the nihilistic depths to which so many modern adventures lead, longing to create and to hold on to something real even as everything melts. (1983: 13–14)

This captures something of the sensibility underlying the film's various arguments about politics and the political. The main focus of overt political discussion concerns the Edward Kennedy-esque Senator for whom Irene and Chip work as speech-writers. Jeff takes particular pleasure in challenging Chip about his job and his politics. At the waterhole, Jeff, stretched out naked on a rock, is confident that 'the whole "working within the system" argument is just the first step towards total co-optation'. Chip, who is also naked, sits with a towel draped over his groin, rubbing sunblock into his nose, his voice taking on a whining quality when he protests that he means 'fighting for what you believe in'. As Chip becomes more irate, so Jeff, having set him off, withdraws, lies face down. Similarly, in the bar, when Chip claims that the Democrats are sincerely-intentioned, Jeff exclaims 'Horseshit!', offers to buy Chip another beer, and then continues with 'That's horseshit, Chip. Carter has about as much sincerity as Ford had brains.' In giving Jeff the best line, the film seems to validate his perspec-tive; but it is more equivocal than that, allowing us to see that Jeff is more interested in teasing Chip than in engaging with him. And Chip does have more insight into politics than Jeff allows, as when he plays at being the Senator while Irene pretends to interview him. His claims to have 'always been a student of the history of the tomato, and a great admirer of some of the outstanding tomatoes of the past' and to 'remember back when Jack Kennedy and I were freshman senators together, sitting down in the Senate commissary, [and being] moved by the fresh red Maryland tomatoes' perfectly captures the meaninglessness of much contemporary public political discourse, later thoroughly lampooned in *Silver City*. Anxiety about commitment to any principle other than obtaining and retaining power is exemplified by his unwillingness to be labelled pro-tomato: 'I don't think it's really a pro- or con- issue. There are mitigating circumstances.' The accuracy of Chip's impersonation is confirmed by Irene's account of drafting and redrafting a speech on the decriminalisation of marijuana until they came up with a version that 'said absolutely nothing'. Chip's motivation for working in a system he can at least partially see through remains unclear, but Irene is outspoken, telling Katie:

> I don't give a rat's ass about the Senator or his career except when you put him up against the alternative … Look, I know people in State agencies, a lot of them came out of VISTA like Mike and Jeff and Maura, and they're doing good stuff – housing, sex education, all kinds of stuff – and they're using the money the State is providing. And these people tell me if the Senator was defeated, they'd be out of business … They're no big fans of the Senator, either, but they need him in order to keep doing the stuff they're doing. I think of myself as an infiltrator. I try to use my job as a form of subversion … I have a very limited, very subtle kind of power, but I do think it's had some influence. I'm able to direct a little bit of the State's power off to the people who really need it.

This clear-sighted perspective on the processes of hegemony represents the limitations of reformism and indicts the perpetuation of democracy as a form rather than a practice. Despite her integration into the party-political system, Irene still sees Amerika lurking behind the image of America. Like schoolteachers Mike and Katie, and drug counsellor Jeff, she still fights to make 'their world' her own. However, there is a simultaneous tendency to assimilate the self into their world, evident not only in the clear and strong limitations on the political effectiveness of Mike, Katie, Jeff and Irene, but also in the aspirations of Maura to escape her shared past with Jeff, of J.T. to become a recording artist, of Irene, Mike and Katie to have children (Katie initially says she would like another 15 years to think about it, but her final line – about unused eggs – suggests otherwise).

Control over reproduction is one of the clearest distinctions the film draws between the working and middle classes. When Maura and Katie meet Howie's wife, Carol (Marisa Smith), Katie expresses a shared sentiment: 'There but for the grace of Ovral-21.' Where Howie and Carol have three children, Maura and Jeff have a shared list of arrests, and Katie, Mike, Irene and Frances have professions. The desire, now they are in their thirties, to have children is akin to Ron's utopian yearning to escape his circumscribed existence in Washington Valley (even while he simultaneously has no desire to leave). Despite their different backgrounds and lifestyles, Ron and Frances find common ground in terms of the similarities between their labour (he is a mechanic, she is training to become a doctor) and of sexual desire. Without denying the very real differences in the fabric of their existence, they are both exploited and know disappointment, but for one night they succeed in making the world their own, even as everything around them melts. This is a fleeting moment, just as the weekend has been a short break from the world, yet this utopian possibility fuels dominant ideology, offering access to the feeling of utopia through the possibility of celebrity (J.T.), relationships (Irene and Chip; Mike and Katie), career (Frances, overjoyed at delivering a baby), sexual pleasure (J.T. and Maura, Ron and Frances) and commodities (Jeff, tempted by heroin).

Lianna (1983)

Lianna, which can be seen as a critical reworking of Annie Hall (1977), tells the story of the eponymous thirtysomething faculty wife (Linda Griffiths) who abandoned her own academic career when she married her teacher, Dick Massey (John De Vries). When she falls in love with her evening class teacher, Ruth (Jane Halleran), Dick throws her out. Forced to fend for herself after losing her social position, she continues her affair but Ruth eventually decides to return to her partner, Jan. In the closing scenes, Lianna achieves a tentative reconciliation with her daughter, Theda (Jessica Wight MacDonald), and her best friend, Sandy (Jo Henderson).

Despite its focus on a single central character, Lianna is, like Return of the Secaucus Seven, concerned with the imbrications of people into social and economic networks. It identifies the violence and desires behind the bourgeois façade and, through Dick's quest for tenure and Lianna's enforced proletarianisation, demonstrates respectability's economic imperative. It depicts the conflicts between the socio-economic system and 'romantic love', emphasising the mutually reinforcing effects of compulsory hetero-sexuality and sexism in everyday life. It has also attracted probably more adverse criti-cism than any of Sayles' other films. Vito Russo argues that 'Lianna basically presents lesbianism as a refuge from the hostilities of heterosexual life. Lianna's husband is such a bastard that the film gives the viewer the idea that if men weren't so odious, women wouldn't turn to each other', going on to quote Rex Reed's ambivalent suggestion that 'Any director who makes a grainy, amateurish home movie about lesbians in Hoboken … must have a death wish' (1987: 280). Although Reed claims Lianna is '100 times better than' Personal Best (1982), the other lesbian romance directed by a straight man that year, and accepts that it 'may be the most sensitive, balanced and sobering view of lesbians the movies will ever give us', he also faults it for never showing lesbians having any fun, describing it as a 'sad, humorless, thoroughly depressing downer' (quoted in Russo 1987: 280). A rather different ambivalence marks Cindy Patton's response to a dozen 1980s films, including Lianna, which

> attempted to show gay and lesbian life as it really is. These films were like manna from heaven for a community of people who had never seen them-selves depicted as 'real people' … There had, of course, been much debate among gay and lesbian critics about these films – they're too stereotypical, they show too much sex, they don't show enough sex, too many upper-class gays, too many troubled gays, not enough of the problems faced by gays. The films which featured entire plots about gay and lesbian life were important. Nevertheless, their plots were still structured around their characters' reac-tions to a homophobic world. (1995: 26)

This ambivalence is as important as it is inevitable: just as a sexuality or a gender contains diversity, so a community is not monolithic, and thus Jane Gaines' contention that 'Visually, *Lianna* is not the film that either a straight woman or a lesbian would have made in celebration of women loving women' (1990: 85) must be greeted with a degree of scepticism as it claims unitary identities for obviously diverse groups. A similar problem emerges in her complaint about the film:

> *Lianna* is not just cautious, it is apologetic about photographing women. The tentative representation of lesbian love-making, for instance, is an attempt not to intrude voyeuristically or shape salaciously ... Showing wholesome lesbian bodies with restraint neither withdraws the image entirely from male view nor subtracts the 'to-be-looked-at' connotations from the female body. But finally, as a film about female desire *Lianna* is incredibly pallid. *Flash-dance* [1983], in contrast, is an alluring inducement to give oneself over to watching gorgeous women dance. (1990: 85–6)

Although Gaines is correct to challenge Laura Mulvey's (1975) influential contention that the female spectator is compelled to view 'the female body on the screen from the male point of view' (Gaines 1990: 84), her ensuing valorisation of the active lesbian spectator whose 'ingenious viewing strategies ... allow for the "clever coexistence of pleasure and displeasure"' (1990: 85, quoting Straayer 1984) as a model for female spectatorship is problematic. She treats explicit eroticisation as *the* source of female pleasure even as it criticises *Lianna* for its refusal of such eroticisation. Ultimately, Gaines' overwhelming displeasure with the film threatens to negate her argument: what, one must ask, has happened to the cleverness of the spectator?

Equally ambivalent, Jackie Stacey finds that 'The final image of Lianna, lonely and rejected, is perhaps preferable to the deaths of the lesbians in *Another Way* [*Egymásra nézve*, 1982] and *The Children's Hour* [1961], the nervous breakdown in *At First Sight* [*Coup de foudre*, 1983] or the rejection of lesbianism for heterosexual normality in *Personal Best* ... However, the shift from the construction of lesbianism as masculine, sick, neurotic or dangerous to one in which it is simply sad and depressing offers little comfort to audiences seeking a more rewarding, affirming or even inspiring lesbian image' (1995: 98). The negative heterosexist associations attached to lesbianism are 'externalized as obstacles to the romance in the film narratives', reinforcing 'definitions of lesbianism as a negative category' by producing 'symbolic barriers to lesbian desire' which are 'too great to resolve in narrative terms' (ibid.).[36] Chris Straayer identifies a related problem arising from the romance form deployed by *Personal Best*, *Desert Hearts* (1985) and *Lianna*. Belonging to the romance genre requires them to 'partake in the dominant hermeneutic impulse of mainstream cinema, the coercive pleasure of coupling' and this 'fosters an understanding of "coming out" that clashes with the political meaning promoted by the gay liberation movement, and also diminishes the many ways that coming-out stories are used in lesbian personal life and social relations' (1996: 23). The 'falling-in-love' narrative effectively 'desexualizes and depoliticizes coming out':

With little variation, lesbian features focus on a lone lesbian couple within heterosexual society. Like heterosexual romances, the films support the notion of a singular destined love for every person. Although the romance genre can afford both sanctified and ostracized heterosexual couples, the lack of any homosexual context in most lesbian films assures that the lesbian couple will be in defiance of otherwise accepted norms. Inadequately determined, the lesbian couple is first awash and then dissolved. And, in a diegesis with only two lesbians, dissolution of the couple is tantamount to the elimination of (lesbian) sex. (1996: 23–4)

Lianna is a partial exception to this rule in that it does depict other lesbians and shows Lianna enjoying a one-night stand. Straayer argues that its 'inclusion of a lesbian context and unsentimental sex attenuates its primary plot of romantic coupling and allows the main character to remain lesbian after de-coupling' (1996: 294 n.20). However, she then describes Lianna's reconciliation with Sandy, who has come to accept her lesbianism, as a 'backward flip' in which 'the coming-out hermeneutic abandons sexuality' (ibid.).

This pervasive ambivalence is unsurprising. It remains unusual to find films which do not pathologise, criminalise, metaphorise or terminate lesbianism. Because *Lianna* does none of these things, it clearly raised hopes that it would do many other things; consequently, many of the criticisms seem to result from its failure also to do the thing(s) the particular critic would have liked it to have done. Patton's complaint about a coming-out film being structured around reactions to a homophobic world is not only inaccurate (Lianna acts as well as reacts) but also a little odd in implying that homophobia should not be depicted (and it is worth noting that *Lianna* contains characters who are not homophobic and others struggling to overcome heteronormative attitudes). For Gaines to criticise its attempt at a sensitive, non-exploitative representation of lesbian sex in an article which itself only tentatively explores the issue of female pleasure is disingenuous. Although Straayer's disappointment at 'lesbian audiences' finding 'female bonding … an acceptable displacement at the conclusion' (1996: 17) of lesbian romances is understandable, to describe the closing reconciliation as an abandonment of sexuality is to equate sexuality with sex and argue for an impossible separatism in which Lianna disconnects completely from the straight world.

Three scenes in particular have attracted negative attention – the sex scene between Lianna and Ruth, their trip to the lesbian bar, and Lianna's emergence into a world full of women – which are best considered through Mandy Merck's discussion of the film:

To a cinema which affects an attitude of high seriousness in matters sexual, the lesbian romance affords a double benefit. It provides a sufficient degree of difference from dominant cinematic representations of sex and sexuality to be seen as 'realistic', 'courageous', 'questioning', '(saved) from Hollywood fudging', 'true to itself' (all terms from reviews of *Lianna*). Yet it does this by offering – quite literally – more of the same (the same being that old cinema equation 'woman=sexuality' which art cinema, despite its differences with Hollywood, has rarely forsaken). (1986: 166)

If Lianna's story is a sentimental education, Merck suggests, her lesson is primarily that of an 'induction into the film's own voyeurism. From her first, wide-eyed gaze at the moonlit posterior of the woman student she discovers with her husband ... to her eager gaze at passing women the morning after her first visit to the lesbian bar, Lianna learns to look ... Lianna's romance with Ruth is conducted through emphatically visual exchanges' (1986: 172). This diegetic exchange of looks is matched by that of the spectator in the scene in which Lianna turns her back to the camera and looks 'with us at [her] own semi-clad' (ibid.) body in a mirror, and in the scene in which she watches a woman dancer (Marta Renzi) rehearsing. Merck also notes that during the scenes of dancing in the My Way Tavern, and during the sex scene between Lianna and Ruth, that diegetic sound is displaced, enabling 'the visual register to assume pre-eminence' (1986: 173). This 'legitimation of the feminine spectacle', she argues, 'makes lesbianism such a gift to art cinema' (ibid.), and asks, 'What are the consequences of a cinema which frees the woman's look in order to vindicate that of the spectator?' (1986: 174). She concludes that although art cinema's lesbians 'survive, they suffer':

> They suffer for their stares in a way which we spectators can escape: our looks are not returned by their mirrors, our curiosity is gratified without jeopardy. Ultimately, these characters suffer as the objects of a cinema which cannot come to terms with its own pleasures ... Despite Dick Massey's classroom quotation of Heisenberg's Uncertainty Principle to debunk the 'purity' of documentary film, *Lianna* – like so much of art cinema – remains studiously unaware of the effects of its own observations. (Ibid.)

Merck's treatment of *Lianna* is problematic, not least because of her attempt to make it stand in for all art cinema, a category she never questions and into which she struggles to fit it.[37] But any more substantial response must begin with the self-reflexive artifice of Sayles' realism – with, in fact, Dick's debunking of documentary realism (by, incidentally, restating the naturalist dilemma of the problematic boundary between observation and intervention).

He says to his class, 'I've heard people complaining about Flaherty staging his footage, about how this is some kind of betrayal, and that there's such a thing as "pure" documentary. Well, there's a law in physics that the act of observing an event can't help but change that event, and a documentary filmmaker not only observes but edits.' He points to 'this little message' written on the blackboard:

> In allowing your workers to be swayed by such propaganda you are surrendering them to the force that has kept Eastern Europe in chains for three decades, the evil forces of the world communist conspiracy. These people are ruthless. They have nothing to lose, but if we unite behind the banners of Christianity and democracy they cannot prevail.

Then circling key words and phrases, and erasing others, he says, 'This is just our raw footage. First we select the parts we want to keep. Anything that doesn't agree with our idea of what the story should be, it goes on the cutting room floor. We change the order of our bits of film, taking it out of real time and into film time, and splice them together for effect.' This process leaves him with the words 'Workers of the world unite. You have nothing to lose but your chains'. In using this sequence to understand the film's treatment of women it is important to recognise that Dick cannot merely erase words. He must rearrange the ones he wants to use into a conventional grammatical structure, but in doing so he can alter the tone of his 'footage' considerably. Which returns us to the three most criticised scenes in *Lianna*.

In the sex scene, the emphasis throughout is on Lianna. Shot through a blue filter, with light streaming into the darkened bedroom through a background window, Lianna and Ruth appear almost in silhouette. Their lovemaking is characterised by slow, careful movements. Light from the window pools on the contours of Lianna's body. Ruth is initially the more active lover, and then Lianna reciprocates. Beyond its restraint, what makes this sequence noteworthy is the peculiar effect produced by its unconventional soundtrack of female voices whispering softly. The sense of strangeness and familiarity generated for an Anglophone audience – both French and English voices are clearly audible – correlates to Lianna's experience. Her first overtly lesbian sexual experience and the first time she has been unfaithful to Dick, it is new and strange to her; yet it is also familiar in that we know that when she was young she experienced a kind of physical intimacy with another girl, that she is familiar with infidelity (albeit as the betrayed party), and she has had sex before (regardless of the differences between heterosexual and lesbian sex, they can and do share some repertoires, investments and significances for the individual. This last point is important in understanding the humanist logic of Sayles' films which constantly struggles to locate individual difference within collective similarity; this is achieved most effectively in *Lianna* not through the combination of strangeness and familiarity in this scene but in the decision to make the focus of the film not so much Lianna's lesbianism as her enforced proletarianisation when she steps outside of the norms sanctioned by dominant patriarchal ideology and institutions). What is significant in this scene is *Lianna*'s attempt, through visual and aural elements (other than dialogue), to communicate both the immediate experience of this moment for Lianna and the complexity of its significance and implications within her life. Moreover, the strangeness of the soundtrack closes down the possibility of sentimental or erotic responses to the images. That the scene has attracted so much criticism perhaps results from its refusal to insist upon and celebrate some fundamental, pristine difference separable from existing social relations.

In the second scene, Ruth takes Lianna to the My Way Tavern. Does it, as Merck suggests, legitimate the feminine spectacle? The scene certainly contains diegetic gazing, and since it is initially constructed from Lianna's perspective, it does appear to isolate and alienate her from the other women in the bar; and, because the objects of her gaze themselves gaze at her, it also seems to reduce her to mere appearance. The scene as a whole, though, is more complex in its construction, repeatedly demonstrating that the gaze does not necessarily always represent the same thing. The first shot inside the bar shows women dancing. Cut to Lianna, who has just entered and nervously gulps as she looks around. Cut to the profile of a woman drinking, who looks out of shot (it is by no means certain she is looking at Lianna). Lianna then looks at Ruth, out of shot to her left. Cut to an uncomfortably close close-up of another woman staring (although again it is not clear that she is looking at Lianna as the next shot is of the bar and women dancing). Not only do the three women shown looking seem to express a different emotion, a different meaning, but the editing makes the significance of each of their looks contingent upon whether it is paired with the preceding or succeeding shot. Lianna's appearance in the bar does not make her the victim of the gaze, or bestow upon her some asymmetrical power of the gaze; rather, she enters into a field in which, courtesy of the editing, the gaze is distributed without being made utterly safe. She complains that everyone is staring, but can only do so because she has been looking at the women around her – a point emphasised when Lianna worries about being recognised by a woman she vaguely knows from the PTA, only for Ruth to tell her that she has raced into the powder room, scared of being recognised by Lianna.

The power of the gaze is also disturbed by apparent chronological disruptions. It is only after Lianna talks about having danced with another woman that we see her dance with someone other than Ruth. This woman seems to be the one whose eyes have several times appeared in a too-close close-up, but as they dance there is suddenly interposed another shot of these eyes. This interruption, which reintroduces an air of threatening strangeness, might seem a consequence of careless editing. However, while they have been dancing, five shots of Ruth watching have also been intercut. Initially happy that Lianna has overcome her nervousness, she becomes increasingly uncomfortable, ambivalent, suggesting that it is now Ruth who perceives this woman as a threat, but more importantly indicating that the gaze is not unequivocal, that the economy of the gaze is more prone to shifts and changes than Mulvey's account permits. This is further demonstrated in the third scene, which immediately follows.

Cut to the next morning, with Lianna walking along a sunny street. A woman approaches, looks at her and smiles as she goes past. Lianna smiles to herself. There follows a brief montage of women – individually, in pairs, with children – whom Lianna watches. This is the learning-to-look of which Merck complains, yet her criticism of this sequence pays scant attention to its tone or what follows. It is important, first, to note the comic effect of this sequence's ironically erected, self-deflating pathetic fallacy: the sun shines *so* brightly on the rather battered urban environment, looking like something from an advert. Such an overblown insertion must be read against the more conventional 'realism' of the film, and thus the learning-to-look it invokes cannot be taken at face value. At the end of the sequence, Lianna catches up with Ruth, who has just left her house, and enthusiastically embraces her. Ruth quickly disentangles herself, warning Lianna that they are in 'the real world' now – even if Lianna has learned to look, normative patriarchal heterosexism will not permit her to possess the power of the gaze. The montage sequence is then retrospectively constructed as an attempt to briefly imagine and inhabit a forbidden utopian space of possibilities, libidinal and otherwise. Like all utopias, it is ambiguous, conflicted,

Lianna: discovering a world full of women

tenuous. That it is imagined in terms of the gaze is both its strength and its weakness, proposing empowerment but only on the pre-existing terrain of power.

This sense of an ambiguous utopian space and relationship is reiterated by the film's return to the theatre where Lianna works as a lighting technician, and where we see a couple rehearse an Apache dance, a set of carefully choreographed, vigorous – if not violent – physical encounters. These overtly symbolic sequences are metaphoric of the various struggles and co-operations within the key relationships in the film, and suggest Lianna's ultimate reacceptance by and of the social group she inhabited before her separation from Dick, including Jerry (John Sayles), Bob (Stephen Mendillo), Sandy and her own children. Straayer's suggestion that in this conclusion 'the coming-out hermeneutic abandons sexuality' reduces identity to sexual identity, and sexual identity to sex, and imagines that identity can exist outside the social rather than as a coming-into-being through material communicative interaction with others.

Baby It's You (1983)

Sayles' next film, a high-school romance set in 1966–67, reworks the conventions of this genre in several ways. Contrary to the pattern established by *American Graffiti* (1973) and *Fast Times at Ridgemont High* (1982), Sayles continues to follow his odd couple after graduation. The first half of the film charts the tentative senior-year romance between the middle-class Jewish-American Jill Rosen (Rosanna Arquette) and the working-class Italian-American Albert Capadilupo (Vincent Spano), better known as Sheik, culminating in a disastrous prom night: Sheik, who has been expelled, is excluded; Jill's friend Jody (Liane Curtis) attempts suicide and reveals that she had slept with Sheik; and after a failed burglary, Sheik flees to Florida. In the second half, Jill goes to Sarah Lawrence College to study drama. A valedictorian in Trenton, New Jersey, she is nobody special there. Frustrated by her lack of success and failure to fit in, she visits Sheik. He is happy washing dishes in a club during the week and doing his act – miming to Frank Sinatra on the jukebox – at weekends. They finally sleep together, an experience Jill finds less than satisfactory. She returns to college, promising but not intending to stay in touch. Sheik's boss hires a real singer, so he quits and comes looking for her. Discovering her no longer to be the person he knew, he trashes her room. She explains that her life, too, is a disappointment. Sheik begins to accept that she is not in love with him. Her date has stood her up, so Sheik escorts her to the dance. The film ends with them dancing to a rock version of 'Strangers in the Night', which segues into a Sinatra version.

Set in a world which commonly displaces differences of social class onto ethnicised cultural differences, *Baby It's You* explores the roots of domestic and gender power relationships, and the interrelation of violence and desire in romance. Its final apparently harmonious shot – Sheik and Jill holding each other, dancing to Sinatra – is ambiguous, impermanent, self-consciously incongruous. It offers a conventional image of romantic resolution that is undercut by the knowledge that their lives will go on without the other. It is about the end of romance – at most, there is friendship, nostalgia and then parting.

Sayles reports that co-producer Amy Robinson, upon whose original story his screenplay is based, 'always said, "The problem with this movie is I think that it's a romance, you think it's a class-conflict movie, and Paramount think it's a teenage sex comedy – so something's got to give somewhere"' (in G. Smith 1998: 80). Robinson's romance and Sayles' class-conflict movie ultimately usurp the teenage sex comedy,[38] articulating through each other a critique of social class and romance, as well as extending Sayles' critique of simulacral commodity culture.

Sayles describes high school as 'the last bastion of true democracy in [American] society, where you have classes and eat lunch with the guy who's going to be picking up your garbage later in life' (in Osborne 1999: 33); but in order to comprehend the seemingly insurmountable class differences which separate Jill and Sheik it is worth beginning with their respective homes. The first shot of Jill's home comes when, returning from school, she walks up the pathway that leads to the steps up to the front door. Snow covers the lawn and shrubbery, but the path is clear; in the left foreground hangs a sign for Eli Rosen, M.D. Drapes are pulled back from the lighted windows to the right of the front door. This dully-coloured house connotes middle-class comfort and, by being set back from the road with its own path and steep steps, isolation from neighbours and community as well as her father's professional distance. Jill enters the house, closes the door behind her. The lounge is clear and relatively uncluttered. A rug covers a large part of the polished wooden floor, and several chairs are grouped around the fireplace. Ornaments and paintings, here and in the dining room, are solid and respectable, suggesting mediocre bourgeois taste. The house stretches out into the background; the camera follows Jill as she moves into the foreground, opening up still more space as she enters the dining room. Her father (Jack Davidson) is sitting on the right-hand side of the screen, reading some papers, his stethoscope on the dining table. Through an open doorway in the background, Mrs Rosen (Joanna Merlin) can be seen working in the kitchen. Jill's position relative to her parents – she stands on the left of the screen, they occupy the right; her father is in the foreground, her mother in the background, with Jill between them – makes her the focus of their attention as they ask about her day. Her parents are united in their regard and physical occupation of one side of the screen, even as they are separated by their differently gendered spaces and activities. The open door which forms a vertical bar separating them also connects them.

Although it is spacious, the house is stultifying, evoking wealth and comfort, complacency and entrapment. The sense of confinement becomes stronger when Jill goes upstairs. Framed by her bedroom doorway and in the diagonal gap between two sets of banisters, the ceiling and the bedroom doorway, she looks downstairs through this gap to respond to her mother's questions about the audition. Jill rejects her mother's suggestion that 'the object is not to have the biggest part' in the play, and is simultaneously squeezed into a tiny fragment of screen, trapped behind bars and caught in the centre of a spotlight-like diagonal space. Jill's discomfort when she goes to college is a result of her enclosure in this bourgeois space and her desire to be at the centre.

After Jill and Sheik have met a couple of times, he phones her for a date. Sitting on her bed, she surprises herself by agreeing. Cut to Sheik's house, the camera square on to the lounge, above and behind the television set, giving a wide shot of the room. The middle of the shot is dominated by Mr Capadilupo (Nick Ferrari), sprawled across an armchair in front of the television. In the background are two doorways. Through the right-hand one, Mrs Capadilupo (Dolores Messina) irons Sheik's trousers; the other leads to Sheik's bedroom, in which he dresses. On the wall between them hangs a big ugly clock, its pendulum swinging. Running along the left-hand wall is a sofa, at right angles to the television and Mr Capadilupo's armchair. 'I'd like to see you move that fast when I need something around here,' he bitches to his son, as his wife sits down, her back to the arm of the sofa so that she can see the television. 'Thataway, guys,' he advises the cop show. 'Kick ass.'

When Sheik emerges to check his appearance in a mirror, the scene alternates between this shot, and another one of his parents. In this other shot, Mr Capadilupo, in medium close-up, dominates the foreground as he continues to watch his show and criticise his son, accusing him of criminal activity, threatening him with violence. Sheik is insolent in return. Mrs Capadilupo is dwarfed in the background; on the table at the end of the sofa is a photograph of her son when he was younger. Sheik kisses his mother goodbye, dons his overcoat and leaves. His father says, 'Dresses like a pimp';

Baby It's You: in the spotlight and behind bars

his mother replies, 'He looks handsome.' Throughout this scene, despite some disapproving glances at Sheik, Mr Capadilupo makes no eye contact with either his wife or son.

The contrast between these two houses and families provides a cogent background for Jill and Sheik and demonstrates the gulf that separates them. Jill is the daughter of a Jewish-American doctor, Sheik the son of an Italian-American garbage collector. Jill's father is timid, eager not to offend, her mother sharp-tongued but caring. Sheik's mother dotes on him, but his father can barely stomach him. Neither set of parents seem to be in a particularly love-filled marriage: Jill's co-operate but lack passion, Sheik's channel whatever passion they have into disagreements about their son. The construction of these family backgrounds in terms of social class, ethnicity and gender relationships hovers somewhere between observation and stereotype, deftly sketching in a complex history not only for Jill and Sheik but also for Americans of their generation. The class and ethnic differences which can be ascribed to parents and homes can also be observed in Jill and Sheik's very different senses of propriety, evident in their dress and their attitudes towards school.

The film opens with 'Wooly Bully' by Sam the Sham and the Pharaohs over the credits, then cuts to a square-on shot down a deserted school corridor, emphasising perspective and order, as the bell rings. A lone figure appears in the distance, and then classroom doors open and students spill noisily out, their voices mingling with 'Wooly Bully'. Jill and three friends appear through the crowd; as they reach the foreground, the volume of the music drops. The petite Jill is neatly turned out, with a long bob and Alice band. The girls chatter enthusiastically, the camera tracking back and around a corner, keeping just ahead of them. A male student says 'Hi' to Jill, who denies knowing him. The girls separate (to go around the camera), and an enormous dark-haired figure in a dark suit and white shirt – Sheik – appears from behind the right-hand side of the camera and bumps into Jill. He fills half the screen. Jill spills past him, and the now-stationary camera holds on him as he turns to look at her. Cut to Jill looking back, with a mildly flirtatious glance; she turns and walks away. Again the camera tracks away in front of the girls, as Jill denies knowing Sheik; in the distance, framed in the middle of the screen, he stands motionless, watching her. The girls, and the camera, stop. They chat some more, obscuring the centre of the screen. When they separate to go to different classes, Sheik is revealed in the background; he has still not moved. As the corridor empties, he strolls, hands in pockets, into the foreground, the camera rising up slowly as he comes into medium close-up. He watches Jill through the wire-meshed glass of the classroom door until the teacher mentions her name, and then wanders off down the next, deserted corridor.

This sequence is suggestive of the difficulties Jill and Sheik will face. She is perpetually surrounded (although this changes at college), while he is always isolated. She seeks peer approval and deploys performance skills – imitating a character from a film, answering sarcastically in class – to get it. As befits her status, she leads her group of friends around the corridor, moving briskly and obediently from classroom to classroom. Sheik, who has just been expelled from his Catholic school, moves against the tide of students (and the direction of the camera) and when he stops in the middle of the corridor other students have to go around him. His physical presence is commanding and immediate, his dress sense so different that it is not at first clear that he is a student. Completely at odds with his surroundings, his casual change of direction indicates his lack of respect for the institution in which he finds himself: he is going to go where he wants. Exercising this autonomy, he drops in on one of Jill's classes, and repeatedly attends the wrong lunch session so as to see her. Significantly, the window in the classroom door through which he looks at Jill is criss-crossed by a wire mesh.[39]

Jill and Sheik are further separated by cultural differences rooted in their respective class, gender and ethnicity. This is manifested through the music associated with each of them. Jill mimes the Supremes song 'Stop in the Name of Love' in front of her bedroom mirror, and sings Phil Spector's 'Chapel of Love' with her girlfriends when they tease her about Sheik. He, meanwhile, is doubly anachronistic, associated with the 'skinny white cool' of both Frank Sinatra (he loves 'Strangers in the Night' and we see him mime 'Mr Success') and Bruce Springsteen. The latter's songs are used throughout the film: when Sheik, self-possessed and the subject of his fellow students' gaze, strides into the cafeteria to find Jill, 'Hard to be a Saint in the City' thumps on the soundtrack; 'E Street Shuffle' accompanies his date with Jill at Joey D's Cocktail Lounge; he convinces Jill to skip school one day and go with him to Asbury Park;[40] 'She's the One' blares out during the aborted robbery; and when he quits his job and goes in search of Jill, the montage is edited to 'Adam Raised a Cain'. The successful image of both Sinatra and Springsteen depends upon a tactical denial of ethnicity, manifested in different ways, which promoted instead a white, working-class masculinity. Sinatra's persona did play on his Italian-American background – the competition with Bing Crosby was as much concerned with ethnicity as their different styles of crooning, and Sinatra's Mafia connections ensured he could not leave it behind – but it was downplayed in favour of an emphasis on a white, working-class identity. In addition to his image of the tender tough guy (which later transmuted into the playboy), throughout the 1950s he also represented an underdog masculinity excluded from consumerism and suburbia. For example, in *From Here to Eternity* (1953), he embodies masculine bravado when his character Maggio, 'small, physically weak, and pugnacious as a Pekinese', resists the 'sadistic, two-hundred-and-fifty-pound army brute played to the vicious hilt by Ernest Borgnine' (Mellen 1978: 240). (When Sheik, out of misguided bravado, physically resists Mr McManus (Sam McMurray), a teacher who used to be a marine, he comes off worse and is expelled.) The whiteness of Sinatra's persona was further anchored through his later associations with the Kennedys and the Reagans, even as Italian-American identity became more generally perceived as 'white' in the second half of the twentieth century. One of the most remarkable aspects of Springsteen's persona, music and performance is the exclusion of non-white elements (beyond the onstage presence of black saxophonist Clarence Clemmons). As Fred Pfeil argues, 'the main point here is how relatively little Bruce's music owes to black-centered blues and R & B, how much to the traditionally white idioms of country blues and ballads. Such influences show up practically everywhere in his music: in the western Frankie Laine or Jimmie Rodgers-style yodelling he trails off the end of a song like "I'm on

Fire"; in the ballad structure of "Spare Parts" … ; in the pulse of the rhythm, timbre and drawl of his voice in a first-person love-trouble tune like "One Step Up"' (1995: 85). Pfeil suggests that:

> The 'Whiteness' of these musical influences contributes to the construction of Bruce's image in a variety of ways, even as they are inflected by other elements of the Springsteen complex. Circumscribed and to some degree masked by Bruce's 'tougher-than-the-rest' voice, and elevated sonically, visually, and/or verbally by … various strategies of ennoblement … they nonetheless function to *dis*affiliate Springsteen's rocking from rock's traditionally uneasy, energetic, and exploitative relationship with 'Blackness'. At the same time, and as part of the same process, they help to reconnect the notion of rock and authenticity to the class signifier to which they were first attached …: the white *working-class* rocker, albeit shorn here of any musical attachment to Blacks. In so doing, moreover, we might say the image of this ennobled yet class-specific rocker simply leaps back over and 'forgets' the 1960s moment when rock largely lost its class accents to become the music of 'its' generation, that is, of college- and draft-age baby-boomers as volatile political subjects and target-rich consumer group: a moment when … rock masculinity draws closer to 'femininity' and 'Blackness' alike while remaining distinct from each. (Ibid.; emphasis in original)

The association of Sheik with Springsteen – which, unlike the association with Sinatra, is completely extra-diegetic – is particularly telling. Like the clean-shaven, shirt-and-sports jacket early Springsteen (before blue-collar *Born in the USA* scruffiness became *de rigeur*), Sheik always dresses up for his performance.[41]

Moreover, just as Springsteen's white idiom strips blackness and related radical connotations out of rock, so *Baby It's You* envisions a late 1960s without protest and upheaval. The politics of the period are reduced to a classroom noticeboard on the civil rights movement and a snide comment by an obnoxious rich white kid in Florida about freedom riders. The nearest we get to sampling the cultural politics for which the period is best remembered is when Jill, at college, smokes pot while listening to the Velvet Underground and Simon and Garfunkel, and when she begins to use contraceptive pills – no more 'going to the chapel'.[42]

The social and cultural distance between Jill and Sheik is made physical on their first date. Having arranged to meet Sheik, Jill paces up and down in front of a liquor store and parking lot. It is dark apart from the storefront; the only sound is the soft tapping of her heels. A cat mewls. Something glass, or maybe metal, rolls around somewhere. Jill seems tiny in this alien environment. Cut to a medium close-up: she looks around nervously, wondering what she is doing there. In the distance, a siren; closer, men's voices. Four young black men come out of the liquor store. Car doors slam. Jill looks off to her right, but it is not Sheik. Two older white men emerge from the parking lot and ogle her as they walk past. A car prowls by; its driver hits the horn and tries to catch her attention with a suggestive look. She looks away. In medium shot, she shrinks back into an urban environment very different to her suburban neighbourhood. This is not her part of town.

Finally Sheik approaches and they exchange greetings. He compliments her. They do not touch; there is a very clear space between them. 'C'mon,' he says, 'Rat's waiting on us', and without waiting for her, he exits the frame. She follows.

In Joey D's Cocktail Lounge, Jill sits beside Sheik in a booth. He is deep in conversation with Rat (Gary McCleery), who is sitting across from him. Jill sits opposite Rat's girlfriend, Joann (Robin Johnson); they do not speak. Jill looks bored and glances around the bar. A couple are necking. No one is paying her any attention. She sips her drink, pulls a face at the taste, stifles a yawn, looks around some more. The necking is getting more passionate. At another table sit a group of would-be mafiosi; one of them notices Jill looking and winks at her. Cut to some time later: Sheik and Rat are talking to the mafiosi; Jill discovers she used to know Joann. Although this sequence lacks the expressive montage of *Lianna*, the bar is nonetheless established as a place in which Jill feels uncomfortable; it is not what her class and ethnic background has taught her to expect from a date.[43]

On leaving the bar, Sheik walks a disenchanted Jill back to her car. He asks for another date. She complains, 'you hardly said two words to me all night', and turns on to the parking lot, increasing the distance between them. His defence is that he wanted her to get to know him before he hit her 'with anything too heavy'. He has no idea how to act around her, and she does not understand why he acts the way he does. He compliments her 'real pretty eyes'; she nods agreement. He tries again, but does little better: 'I bet you don't even have to act up there on stage. People just stare at your eyes.' 'I hope not,' she replies. Throughout this exchange, Jill has either had her back to Sheik or, facing him, leans back away from him against her car. 'I never went out with anyone like you before,' Sheik says. He closes down the space between them, holds her chin up, leans in and kisses her. She offers him a lift home, but he says he prefers to walk; more likely, he does not want her to see where he lives. 'Have you ever seen Trenton late at night?' he asks. 'It looks like a whole different place'. Jill replies, 'I got to get home', and stretches up to kiss him again, but he has looked away and misses this gesture. They part, the physical gap reopened between them.

This sequence further delineates the different worlds from which the protagonists come, but also charts their tentative, uncertain attempts at contact, with the missed second kiss a tender signifier of the ultimately unbridgeable gulf between them. Central to this failed connection is the romanticism of the characters: for a time at least, Jill finds Sheik different, exciting, forbidden, while Sheik places her on a pedestal and, as his raptures about nocturnal Trenton suggest, is susceptible to romantic idealism. That the conflict between their class, ethnic and cultural origins is the unresolved problem at the heart of their relationship is captured three scenes later. In the next two scenes, Jill's friends tease her about her date, and Sheik strolls into Mr Ripeppi's (William Joseph Raymond) class just to sit near her. In the next scene, Jill and Sheik wander around the schoolyard, holding hands. 'If you get in,' he asks about her college application, 'are you going to go?' She replies that of course she will. 'It's not like a rule or anything,' he protests, unable to understand why anyone would want to go to university. The physical space between them has been bridged, but the cultural gap remains immense. Then an idea hits Sheik: she could go to college in Florida, where Frank Sinatra now lives, and he could go with her to pursue his own career. But most of this is left unsaid. The bell rings and she heads off to class. Cut to a high-angle shot down into the schoolyard. The last students swirl away into a building, and Sheik is left there alone. He strolls off in the other direction – he always seems to be alone or going in a different direction – and straight into a collision with Mr McManus. (Significantly, the next scene begins with Jill imitating Joann's accent, simultaneously trying on an identity which might fit better with Sheik while using Joann merely as a case study, a found object, to make use of in her pursuit of a career.)

Despite their differences, Jill and Sheik are obsessed with image and performance. Jill knows how to act (in both senses) at school, but not at college. At school, she fits in and is cast as Kitty in William Saroyan's *The Time of Your Life*; at college, she neither fits in nor takes the lead. At her lowest ebb, she phones Sheik in Florida, and tells him, 'I don't know how you're supposed to act'. This ambiguity requires no clarification because it is true in both senses. Sheik tells her he is singing in a club, and when she visits the illusion is momentarily sustained by a tracking shot which does not immediately reveal that he is miming to a jukebox. When Jill, who believes in training and rehearsal, asks about his voice, he cites Dean Martin as an example of how style is more important than voice. And in defence of his job, he reminds Jill that Jerry Lewis started out lip-synching to other people's records. Although the chain Sinatra-Martin-Lewis makes a kind of cultural sense, it is also ludicrous, and so when we see Sheik's apartment decorated with photographs of Sinatra and Jill, we know that neither of the ideals in his life are attainable for him. Similarly, at the conclusion of the film, Jill seems just as distant from the success of which she dreams. This is what they share, this is why they dance together and this is why the rock version of 'Strangers in the Night' segues into Sinatra's version, which they did not get to dance to at the prom. Despite its promises, the American Dream is precisely that: a dream, a hope-filled delusion.

The Brother from Another Planet (1985)

Towards the end of *Baby It's You*, as Sheik is racing back from Florida to see Jill, he drives into New York and for a brief moment the Statue of Liberty can be glimpsed through a gap between houses. In a movie concerned with, among other things, the unattainability of images – Sheik's desire to be like Sinatra and with Jill; Jill's desire to fit in at Sarah Lawrence and become a star, an image – this momentary sighting does rather more than function as a shorthand signifier of Sheik's location: it ties the protagonists' thwarted desires and ambitions into American ideology and suggests that the dominant ideological image of America is as illusory and unattainable as those things for which Jill and Sheik yearn. In the opening scenes of *The Brother from Another Planet*, the Statue of Liberty is heavily ironised in precisely this manner, but before discussing the film's critical vision of the contemporary US, it is necessary to consider the role and functions of the alien in science fiction films, beginning with a consideration of the opening sequences of *The Brother from Another Planet* and Barry Sonnenfeld's *Men in Black* (1997), both of which are concerned with extra-terrestrials as immigrants and assign significant, and superficially contrasting, roles to Men in Black.

After crashing his fleetingly-evoked spaceship into the stretch of water between Bedloe Island, home of the Statue of Liberty, and Ellis Island, home of the immigrants' Detention Center, the Brother (Joe Morton) levers himself out of the water and half-crawls, half-flops onto dry land. It is night time, and the Statue of Liberty is an out-of-focus but nonetheless recognisable vertical smudge behind him. Cut, and the Brother stands up into the new shot, intruding into the frame and thus emphatically entering America. Now the Statue of Liberty is in focus behind him, but still he does not see it, and then the focus shifts and it becomes a smudge once more. He turns to his right. Now in profile, his eyeline is on the same level as the yellow lozenge of light at the top of the Statue's torch, but still he does not see it. The camera reframes his body so as to reveal that instead of a foot his right leg terminates in a bloody stump. It is a fresh injury from which blood is still pouring. Either he has lost his foot in the crash or, as his later comparison of himself to a picture of a runaway slave implies, he has severed it in order to remove a fetter. When he reaches down to touch the wound, his hand glows with a healing orange light.

He hops towards the Detention Center. Inside is a vast and empty space; every noise echoes. He rests a hand on a wall to support himself, and in response to his touch a disembodied voice calls out. Startled, he lets go of the wall, then tentatively touches it again. More voices reverberate around the hall. He hops into the middle of the deserted space, but when he sits down on a bench the voices start up again. He hops away, and as he looks around at the arched roof a disorienting babble of voices erupts from nowhere. The Brother lets out a silent scream and collapses to the floor.

The opening credits follow, and then the film cuts to the following morning. The camera pans across the Manhattan skyline, starting with the twin towers of the World Trade Center and ending on the Brother as he looks across at the city, the Statue of Liberty an out-of-focus smudge behind him. A boat's siren causes him to turn towards the statue, and the Brother's point-of-view shot of the boat is followed by a close-up of his face in which the direction of his gaze seems to change slightly. It is initially implied that the following in-focus shot of the statue is also from his point of view, but he then steps into the frame as the statue goes out of focus, retrospectively placing the shot's apparent origin under erasure. This recurrent failure of the Brother to see the Statue of Liberty, and the persistence with which it is made visible to the audience before being denied to the Brother's gaze, is a nagging feature to which I will return.

Men in Black opens with a computer-generated bug, which has soared and swooped over the desert during the opening credits, splattering across the windscreen of a van which is smuggling a dozen illegal immigrants into the US. Stopped by the Border Patrol, the driver, Nick (Jon Gries), claims that he has merely been fishing across the border in Mexico. When Immigration and Naturalization Service (INS) Agent Janus (Fredric Lane) opens the van and discovers the immigrants, he says that he would have thrown them back. A black car pulls up and two Men in Black step out. Claiming to be from Division 6, they take command. Kay (Tommy Lee Jones) questions the immigrants. Having picked out the most stereotypical Mexican – he is

The Brother from Another Planet: not a point-of-view-shot

dressed in a shapeless blanket-like poncho over an equally shapeless gown, with a lank and greasy mass of hair and a scruffy moustache and beard – Kay tells the others to continue on their way. Kay and Dee (Richard Hamilton) march their prisoner off into the desert. Away from the Border Patrol, Kay pulls a knife on the Mexican and cuts open his disguise, revealing the extra-terrestrial Mikey (John Alexander). The most Mexican of the Mexicans is, it seems, truly alien. Kay and Dee scoff at Mikey's claim to be a political refugee, and point out that his very presence has broken seven treaties. Suddenly, Mikey spots Agent Janus, who has witnessed the end of this exchange, and charges at him. Kay shoots Mikey with a futuristic silver handgun. Mikey explodes in a cloud of blue alien gloop that drenches Janus and much of the surrounding area. Kay then uses a Neuralyzer, a device given to the Men in Black by some friends 'from out of town', to erase the Border Patrol officers' memories of the night's events.

Writing about the peculiar relative absence of the nation, nationality and nation-alism from science fiction's future visions, Istvan Csicsery-Ronay, Jr identifies several major strategies by which the genre expunges 'nations as agents or subjects of future history and national cultures as historical forces', including, of greatest relevance here, that of '*biological displacement*' (2002: 223; emphasis in original). By abjuring national identity in this way, science fiction is able to elide 'the distinction between national culture and race' and to let the 'political-cultural problems of nationality and ethnicity … slip into the context of racial difference' (2002: 228). The main device science fiction uses to achieve this is the alien, and because this figure is 'ontologically other only by virtue of its being biologically Other', its depiction is typically built upon a 'fundamental ambivalence' (ibid.). According to Csicsery-Ronay, Jr, science fiction tends to imagine 'alien-human difference as analogous to terrestrial racial difference', depicting alien-human 'biological relations … as a nebulous kind of species difference' and thus permitting 'much the same imaginary sleight-of-hand as the concept of race' (ibid.). This allows

> the dominant members of a culture to see aspects of themselves objectified in Others while also disavowing them, by placing the Others beyond a nonne-gotiable *essential* line of separation. As a result, human national-political, ethnic, class, and gender differences are distanced beyond mediating human

institutions. Rapprochement is only possible accompanied by the anxiety that differences may prove to be intractable and even dangerous; or at the risk of violating a taboo about which the central protagonists are deeply ambivalent and the audience is ontologically confused ... Race insinuates the model of species difference into relations among members of the human species. It purports to name qualities deeper than expression, and consequently deeper than culture and politics. Race implies forces that cannot be examined in oneself and yet that may manifest themselves at any time. The insidiousness of race lies precisely in this precondition for its being imagined at all, lying beneath all conscious articulations, all sharing of premises, all decisions. When race is in play, it implies that nature supersedes culture. (Ibid.; emphasis in original)

The encounter with the alien has been a science fiction staple since the origins of the modern genre in H. G. Wells' work of the 1890s. Ziauddin Sardar traces the dominant imagery of this encounter back to the origins of European identity in the fight against Islam in the eighth century. 'This war of the worlds,' he writes, 'began with the battle of Tours in October AD 732 near Poitiers in western France' (2002: 7), and in it we see again 'the armies of Charles Martel turning the tide ... Charlemagne and his paladins at Roncesvalle mustering for the first time a common sense of European identity, gathering the armies of Western Christendom to confront the Muslim hordes' (2002: 6). Evidence for Sardar's claim can be found in the 'alien' invader of Richard Marsh's *The Beetle* (1897), a monstrous threat to Imperial Britain which has much in common with Bram Stoker's eponymous *Dracula* (1897) and the Martians of Wells' *The War of the Worlds* (1898). As Rhys Garnett observes, Marsh's 'alien intruder is variously described as an Algerian, an "arab of the Soudan", an "unbaptised Mohammedan", and an "Egypto-Arabian" and, later, as "Oriental to his finger-tips" yet "hardly an Arab ... not a fellah", perhaps "not a Mohammedan at all" and, because of his "thick and shapeless lips", as having "more than a streak of negro blood" ... Because he is none of these things specifically, he is all of them approximately' (1990: 34–5). Imagining Otherness in terms of racialised difference has long been a major strategy of both literary and cinematic science fiction, although it is perhaps more prevalent in visual science fiction, which depends more heavily upon the immediacy of the image (see, for example, the *Alien* (1979–), *Predator* (1987–), *Star Trek* (1966–) and *Star Wars* (1977–) franchises).[44] Although *The Brother from Another Planet* invites comparison with a number of contemporaneous science fiction films,[45] I am here more concerned with considering it alongside other science fiction films overtly concerned with the supposed threat to American society posed by the immigration of non-white illegal aliens. For example, in *Independence Day* (1996) – like *Men in Black*, a NAFTA-era film with important scenes set closer to Mexico than Canada – the US president, a Gulf War veteran, organises global war against the aliens because he has received the awful revelation that the aliens are migrant labourers and therefore they must be destroyed: 'I saw its thoughts. I saw what they're planning to do. They're like locusts. They're moving from planet to planet, their whole civilization. After they've consumed every natural resource they move on. And we're next. Nuke 'em. Let's nuke the bastards.'[46] The assertions that it is migrant labour – rather than migrant capital – that destroys environments, communities and the more positive aspects of civil society, and that only the labour embodied in commodities and surplus-value (profit) have the right to cross national boundaries, are vital components of the neoliberal ideology which was coming to prominence when *The Brother from Another Planet* was made and which *Independence Day* and *Men in Black* reproduce.

As indicated above, *Men in Black* deserves closer attention as the gaps and contradictions in its ideologically-complex opening sequence are often revelatory. Although Janus's response to Nick's lie about fishing is intended to be jokey, taken alongside Kay's reference to out-of-town friends it suggests a lot about contemporary Western immigration policies which often claim not to be racist, but which nonetheless distinguish between unskilled 'economic migrants' from the 'developing' world and skilled 'immigrants' from the 'developed' world. Considering that immigration is a discourse riven with euphemisms, Mikey may indeed be a political refugee, despite the scepticism with which his claim is met. That he has broken a number of treaties may criminalise him – in a telling ambiguity, it is unclear whether it is his presence on Earth or in America that is the problem – but there is absolutely no reason to suppose that secret treaties enforced by a covert paramilitary organisation are just. In this context, it is significant that in order for the Men in Black to be presented as heroes, Kay is shown to be unconcerned about the Mexican immigrants whom he only ironically describes as 'the dangerous aliens'.[47]

By dismissing the immigrants to focus on Mikey, *Men in Black* performs precisely the disavowal Csicsery-Ronay, Jr describes, transforming national culture and 'the political-cultural problems of nationality and ethnicity' into an image of racial difference imagined as species difference. That the rest of the film should be so concerned with the recruitment, training and first mission of Kay's new partner, the African-American Jay (Will Smith), is indicative of the extent of the film's disavowal mechanisms.[48]

The expensive computer-generated imagery (CGI) which dominates *Men in Black* could not be more different from *The Brother from Another Planet*'s very cheap – and scarce – effects. The latter's cheerfully low-budget opening effects sequence, in which the Brother's spaceship falls from the sky, constitutes a declaration that the film is unconcerned with the hegemonic aesthetics of post-*Star Wars* blockbuster science fiction, an aesthetic so dominated by spectacle that science fiction films often now seem to be little more than extended advertisements for cutting-edge cinema technologies. Moreover, *The Brother from Another Planet*'s retreat from special effects is accompanied by a rejection of the frequently unreflexive imagery of cinematic science fiction. As the title of this film, its opening Afro-Caribbean music and our first glimpse of the Brother tell us, race will not be displaced onto the figure of the alien. Racial difference will not be imagined as species difference but rather species difference as racial difference. In stark contrast to *Blade Runner* (1982), the alien will have the appearance of the Other it is supposed to displace. This makes the significance of the opening sequence clear. For a black person to enter the US via the traditional route of European immigration is rare enough, but in a racially-divided society it is a fitting irony that he should repeatedly and so insistently not see the symbol of freedom intended to welcome the 'huddled masses'.

The Brother's collapse in the Detention Center is the first of several occasions in the film in which racial and class history is inscribed in the physical structures and spaces of the city. This is exemplified in the scene on the subway in which the Card Trickster (Fisher Stevens), who has just shown the Brother an elaborate trick, offers to perform a rather more impressive piece of conjuring: making all the white people disappear. This is achieved simply by pulling into a station; and, sure enough, all the white people disembark before the train continues on into Harlem. However, we do see some white people in Harlem. Two guys from Indiana in town for a 'Self-Actualization conference' suddenly find they have wandered by mistake into this predominantly non-white part of the city. A white cop on his first day in the precinct sits next to the Brother and tells him about the cannibalistic horror stories with which his partner has been tormenting him. These white men in Harlem have a vital function in the film's analysis of oppression and exploitation inasmuch as their comments can be easily identified as racist; but, as characters, even ones so briefly sketched in, they are rather more complex. Clearly, their racism is not intentionally malicious: they are naïve, insensitive – ignorant, even – but their racism is unintended. By deploying such characters, *The Brother from Another Planet* demonstrates the pervasiveness of racism in America without making it the sole explanation for oppression. Rather, the major root of that oppression is located in American ideology as an articulation of capitalist social relations and commodity culture. As Virgil (Sidney Sheriff, Jr) instructs the Brother on their nocturnal tour of Harlem,

> Children withering away up here, brother, worshipping the idol of capital, lusting after the false salvation of the here and now. Black brother and sister perishing up here, man, waiting for scraps from oppressor's table. Oppressor got us a ho's bed, doing tricks to get reward. Oppressor need a slave, him find it here. Oppressor need a harlot, him find it here.

This key speech, which utilises the imagery of racial and sexual oppression, locates the source of oppression outside of specifically racial and sexual contexts by personifying capital itself as the 'oppressor' (while retaining the sense that the oppressors within the system are, to the extent that they can be individualised, almost certainly white and male). Just as the runaway slaves recalled in the scene at the Harriet Tubman exhibition sought freedom in Harlem – the 'Promised Land' ironically invoked in the film's closing moments by the African-American spiritual of that name ('still not there', it continues) – so various characters seek the Promised Land promised but not delivered by commodity consumption. The main group of such characters are the regulars at Odell's bar. Tolerant acquaintances rather than friends, there is little in their interactions to suggest genuine human solidarity. They seem to meet as much by chance as desire for contact, although the bar itself offers them an important haven from the world. That the promised land their ancestors sought should be reduced to a bar is an ironic indication that of the many aspects of American life from which African-Americans are still excluded, consumption is not one of them (as long as, like everyone else, they can pay). The strength of this critique lies in the fact that it does not condemn the habitués of Odell's bar – in fact, it treats them affectionately as figures of community, however diminished – but treats alcohol as a commodity like any other (including the narcotics for which the junkies fight and die, and the near-orgasmic pleasure sought from video games by the perpetually-bored Ace (Liane Curtis)). What each of the 'drugs' have in common is the commodification of desire – one aspect of the compulsion to repeat with which capital instils us and something to which the Brother himself succumbs.

Almost an hour into the film, the Brother, who has been making a meagre living squeegeeing windshields, wanders down a city street munching on an apple and a cabbage. The camera tracks away from him, keeping him in long shot. He is briefly surprised by a woman wearing deely-boppers. He liberates a dog someone has chained up. Suddenly, he notices something off to his right, and the camera pans to follow him, still tracking back as he passes from a long medium shot to a closer medium shot. He stops in front of a wall covered in (at least 64) posters advertising a new album by Malverne Davis. There is a medium shot of him facing the wall, a background composed of nothing but the replicated image of Malverne. Cut to a medium shot of the Brother, the camera slowly tracking into his face; cut to a reverse shot, the camera slowly tracking in on one poster. The camera tracks in closer to the Brother, and then to the poster; and again, getting closer to both. The Brother blinks, a faint smile growing on his face. On the soundtrack, we hear 'Two People in the World' by Little Anthony and the Imperials. After the final reverse shot of the poster, there is a 15-shot montage sequence of the Brother beginning to notice the sexualised images of women which fill the city: advertisements for beer and Jamaican holidays, strippers, pornographic films and magazines, fashion and lifestyle magazines and several more images of Malverne.[49] Finding Malverne's new album displayed in a record shop window, the Brother buys a copy. He extracts the record, touches it and then discards it along with the polythene wrapper. He walks down the street, the album sleeve held high, admiring her image.

This sequence represents a turning point in the film: suddenly the Brother begins to care about his appearance and express strong emotions, such as his desire to see Malverne and subsequent frustration when the doorman will not let him into the club where she is performing. He becomes a rather more active figure, first meeting and sleeping with Malverne and then tracing the drugs plaguing his neighbourhood back to Mr Vance (Edward Baran).

The liaison between the Brother and Malverne is worth considering in detail as it is simultaneously the film's most successful attempt at depicting genuine human contact and, because of its transitoriness, a doleful indictment of the commodification to which capital subjects us. The neatly turned-out Brother sits alone in the club, content to watch Malverne singing. She is a sort of Diana Ross figure, but one whose success faded after splitting from her group and is now just trying to continue making a living. After her opening set, she joins the Brother at his table and recruits him into the fiction that he is her gentleman friend, so as to ward off the advances of the club owner, Mr Price (Carl Gordon). When the sleazy Price joins them, he is dismissive of the mute Brother, and attempts to use his position to proposition Malverne, reminding her that she is no longer 'flying high'. Because he now owns the club and she now works for him, he seems to feel he in some way owns her, and it signifies something of her status in his eyes that she is not alone when she complains that he has 'been on my ass' (both the bouncer (Randy Frazier) and the waitress (Dwania Kyles) use the same expression to describe his treatment of them). Malverne tells Price that she and the Brother have already made plans for the evening, and after he leaves Malverne reasserts the independence that has characterised her thus far, saying, 'I will never tumble down that low.'

The scene cuts to a bathroom in which Malverne, dressed in a negligé, peels off her fake eyelashes and hair extensions. When she enters the bedroom and asks the Brother whether he is still interested, he applauds this stripping away of the image. As they begin to kiss, Malverne says, 'Let's forget about that woman you saw onstage. It's just you and me, okay?' Aware of her own commodification, Malverne insists that he remembers that she is not her image. We do not see their lovemaking; the film excises it from the visual field, refusing to reduce this potentially utopian moment to a consumable image, merely hinting at its passionate nature and, through their physical proximity next morning as they sit alongside each other on the end of the bed, at the intimacy it has engendered between them.

Ultimately, though, Malverne is unable to escape her commodification for any longer than their night together. She is a commodity in the sense that capital reduces all workers to their exchange value: the 'modern working class ... who live only so long as they find work, and who find work only so long as their labour increases capital ... who must sell themselves piecemeal, are a commodity, like every other article of commerce, and are consequently exposed to all the vicissitudes of competition, to all the fluctuations of the market' (Marx & Engels 1976b: 490–1). Like all commodities, she is unable to provide more than a fleeting satisfaction of the Brother's desire because her job requires her to leave the next day and she has no idea when she will be back in New York. Just as the Brother's desire for her was prompted by her commodification, so she too is subject to her commodity status.

And, ultimately, it is rage against the commodity form – particularly when it proves fatal – that drives the Brother to seek out and kill the drug kingpin, Mr Vance. This expansion out from narcotics to the commodity form is not only supported by the montage sequence described above, but also by one particular shot when the Brother is following the trail of the drugs. On a patch of waste ground outside the city, he watches a deal in progress. In the background, are the twin towers of the World Trade Center, a more convincing emblem than the Statue of Liberty of the society in which he finds himself. In the opening sequence, the interplay of clarity and obscurity as the Statue of Liberty slips in and out of focus, of visibility for the extra-diegetic observer and invisibility for the diegetic observer – this shifting presence-absence on the New York skyline – emphasises the significance of the Statue of Liberty for the film's meaning even as it renders that significance ambiguous. In focus, its meaning seems certain, as fixed as its presence; out of focus, that meaning becomes uncertain, fluid. This brings us to the second commodified woman-image that I wish to discuss, the Statue of Liberty.

Linda Zerilli persuasively argues that the Statue of Liberty is not the bearer of a single, uncontradictory, ahistorical and universal meaning. Rather, it has always been caught up in the ideological wrangling 'over the meaning of the American founding' (2000: 171) and American national identity. As a 'political symbol' and 'national monument', it is without parallel in the 'creation stories that Americans tell themselves about the beginnings of their democracy' (ibid.); but the certainty over its meaning characteristic of much popular commentary serves to assuage 'political anxieties' (2000: 169). Its 'official meaning' at its unveiling did not include immigration, which was deeply contested and opposed 'through the late 1930s' (2000: 177). It was only after the passing of the draconian and racist 1924 Immigration Act, which massively reduced the number of immigrants entering the US, especially from anywhere other than North-Western Europe,[50] that the Statue of Liberty 'came to enshrine "the immigrant experience as a transcendental national memory. Because few Americans were immigrants, all could think of themselves as having been immigrants"' (ibid., quoting Higham 1975: 81). It is unsurprising that the figure of the immigrant should become the totemic national symbol after so many 'actual immigrants had been denied entry' because, Zerilli argues, the diversity of the American population is only partly a product of immigration, being equally derived from the terrorism of 'conquest, invasion, and enslavement' (2000: 177).[51]

Although formally accepted by Congress in 1877, the component parts of the Statue of Liberty spent a number of years stored in crates until Hungarian immigrant Joseph Pulitzer used his newspaper, the *World*, to raise funds from 'working-class and immigrant readers' (Zerilli 2000: 173) to construct a pedestal on which to erect it. Zerilli argues that these largely impoverished sectors of society were 'inspired by the revolutionary spirit' that was lost after the Founding to transform 'Bartholdi's folly' into 'a site of intense mass-affect', known as 'our Lady Liberty' (2000: 174). The shift the Statue of Liberty made from symbolising 'transnational republicanism' to 'immigration' was just the first of several. It later became symbolic of a US 'threatened by the wrong kind of immigrants', of 'national heritage', of 'democracy' (ibid.). Moreover, from the moment of its unveiling, to which no women were invited, its meaning was contested; as a suffragette statement declared, 'In erecting a Statue of Liberty embodied as a woman in a land where no woman has political liberty, men have shown a delightful lack of consistency which excites the wonder and admiration of the opposite sex' (see Zerilli 2000: 171–2, quoting Shapiro 1986: 65). Zerilli critiques the notion, challenged by the suffragettes, that 'sexual difference is the stable, prepolitical ground' on which 'the far more volatile (because political) institutions of democratic equality' (2000: 183) could be constructed. However, she does also refer to two images of black women posing as the Statue of Liberty: Thomas Worth's 1884 'Liberty Frightenin' the World' and Jean Lagarrigue's 1972 picture of Angela Davis. Like the argument about sexual difference, these appropriations confront the way in which racial difference functioned as what Csicsery-Ronay, Jr calls a 'nonnegotiable *essential* line of separation' (2002: 228; emphasis in original) capable of authorising 'in advance political arrangements' (Zerilli 2000: 185).

This overview of some of the meanings and the images of the Statue of Liberty is important because, as Zerilli notes, it 'was an image before she existed as an object' (2000: 175). Stored as a collection of parts, some of which were put on public display, the Statue of Liberty circulated as an image. It is unsurprising that such a potent symbol should have subsequently been used to advertise all manner of commodities, including war bonds, Coca-Cola, Sure deodorant and the Modern Language Association, because from the very outset the Statue of Liberty itself was a commodity. Zerilli refers not only to a variety of souvenirs (including photographic and ornamental reproductions) sold on both sides of the Atlantic to help fund its construction and a range of products which used its image, but also to the world's fairs at which parts of it were displayed in all its 'fragmented, fetishistic glory' (ibid.).[52] Such expositions were both a 'testament to the imbrication of commodity culture and liberal nationalism' (ibid.) and the site at which, Anne McClintock argues, 'a crucial political principle took shape: the idea of democracy as the voyeuristic consumption of commodity spectacle' (see ibid., quoting McClintock 1995: 59). Nowhere has this version of democracy been more apparent than in the Statue of Liberty's 1986 rededication ceremony, which turned the object back into pure image (see Nye 1994: 257–80).

So even though the Brother never actually sees the Statue of Liberty, its presence in the opening sequence becomes relevant not only to the story of an illegal alien entering the US but also to understanding the nature of the society into which he assimilates himself. Although not overtly sexualised like the many other images of women he notices adorning New York, the Statue of Liberty is merely the first spectacle offered for voyeuristic consumption.

I want to end this chapter by returning to the opening sequence and the fact that the Brother never speaks. When he touches surfaces in the Detention Center, he is overwhelmed by the sound of immigrants' voices, a babble of disorientated, confused and anguished European tongues that seem to have been recorded in the very stones of the building. According to Bakhtin, the sociohistorically-specific 'living utterance … cannot fail to brush up against thousands of living dialogic threads, woven by socio-ideological consciousness' (1981: 276). The Brother's touch, which has already been shown to have healing properties, plucks at this dialogical web, activating the lived social being and history inscribed into the physical structures and spaces of the city. Screaming silently at this encounter with the radical otherness of the alien, the Brother collapses.

Bakhtin argues that the lively instability of heteroglossic language is dialectically determined by an anti-authoritarian, centrifugal dispersal and a centralising, centripetal impulse concerned with limiting, rationalising and instrumentalising language, with crystallising its variety into a unity. This dialectical process involves not merely a centripetal-centrifugal tension but also the operation of the dialects and languages of various social groups in relation to each other; and its processes of contradiction and sublation are described by the boundary along which different language-worlds meet and mutually shape each other. Ellis Island, for all its differences from the ports through which African slaves passed, is nonetheless a site through which labour passed and was more or less effectively stripped of language, custom and identity (and often even assigned new names). A traumatic locale, it should be no surprise that the Brother finds traces of these discarded 'Othernesses' lingering there, and in a film which delineates the failure of the US to be the Promised Land, the Brother's silence should perhaps be seen as a refusal to speak – a refusal best understood through Alan N. Shapiro's discussion of the logic underlying *Star Trek*'s universal translator.

While promising communication with the radically alien Other, the universal translator is 'conceived from the start on the model of communication with a computer, not a real Other' (Shapiro 2004: 136). It is postulated on 'a universal cybernetic grid to which all languages are programmable or convertible' and which misses 'any valuation or regard for the radical otherness of the languages of others', running 'counter to any alternative effort of trying to learn the language of others, to see what it is that I can learn from their radical non-compatibility with my own communications protocols' (ibid.). Failing to respect 'that which in their speech is untranslatable, that which in each language is singular and unreconcilable with other languages', the universal translator presumes 'it is possible and desirable to commute the grammars and signifying terms of all languages into each other' and 'absorbs the meaning (or dispersed "non-meaning") of the alien's message into the self-fulfilling prophecy or tautological circuitry of the translation model' in which 'it all comes out as our – projected universal – language' (ibid.). Shapiro locates the 'rationalist telos of translator objectivity' in the 'moral disinterestedness' of transcendent reason detached from sensuous experience (2004: 144). This disembodiment parallels that of capital's suppression of its production by labouring bodies and *langue*'s suppression of socio-historically particular and intersubjectively constituted speaking subjects. Like Alpha 60, the tyrannical computer in *Alphaville* (1965) which devotes an hour each day to tabulating poetry because despite being meaningless it might one day prove useful, the universal translator 'exterminate[s] or processe[s] all radical otherness through its universal conversion tables', evolving, 'in its concrete use, into a machine for the accumulation and whitewashing of all the "alien information" with which it comes into contact' and leaving behind not otherness but 'its burlesque resurrection in systems of recurring and simulated differences' (2004: 144–5).

The Brother, after waking up in the Detention Center, makes his way into the city. The quietness of the early morning streets is interrupted by a blast of hip-hop. In the following montage, the city comes alive with noise: Latino music, the sound of cars, the voices of people hurrying to work and of a black muslim who addresses the Brother. The self-consciousness with which this melting pot is evoked is crystallised in a Korean shopkeeper, whose words are left unsubtitled but who suddenly breaks into English to call out for a policeman when she thinks the Brother is robbing the store (the Brother understands none of these words, regardless of which language they are in, but he does immediately recognise what the policeman's badge and gun signify). While some characters, assuming the Brother must be Puerto Rican or Haitian, address him in Spanish and French, all of them project their own meanings onto his silence, assimilating him to their language-worlds, stripping him of his alien otherness, his difference, rather than seeking to learn from the non-compatibility of communication protocols his silence foregrounds. Conversely, the Brother does not force his language into some cybernetic equivalisation with the terrestrial languages he encounters.

The use of Ellis Island, along with the shopkeeper's summoning of the police in English, identify the dominant language with the authoritarian centripetal tendency which seeks to confine heteroglossia, even as the multilingualism of the people the Brother encounters represents the anti-authoritarian centrifugal tendency. This dialectical tension is evident throughout the film. The alien Men in Black pick up a copy of *English as a Second Language* and immediately begin to speak in the draconian voice of the INS and FBI. The bilingual Hector (Jaime Tirelli) pretends not to speak English when questioned by them, answering in a torrent of Spanish in which the only discernible English dismisses them as 'Roy Orbison y Johnny Cash'. The social worker Noreen (Maggie Renzi) turns away their questions by adopting the language of officialdom, inter-agency co-operation and form-filling. Odell demands to see their badges if they are dicks (detectives), prompting hilarity among the customers when they reply, 'What makes you think we're dicks?' This lively linguistic texture – what Bakhtin would describe as the system of languages welcomed into the film – resists the centralisation of language because it is the specificity of any alien language which the universal translator must strip away in order to equivalise. This everyday linguistic resistance and excess, generated by sociohistorically-specific intersubjective speech-acts, is captured with remarkable subtlety in the first bar scene, in which Odell, his wife and four customers ponder the problem presented by the Brother. For the most part, these characters talk near rather than to each other, carrying on their own habitual monologues which occasionally prompt dialogue between their language-worlds, weaving the fabric that makes them a community which exceeds the cash-nexus that bring them together in this space.

Shapiro roots his analysis of the universal translator in the real-world mass-extinction of languages: of approximately 6000 terrestrial languages, 95% are likely to cease being spoken in the next half-century, with 'only about three hundred ... safe in the long run from the effects of cultural globalization, electronic media expansion, decline of family and community traditions, and government or majority persecution of minorities' (2004: 131). He argues that the consolidating world market, dependent on global digital technology and swamped with global media culture, carries like a virus within it pan-English, a globalised mutation of American English, whose ascendancy 'makes all languages (including, perhaps, English itself) into endangered languages' (2004: 132) . Shapiro imagines a German speaker who 'freely supplements her speech ... with substitute or designer words pulled down from the terminological celestial sky, the ur-language of pan-English' when she talks about 'business management, computer software, digital technology, telecommunications, financial markets or services, fashion, "avant-garde" music, televised sports, window shopping, consumer appliances, home accessories or "personalized" emotions (Ich habe ein Happy Feeling)' (2004: 133). He argues that such linguistic appropriations are in fact signifiers of a desire to belong to a 'globalized professional, technical or consumer' class, and science fiction's fantasies of disembodiment, especially in and since 1980s cyberpunk, have typically been concerned with separating consciousness from sensuous and historical being and entering into the space of, and becoming, circulating information-capital (see Vint & Bould 2006). Like the Korean shopkeeper who calls 'Police!', thus entering into the dominant language, this can be seen as an inversion of Althusserian interpellation, a hailing of rather than by ideology, a self-amputation of one's own radical alien particularity and an entry into the 'cyber-consumerism of difference', the control strategy which rethinks 'energetic turbulence and recombinant mutation as infinitely productive' (Shapiro 2004: 123) for capital.

While the Brother's silence resists the centripetal forces that would render him not-alien, it also 'brush[es] up against thousands of living dialogic threads, woven by socio-ideological consciousness'; his refusal to speak, even more than his occasional mimed expression and rudimentary signing, is a 'living utterance' given 'meaning and shape at a particular historical moment in a socially specific environment' (Bakhtin 1981: 276). In the era of globalised capital, his silence says it all.

CHAPTER FOUR

It's a Free Country: *Matewan, Eight Men Out, City of Hope* and *Passion Fish*

The central concerns of this chapter are the ways in which Sayles' films address the class structure of capitalist modernity and postmodernity. *Matewan* strips away the ideology of social classes to reveal capitalism's more fundamental distinction between and construction of economic classes. *Eight Men Out* and *City of Hope* return to this distinction after various iterations of the processes of capital in order to produce visions of modernity and postmodernity respectively. *Passion Fish* turns from the large social canvas to a microcosmic investigation of social and economic relations under capital. I begin by situating *Matewan* as a melodrama, the primary mode in which Sayles works, establishing a generic framework within which to consider all of his films. While embracing the simplicities of the melodramatic form, each of the films discussed in this chapter build complex social worlds – intensive totalities – from basic determinants and thus imagine the subjects of a 'two-sided' Marxism. My treatment of *Eight Men Out* and *City of Hope* requires lengthy plot description so as to demonstrate the complexity of the social worlds generated by these determinants and the interactions of multiple, simultaneous determinants within them. This dialectical formation of intersubjective being is examined more closely in *Passion Fish*, with its intense focus on two principal characters. Before tracing its development through the film, I will briefly outline Hegel's Master/Slave dialectic, one of the subtlest tools we have for thinking about the inter-dependence and mutual development of subjectivity. This sense of how subjects are constituted underpins all of Sayles' films, albeit more typically in the broader strokes and at the greater remove required by large ensemble casts.

Matewan (1987)

In the early 1920s, the Union of Mineworkers made a short film called *Smilin' Sid* to tell the mineworkers' version of the attempted unionisation in West Virginia which escalated into the Virginia Coalfield Wars (in which state troopers and militia turned machine guns on a miners' march and in which Billy Mitchell, assistant chief of the air service, advocated dropping gas on the striking miners).[53] The only copy of the film is believed to have been stolen by coal company agents and has not been seen since. Likewise, in the era of Reaganite union-busting and the overturning of long-standing anti-trust legislation, *Matewan* recovered this lost piece of history so as to counter the interlocking propagation of a brutally anti-worker agenda by government and business (including a complicit media). However, the politics informing it result not in crude propaganda but a complex evocation of collective lives, of the material basis and narrative construction of history.

When local miners strike in protest over the Stone Mountain Coal Company again lowering the price per ton of coal, union organiser Joe Kenehan (Chris Cooper) arrives in Matewan and settles into the boarding house run by Elma Radnor (Mary McDonnell), whose teenage son, Danny, is already a miner and a preacher. That night, Kenehan attends a miners' meeting at the restaurant run by C.E. Lively (Bob Gunton), where they are joined by Few Clothes (James Earl Jones), the leader of newly-arrived African-American miners brought in, unwittingly, to break the strike. Used to being called 'nigger', he takes exception to being called a 'scab'. Kenehan argues that *all* the miners – including the 'scabs' – must walk out and be welcomed into the union. As this message spreads, Sid Hatfield (David Strathairn), Matewan's chief of police, warns Kenehan not to bring trouble on his people. A mysterious figure writes to the Baldwin-Felts Agency, identifying Kenehan as a 'red' and requesting help. They send Hickey and Griggs (Gordon Clapp), who try to evict striking miners from company-owned housing. Few Clothes and Fausto Maggdino (Joe Grifasi), the leader of the Italian-American miners, join the strike; the other 'scabs' follow suit.

While the strikers remain wary of the other ethnic groups, harassment by the Baldwin-Felts agents escalates. The treacherous C.E. intercepts a letter from the young widow Bridey Mae (Nancy Mette) in which she declares her 'heartfelt desires' for Kenehan, and he uses it to manipulate her into accusing Kenehan of rape and being a company spy. The miners' plan to kill him is called off at the last minute when they discover he has been set up, after which the strike spreads to other hollows. The different ethnic groups begin to merge, symbolised by a baseball game and by the beginning of a friendship between Mrs Elkins (Jo Henderson) and Maggdino's wife, Rosaria (Maggie Renzi), but when the young Hillard Elkins (Jace Alexander) is tortured and murdered by Hickey and Griggs, the strikers take up their weapons. A shoot-out with Baldwin-Felts' hired guns ensues, and the pacifist Kenehan, trying to prevent it, is killed. *Matewan* ends with the image of a miner walking towards the camera. Pappy's (JK Kent Lilly) voice-over, which has intermittently narrated the film, sums up the aftermath of the massacre before the conjunction of the image and the first-person narration reveal that Pappy is Danny, grown old but still a miner and still a union man.

Sayles' screenwriting-for-hire demonstrates a sure grasp of genre, particularly science fiction and horror, but the genre or mode with which he has the clearest affinity is melodrama. Theatrical melodrama emerged in the wake of the eighteenth century bourgeois revolutions. As feudal hierarchies were removed, tragedy's emphasis on people of rank was replaced by the sentimental drama of the bourgeois family. In turn, the sentimental drama, which lacked 'heroic dimensions, overt excitement', 'cosmic ambition' and 'violence' (Gledhill 1987: 17), merged with popular theatrical traditions of spectacle, performance and music to become melodrama. It adopted a Manichean outlook, derived from Gothic fiction and articulated around the polarised capitalist class structure which had replaced feudalism. In the US, this opposition was typically articulated as city versus country rather than bourgeoisie versus the proletariat, with the country 'invested with America's founding ideology, egalitarianism' and the 'rural past' offering the opportunity for 'regeneration' (1987: 24). This mystification of economic class began because 'melodrama's stress on unpremeditated feeling as an index of moral status and social value' (ibid.) enabled American nationalism to disavow economic inequalities – a clear example of the bourgeois eradication of 'the fact of class conflict from the consciousness of society' (Lukács 1971: 62). Christine Gledhill argues that by pursuing a 'nostalgic mode … a national identity convinced of its radicalism' was able simultaneously to admit to, but displace 'into the past, the inequalities emerging with industrialisation' (1987: 24; 25). Such disavowals and displacements were possible because melodramatic conflicts were less concerned with 'the triumph of virtue [than with] making the world morally legible' (1987: 32–3). The melodrama focused on the post-feudal individual, which bourgeois ideology endowed 'with an unprecedented importance', while simultaneously concealing 'that the same individuality was annihilated by the economic conditions to which is was subjected' (Lukács 1971: 62).

Matewan works within this melodramatic tradition (which fed into the naturalism which emerged in the late nineteenth century), simultaneously refuting and reinforcing aspects of its Americanisation. It attempts to make capitalist modernity morally legible through class conflict, but in an embattled rural setting where democracy might be regenerated through the miners' mass action and self-realisation. It is nostalgic for the possibility of virtue triumphing, even as it questions what that might involve. While the miners' unpremeditated feelings render them believable, it is Kenehan, whose feelings are educated by experience, who possesses true moral stature, and although his death might seem to indicate the defeat of virtue, Danny, through his adoption of Kenehan's unionism and his refusal to shoot hired gun Doolin (Michael Mantell), represents the triumph of both unpremeditated feeling and virtue.

Melodrama – 'a modality of narrative with a high quotient of pathos and action' (Williams 1998: 51) – should not be regarded as a 'specific genre' but as 'the fundamental mode of popular American moving pictures' (1998: 42):

the basic vernacular of American moving pictures consists of a story that generates sympathy for a hero who is also a victim and that leads to a climax that permits the audience, and usually other characters, to recognize that character's moral value. This climax revealing the moral good of the victim can tend in one of two directions: either it can consist of a paroxysm of pathos (as in the woman's film or family melodrama variants) or it can take that paroxysm and channel it into the more virile and action-centered variants of rescue, chase, and fight (as in the western and all the action genres). ... if melodrama was misclassified as a sentimental genre for women, it is partly because other melodramatic genres such as the western and gangster films, which received early legitimacy in film study, had already been constructed ... in relation to supposedly masculine cultural values. (1998: 58; 50)

Michael Walker also distinguishes between action melodramas and melodramas of passion. The former pit the hero against the villain, relegate the love interest to a marginal position, and rely upon 'the excitement and suspense of action and conflict' (1982: 17) to generate the strongest emotions in characters and viewers alike; the latter are not especially concerned with 'the external dynamic of action but with the internal traumas of passion (the emotions), audience involvement being held and articulated through the "agonies and ecstasies" of intense personal feelings and relationships' (ibid.). These melodramatic structures, which Linda Williams describes as a 'dialectic of pathos and action – a give and take of "too late" and "in the nick of time"' (1998: 69), are likely to be found operating in any individual text, including *Matewan*. Its social critique does not resort to the kind of alienation devices employed by Douglas Sirk but instead depends on generating emotion, involving rather than distancing the viewer. Its dénouement successfully integrates the traditional oppositions of critique/emotion and action/pathos, realising the hero-victim's moral value through a paroxysm of violent action (the shoot-out) and a paroxysm of pathos – Elma shoots Hickey through her clean washing; Mrs Elkins repeatedly shoots the corpse of her son's murderer; Mayor Cabell Testerman (Josh Mostel) bleeds to death in the street, protesting that he 'only wanted to talk'; Elma discovers Kenehan has been killed in the crossfire; and Pappy's final voice-over says, 'We buried him with our own. My mama she thought he wouldn't never stay, but now he's with us for always, alayin' up here in these West Virginia hills.'

Williams argues that in American film, 'realistic cinematic *effects* – whether of setting, action, acting or narrative motivation – most often operate in the service of melodramatic *affects*' (1998: 42; emphasis in original), as is demonstrated by the physical construction of Matewan and the ways in which it is shot. For example, the film starts with Sephus (Ken Jenkins), working in the confined mineshaft, drilling a hole and planting a charge; the cramping of this realistic space is emphasised by his framing in the corner of the screen. This physical confinement, forced upon the miners by the maximisation of surplus-value, takes on socio-economic and psychological dimensions as they pass, their condition generalised by their synecdochic trudging feet, beneath the guards' guns and through the narrow channel between coal cars, alongside the railway line which expropriates the wealth they produce, and past battered homes. The surface realism of these images produces an emotional affect, a sense of entrapment in this physical, economic and psychological landscape, reinforced by the recurring weatherworn green-and-white Company livery and the tight shot compositions (dictated by a miniscule set- and location-dressing budget). In contrast, the interior of the Radnors' boarding-house is filmed with a warmth that other settings lack, even after Kenehan moves out to make room for Hickey and Griggs. When Kenehan dines there, the scene is orchestrated to create a sense of harmony with these warm surroundings; when Hickey and Griggs dine there, the warmth of the image is persistently undercut by tensions in the dialogue, framing and editing.

It is particularly appropriate that Sayles' affinity for melodrama should come to the fore in *Matewan* and *Eight Men Out* because melodrama is 'a quintessentially modern (though not modernist) form arising out of a particular historical conjuncture' (Williams 1998: 51) and both films directly address capitalism's modernising imperative. Melodrama constructs secular modern worlds 'grounded in the conflicts and troubles of everyday, contemporary reality' and which dramatise 'the problems of this reality – problems such as illegitimacy, slavery, racism, labor struggles, class division, disease, nuclear annihilation, even the Holocaust' (1998: 53); and at the same time defies secular modernity by demanding that it 'yield signs of moral legibility' (ibid.). By combining realism and sentiment, spectacle and action, melodrama reveals misrecognised, concealed, overlooked or misunderstood virtue 'in a world where virtue has become hard to read' (1998: 54), and establishes moral legitimacy through suffering. However, as Williams notes elsewhere, melodrama, unlike tragedy, 'does not reconcile its audience to an inevitable suffering' but often encourages the audience to question the fate its hero accepts (1987: 320). In *Matewan*, suffering is generalised – as Pappy comments, '"All we got in common is our misery," Joe Kenehan used to say, "and the least we can do is share it"' – while several of the miners and their families are transformed from believing in to rejecting its inevitability. This potential homology between characters and audience underpins the film, particularly in the distance it establishes from Kenehan's fatalism (the 'cold comfort' of people knowing he is unarmed when he stands up to Hickey; the desire for his assassins to come quickly because he does not 'want any more shooting in woods'). This distance is important because of the powerful foreshadowing of Kenehan's death, which renders the refusal to show it peculiarly affecting.

Melodrama constitutes a negotiation of the 'moral feeling' (Williams 1998: 61) that capitalist modernity would deny. *Matewan* refuses to treat moral feeling as ahistorical, personal or transcendent, or to isolate it from historical conditions and processes. While its depiction of the suffering and injustice inflicted upon the miners and their families might move the viewer, and the conspiracies and machinations it maps might make the particular narrative twists and turns credible, it also offers opportunities to reflect upon less proximate but nonetheless ubiquitous causes within the logic and structure of capitalism. This is most obvious in the degree to which Kenehan's analysis does not necessarily contradict the complex social relationships around which the narrative is structured. Critics often reduce melodrama to a sentimental Manicheanism, in which virtue and vice are eventually and respectively rewarded and

Matewan: there's them that work and them that don't

punished, but such generalisations miss 'the complexities of tone' found in individual melodramas:

> The peculiar fusion, in different combinations and/or rapid succession, of sentimentality, wistfulness, comedy, moral earnestness, pathos, passion, triumph, despair, high drama and sheer corn (a by no means comprehensive list) makes the tone of melodrama difficult to 'catch' and respond to; indeed, the high brow reaction (intellectual 'sophistication' tyrannising emotional response) commonly rejects these different textures ... *Most* melodramas may be optimistic, but melodramas *can* be highly pessimistic, with unhappy or even bitter endings. (Walker 1982: 12–13; emphasis in original)

Just as *Matewan* exemplifies tonal complexity, textural variety and emotional and intellectual ambiguity, so its social vision, which is based on the fundamental distinction Kenehan describes between 'them that work and them that don't', eschews the reductiveness of economistic, one-sided Marxism by insisting on its characters as subjects-for-themselves as well as subjects-of-capital, whether articulated through the miners' withdrawal of labour or the cultural differences between them. This is not to claim that *Matewan*'s characters are all of the well-rounded variety typical of Sayles' later films. Walker argues that melodrama contains both 'melodramatic' characters, who without self-awareness straightforwardly express 'ideological projects, tensions or contradictions' (1982: 4), and self-aware 'tragic' characters who 'must in some sense come to understand the nature of the forces which impel them, the choices which confront them' (1982: 5). *Matewan* depicts a melodramatic world, divided into oppressor and oppressed, in which Kenehan in particular is whole and undivided, representing a specific ideological position, while both Danny and Elma are internally divided and must come to terms with themselves and the choices which they face. Significantly, Elma is finally able to externalise the source of the relentless drudgery in the figure of Hickey, whom she kills, ostensibly in order to save an injured miner, whereas Danny recognises himself in hired gun Doolin, a fellow worker, and allows him to escape. By making these final choices, Elma and Danny come to understand the melodramatic world they inhabit. Hence Danny's commitment to Kenehan's ideological position, and Elma's mourning and regret over Kenehan's corpse.[54]

James Smith (1973) adds another set of distinctions to the analysis of melodrama, arguing that there are melodramas of triumph, in which virtue is rewarded and evil punished; melodramas of defeat, which typically end with the death of the hero or heroine as 'the "logic" of the villain's superior strength' is pursued to its conclusion (see Walker 1982: 13); and melodramas of protest, 'which set out to attack established ideology, to expose injustice, to champion reform or even to incite revolution' (ibid.). The melodrama of protest – Walker cites *Bronenosets Potyomkin* (*Battleship Potemkin*, 1925), *Mrs Miniver* (1942), *This Land is Mine* (1943), *Roma, Città Aperta* (*Rome, Open City*, 1945), *Z* (1968) and *Yawar mallku* (1969) as examples – constructs a completely polarised world and 'unequivocally' enlists the viewer's

> sympathies … with a group of people – defined by race, nationality, class or political creed – who are 'innocents', victims of persecution, exploitation or oppression. The oppressors/exploiters are usually heavily caricatured … They all use the death of the 'innocent', or, indeed, innocents … as an emotional device, to rouse not just the people in the film, but those in the audience as well. (Ibid.)

Smith claims that 'the melodrama of protest must end in triumph or defeat', but, as Walker notes, only one or two of his examples do so, with a conclusion that 'affirm[s] the determination to fight on' being more common (1982: 14). *Matewan*, then, is probably best understood as a melodrama of protest: the long history of miners' unnecessary deaths precedes the story, motivating the miners to contemplate unionisation and strike action; the murders of various miners and, especially, of Hillard have a profound emotional impact on both characters and viewer; and the unseen death of Kenehan leaves the viewer with a sense of injustice over the unnecessary death of a good man, made all the harder to bear by Elma's response. That the film ends with Danny many years older, still a miner and a union man, replaces 'triumph or defeat' with an affirmation of ongoing struggle.

In addition to negotiating broader melodramatic characteristics, *Matewan* deploys several of the 'standard' melodramatic elements Walker identifies, including a hero falsely accused (but of betrayal rather than murder); a preference for a low-class setting; a polarity between country and city; moral preaching; ideological institutions taking over the function of the villain (the Baldwin-Felts agents represent American capital's repressive apparatus); and the return of a figure out of the past (Kenehan effectively replaces Danny's father, a union man killed in a mine disaster). *Matewan* also advances its narrative through several overtly melodramatic plot devices, such as its use of letters.

When Kenehan arrives in Matewan, he diverts the miners from the violence against the 'scabs' advocated by C.E., arguing that in a world divided into those that work and those that do not, other workers are not the enemy. Although this issue, a simplified version of Marx and Engels' 'antagonism of capitalism and wage-labour' (1976b: 499) which rings true with the IWW's (Industrial Workers of the World) populist syndicalism, is left unresolved, there soon follows a nocturnal scene in which a white fiddler, a white guitar-picker and a black harmonica-player pick up on a tune played by an Italian-American mandolin-player. These four men and three musical traditions do not share the frame, but there is nonetheless a sense of something shared that goes beyond the differences between them. As if sensing the trouble that such hinted-at unity might produce, Sid confronts Kenehan, and then there is a cut to a hand in a circle of light writing the first of the film's several letters. It requests help from the Baldwin-Felts agency, and in the next shot Hickey and Griggs arrive. Music merging under cover of darkness is contrasted with the circle of light in which the letter is written. The former, a tentative communication between individuals and communities, contrasts with this secretive communication in the service of power from someone who must conceal his identity. Music (and, later, baseball) represents a positive use of technology to develop this community;[55] the secretive transmission of information represents (like the train it summons, shot from a low angle, like the agents' 'offence to the ear' car, like the guns and dynamite Kenehan abjures) the negative intrusion of power into this community. This is not a critique of technology *per se*, but of the modernity's double-edge, vividly described by Marshall Berman and which *The Lady in Red* and *Eight Men Out* address more explicitly : 'the glory of modern energy and dynamism, the ravages of modern disintegration and nihilism, the strange intimacy between them: the sense of being caught in a vortex where all facts and values are whirled, exploded, decomposed, recombined; a basic uncertainty about what is basic, what is valuable, even what is real; a flaring up of the most radical hopes in the midst of their radical negation' (1983: 121).

The letter to the agency is the only one that unequivocally reaches its intended destination. Twice letters of authorisation and writs presented by Baldwin-Felts agents are refused, by Sid and Cabell, but more ostensibly melodramatic is C.E.'s interception of Bridey Mae's letter to Kenehan. With the information it contains, C.E. is able to persuade her to falsely accuse Kenehan of rape.[56] He then presents the miners with a bogus letter to Kenehan from the Baldwin-Felts agency, and convinces them that their supposed betrayer must be killed. This melodrama of misplaced, refused, intercepted and forged letters is a familiar one, but what is most significant about them – the one that brings Hickey and Griggs to Matewan, the one that is intercepted and the one that replaces it – is that the narrative hinges upon these other texts being inserted into it. Without the first, the narrative would stall in the absence of clear antagonists; without the latter pair, the war of attrition on the miners would continue without the strike spreading to other mines.

These letters are not the only texts interpolated into the film. The texture of daily life, and the thematic texture of the film, is developed through the telling of stories: Kenehan's account of the Mennonites tortured for going on strike in Leavenworth on a matter of religious conviction; Hickey's story of his wartime 'heroism'; the deceptions of Bridey Mae and C.E.; and, especially, the two sermons delivered by Danny. In the first of these sermons, delivered in response to the preacher's demonisation of Bolshevists, socialists, communists and union men, Danny offers an alternative moral to a parable told by Jesus, directly challenging the public transcript of apparent conformity to the hegemonic framing of labour by declaring the hidden transcript of resistance.[57] In the second sermon, he alters the story of Potiphar's wife, departing from the biblical text; by talking in an idiom which the congregation share (and which Hickey and Griggs are proud not to), he warns the miners of their error and averts Kenehan's murder. Danny's subversions of textual and institutional authority offer a *mise-en-abyme* of the film: stories are never neutral, they are always told with a purpose, and what *Matewan* attempts to do is to interpolate a story (and the class conflict it represents) typically excluded from American history, and it does this by rejecting textual authority – introducing fictional characters, altering the chronology of actual events – so as to speak more clearly.

Do these factual inaccuracies matter? Christopher Ricks suggests that the 'crucial question is that of the terms on which a work ... offers itself ... By proffering factuality, a work is released from certain obligations – for example, our tests of plausibility rightly become different and may even lapse. But ... a work which proffers factuality will enter into other obligations' (1998: 286–7). Despite its factual basis, *Matewan* self-consciously presents itself as not proffering factuality,[58] favouring instead generic verisimilitude and classical narrative's inherently melodramatic form. Moreover, it signals three times that it is a *story* – Danny's construction of the events, recollected in old age, which produced his lifelong unionism – that is being told. His voice-over's personalisation of history embeds this particular narrative in a longer history of struggle *and* justifies departures from the scant historical record. *Matewan* is Danny's final sermon.

Asked about factual accuracy, Sayles says:

I choose different formats for different projects ... One of the things that you have to do is say, 'Okay, am I going to recreate this entire historical world, or am I going to take one episode that stands for it?' In making *Matewan*, I chose to focus on the Matewan Massacre because it seemed to me that this episode epitomized a fifteen-year period in American labor history. To make it even more representative, I incorporated things that weren't literally true of the Matewan Massacre – such as the percentage of miners who were black – but *were* true of that general fifteen-year period. I wanted to be true to the larger picture, so I crammed a certain amount of related but not strictly factual stuff into that particular story ... The struggle you often see in the making of an historical film is the struggle between how much of a viscerally page-turning, emotionally stirring story you want and how much you want people to think about what's going on ... I try not to condescend to [the audience], and implicit in that is a presumption that they will take some responsibility not to believe everything they see and also to see more than one thing. If you're not going to condescend to people, you do have to ask that. Because if you are going to condescend and spoon-feed them everything and simplify everything, then you're saying the people aren't capable of complexity, they're not capable of reading two versions and making up their own minds about which one to believe. That can be a very dangerous point of view. (In Foner 1996: 13; 28; emphasis in original)

This invocation of the complexity is particularly apt in relation to *Matewan*, whose narrative emerges from simple, uncomplicated elements (and whose delineation of class relations is processed through increasingly complex iterations in Sayles' subsequent films). For example, it opens with Sephus inserting a charge in the coalface and lighting the fuse; he is joined by Danny, bringing news of another reduction in the tonnage rate. This pre-title sequence ends with a close up of the fuse, 'sizzling a fraction of an inch from the face, then disappearing inside – KABOOM!!! There is an enormous EXPLOSION – ' (Sayles 1987a: n. p.). This simple, diegetically-motivated image visualises the notion of the miners' short fuse, and of their increased exploitation exploding into industrial action. This principle of simplicity is also exemplified by the different instruments and kinds of music the three ethnic groups use; and as they learn to play together, so they learn to identify with one another, retaining their particular identities while joining together in a larger identity. However, the limits to this emergent class-consciousness are suggested by the ease with which C.E. divides the Italian- and African-Americans from the West Virginians and by the way in which the black harmonica-player is never in the same frame as the other musicians. Without contradicting Kenahan's analysis of capital-labour relations, such moments indicate that life in capitalist modernity cannot be reduced to one-sided Marxism's economic determinism: despite its generic quality, the extraction of surplus-value also has culturally specific features. Marx argued that:

In the social production of their existence, men inevitably enter into definite relations which are independent of their will, namely relations of production appropriate to a given stage in the development of their material forces of production. The totality of these relations of production constitutes the economic structure of society, the real foundation, on which arises a legal and political superstructure and to which correspond definite forms of social consciousness. The mode of production of material life conditions the general process of social, political and intellectual life. It is not the consciousness of men that determines their existence, but their social existence that determines their consciousness. (1987: 263)

This model is typically criticised as representing a static, reductive economic determinism, a misunderstanding that Marx anticipated, insisting that the relationship between base and superstructure must be understood as being 'historical, uneven, and compatible with the effectivity of the superstructure' (Larrain 2001: 46) and arguing that if 'material production itself is not conceived in its *specific historical* form, it is impossible to understand what is specific in the intellectual production corresponding to it and the reciprocal influence of one on the other' (Marx 1989: 182; emphasis in original). This not only indicates Marx's clear sense of the base and superstructure being in a state of constant change, but also contends that the superstructure (intellectual production) influences the base (material production). Elsewhere, he acknowledges that changes in the base do not necessarily – or perhaps ever – produce straightforward superstructural changes (see 1986: 46). Although he did not have the requisite vocabulary available to him, it is evident that Marx considered determinism to be complex, for the 'effects' of 'causes' to always be mediated by their sensitive dependence upon initial conditions. Engels, too, insisted that 'if someone distorts this by declaring the economic moment to be the *only* determining factor, he changes that proposition into a meaningless, abstract, ridiculous piece of jargon' (2001: 34).

When explaining the miners' position as labour, as subjects of capital, Kenehan distinguishes between 'them that work, and them that don't', an appropriately vulgarised version of Marx's observation that capitalist production 'under its aspect of a continuous connected process, of a process of reproduction, produces not only commodities, not only surplus-value, but it also produces and reproduces the capitalist relation; on the one side the capitalist, on the other the wage labourer' (1996: 577). Despite Kenehan's colloquial compression of the nature of, and relationship between, proletarian and capitalist classes, the immediacy and clarity of his phrasing does not detract from his appreciation of labour's position as a commodity to be bought, used up and discarded by capital. Mike Davis notes that the increasing contemporary

> proletarianization of the American social structure has not been matched by an equal tendency toward the homogenization of the working class as a cultural or political collectivity. Stratifications rooted in differential positions in the social labor process have been reinforced by deep-seated ethnic, religious, racial, and sexual antagonisms within the working class. In different periods these divisions have fused together as definite intra-class hierarchies (for example 'native + skilled + Protestant' versus 'immigrant + unskilled + Catholic') representing unequal access to employment, consumption, legal rights, and trade-union organization. The political power of the working class within American 'democracy' has always been greatly diluted by the effective disenfranchisement of large sectors of labor: blacks, immigrants, women, migrant workers, among others. (1999: 16)

Because Kenehan recognises workers as a class, he can cut through prejudices about ethnic and geographic identities that capital is always ready to manipulate and find the identity shared by all workers as labour. His words are lent weight by his later descriptions of World War One as 'just workers killin' workers' and of his two years in Leavenworth as a conscientious objector being 'worth it' because they kept him 'from killin' some poor stiff who got pushed out on a battlefield by rich folks and politicians'. Kenehan also draws attention to state and federal government's bolstering of capital, serving its interests over those of the workers – a point reinforced by Sephus's scepticism about his country when Kenehan argues that the union is a democracy 'like the United States is a democracy'. The particular forms taken by these ideological and repressive apparatuses, both individually and in combination, are therefore determined, albeit in complex ways, by the conflict in the economic base. This complexity is demonstrated by Sid and Cabell, both of whom, if the base-superstructure model was reductively determinist, would support the coal company and the Baldwin-Felts agents. That they do what they can to protect the citizens of Matewan even though they do not, apparently, support the strike, but restrict their actions to their sanctioned spheres of action (the town limits), typifies the conflicted positions that can arise from an apparently straightforward causative mechanism when it is complexly mediated.

This apparent complexity proves an obstacle to the development of class-consciousness. Prior to Kenehan's arrival, there is no community between the West Virginian miners and the African- and Italian-Americans; there is competition between neighbouring hollows; the only political organisation is the nebulous group who meet under C.E.'s watchful eyes. Uncertain of their class interests, the people of Matewan have no voice other than marginal participation in county, state and federal government – a participation which, even if they pursue it, results in their subordination to a political system unconcerned with their class interests. The drama of *Matewan* is, then, the drama of a class discovering itself, of class-consciousness emerging.

Eight Men Out (1988)

In *The Lady in Red*, Polly and Dillinger joyfully play baseball in a luminously-shot rural setting, and *Matewan*'s striking miners, beginning to identify themselves as workers regardless of ethnicity, play the same game together, democratically participating as subjects-for-themselves rather than subjects-of-capital. *Eight Men Out*, adapted from Eliot Asinof's account of how and why the Chicago White Sox threw the 1919 World Series, turns these idyllic images on their head, recovering history so as to tell a different story about the 'Black Sox scandal', which makes clear the role played by the owners, gamblers, legal system and mass media. Only in this larger context can the players' actions be understood.

Despite being set a year earlier than *Matewan*, the urban setting of *Eight Men Out* offers a more complex picture of capitalist modernity than its predecessor. It is Chicago, 1919. Two young boys, Peewee (Brad Garrett) and Bucky (Tay Strathairn), race through the streets to Comiskey Park to watch the White Sox. In an impressively concise expository sequence, the audience is introduced to journalists Ring Lardner (John Sayles) and Hugh Fullerton (Studs Terkel), White Sox owner Charles Comiskey (Clifton James), two minor gamblers – ex-pitcher 'Sleepy Bill' Burns (Christopher Lloyd) and ex-boxer Billy Maharg (Richard Edson) – and the key White Sox players: pitchers Eddie Cicotte (David Strathairn), Claude 'Lefty' Williams (James Read) and Dickie Kerr (Jace Alexander); first baseman Arnold 'Chick' Gandil (Michael Rooker), second baseman and team captain Eddie Collins (Bill Irwin), third baseman George 'Buck' Weaver (John Cusack), short stop Charles 'Swede' Risberg (Don Harvey), center fielder Oscar 'Happy' Felsch (Charlie Sheen), catcher Ray 'Cracker' Schalk (Gordon Clapp), left fielder 'Shoeless' Joe Jackson (D. B. Sweeney) and manager William 'Kid' Gleason (John Mahoney). Although they play well together, many of the players do not like each other – the ribbing and mocking, especially of the illiterate Jackson, is far from good-natured – and they are not well-paid. While the assembled journalists carouse at Comiskey's expense, the winning White Sox find that he has sent them bottles of flat champagne instead of a promised bonus.[59]

The next sequence, the Sox's bar-room celebrations, quickly sketches in more detail about individual players and how they relate to each other, as well as depicting the free intermingling of sportsmen, gamblers and journalists. Gambler Joseph 'Sport' Sullivan (Kevin Tighe) listens while Gandil discusses, hypothetically, how easily the upcoming World Series against the Cincinnati Reds could be fixed, with bribes for just half-a-dozen players. Burns then approaches Gandil and Risberg, and they agree to fix the series, planning to take both gamblers' money. When Comiskey refuses to pay Cicotte a $10,000 bonus for pitching thirty victories (he pitched 29, but had been deliberately rested for a couple of weeks),[60] he joins the conspiracy; Williams is soon recruited, too. Meanwhile, Burns and Maharg ask Abe Attell (Michael Mantell) to take their proposition to wealthy gambler Arnold Rothstein (Michael Lerner); when Rothstein refuses to become involved, Attell calls in debts owed to Rothstein to finance the fix himself. Sullivan then persuades Rothstein to fix the series, and puts the money on Cincinnati, giving the players just enough to 'know they're hungry'.

Gandil recruits Felsch while Risberg half-cons, half-bullies Jackson into joining them. Weaver wants nothing to do with the fix, but cannot bring himself to tell manager Gleason about it. While Attell is elusive about their money, Gandil pays Cicotte from the money Rothstein gave Sullivan, ensuring the first game of the series is thrown. Suspicious, Lardner and Fullerton agree to keep separate scorecards of every play to see if they identify the same ones as dishonest.[61]

Game one. Gleason insists the reluctant Jackson plays. In New York's Ansonia Hotel, each play is simulated on a wall display and Rothstein watches until Cicotte gives the signal that the fix is on. After the 9-1 defeat, Lardner asks Cicotte if the match was fixed. Cicotte denies it. Williams pitches the second game, throwing it 4-2. After the game, a furious Schalk attacks Williams, and Gleason attacks Gandil. That night, outside the hotel a White Sox player is burned in effigy. There follows a carefully choreographed sequence in the hotel: Gleason tells Comiskey about the suspected fix; Comiskey and John Heydler (Eliot Asinof), the President of the National League, try to tell Ban Johnson (Clyde Bassett), the President of the American League, but he does not believe them. Burns and Maharg try to get more money for the players, but Attell gives them only $10,000 because all the rest is 'out on bets' and he does not intend to give them any more.

Kerr, who is not in on the fix, pitches game three. His and Weaver's example, and the absence of further money, inspires the other players, and they win 3-0. Burns and Maharg lose all their money, and Attell is in trouble, too. Cicotte pitches game four, losing 2-0; Williams pitches the fifth, losing 4-0. Walking home, Weaver runs into Peewee and Bucky and tells them that 'a guy's gotta stick up for his friends'. Kerr pitches game six, winning 5-4.

Cicotte and Williams realise that they do not actually care about the money as much as they do about the game, and Williams and Felsch tell Gandil that they are going to play to win. Cicotte persuades Gleason to let him pitch, and they win the seventh game 4-1. They are now 4-3 down in the nine game series. Rothstein sends henchman Monk Easton (Stephen Mendillo) to pressurise Sullivan, who in turn sends a hired killer (Danton Stone) to threaten Williams' wife. In game eight, he gives the Reds an insurmountable lead by pitching 'nothing but fast balls – slow ones' until he is relieved. The Sox lose the game 10-5 and the series 5-3. Gleason cannot comfort the inconsolable Weaver.

Collins tells Comiskey that the series was fixed. Comiskey's lawyer, Alfred Austrian (Michael Laskin), argues that from a business perspective the guilt or innocence of the players is irrelevant. Comiskey and the club owners ask Judge Kenesaw Mountain Landis (John Anderson) to clean up the game; he agrees to accept a well-salaried life-time appointment as baseball commissioner.[62] Lardner suggests that the way to clean up baseball would be to start with the owners. Cicotte, Jackson and Williams sign confessions; as Jackson leaves the court building among a throng of reporters, PeeWee asks him to 'Say it ain't so, Joe'. Austrian introduces the eight indicted players to their high power defence team, but refuses to tell Weaver who is footing the bill. Rothstein's lawyer (John D. Craig) convinces Austrian to hand over the confessions. Weaver's request for a separate trial is denied. Talking to his wife, Rose (Maggie Renzi), Cicotte identifies Comiskey, Sullivan, Attell and Rothstein as the real conspirators, yet of these only Comiskey and Sullivan appear in court – and then as prosecution witnesses. Weaver tells PeeWee and Bucky that life becomes complicated when you grow up, and his mistake was not growing up. When the players are acquitted, Lardner notes that 'That was a bigger fix than the series'. But as the players celebrate, Landis states that 'regardless of the verdicts of juries, no player who throws a ball game, no player that undertakes or promises to throw a ball game, no player that sits in conference with a bunch of crooked players and gamblers where the ways and means of throwing a game are discussed and does not promptly tell his club about it, will ever play professional baseball'. A brief coda shows Jackson playing under an assumed name for a semipro team in Hoboken, while a broken Weaver watches incognito. The crowd remember the 1919 White Sox as 'those bums who threw the World Series'.

This complicated plot not only challenges what we thought we knew about the Black Sox scandal but also, by refusing to pass judgement, challenges audiences to reconsider the ways in which we make sense of a world relayed to us through media which are organised in such a way that 'objectivity' and 'truth', if they are even viable categories, are not primary concerns (despite frequent claims to the contrary). In a way, *Eight Men Out* can be seen as the story behind the headlines and newspaper reports, a story in which news media were uninterested or had no capacity to relate. But it does not end there. The film is a simplification of a book pieced together from the not entirely accurate memories of those involved. History is unrecoverable; there are only narratives, some of which might get us closer to what actually happened, hence the film's preoccupation with 'the social construction – the making and meaning – of [the players'] actions' (David Scobey, quoted in Ryan 1998: 155), with challenging common constructions and offering the possibility of different constructions which counter the eradication of 'the fact of class conflict from the consciousness of society' (Lukács 1971: 62). Although Ring Lardner's occasional laconic witticisms come close

Eight Men Out: anything can happen in this game

to voicing this fact, it is the film's artful construction which produces such an analysis. Take, for example, the sequence following the Sox's seventh-game victory, beginning in their dressing room.

In the foreground, facing the viewer, a photographer and his assistant prepare to take a photograph. Behind them are a number of reporters, including Fullerton in the centre and Smitty (Jim Desmond) to his left. The flashbulb flares; the photographer and his assistant depart. Cut to a reverse shot of Kid Gleason, the subject of the photograph, in mid-shot facing the reporters, still wearing his uniform. On either side, the outline of a reporter's head and shoulder enframes him, as does the stovepipe to his right. Visible through the gap between the stovepipe and Kid are two more reporters, one in a straw boater, facing the audience. Weaver is just discernible in the background. Kid is proud of his team, but the Sox logo on his puffed-up chest looks, on Weaver's shirt, more like a dollar sign. Kid is in mid-flow: '…and I figured I oughta stay with my blue chip ball players. You have faith in your fellas, they come around.' Goofing around, Weaver throws a towel at another player, one of several tiny details in this sequence which shows the players to be more than just the 'horses' both Sullivan and Comiskey describe or the investment to which Gleason compares them. Cut back to the reporters. Smitty says, 'The Reds only need one more game to take the series. Now it's do or die for your club.' In a slightly closer medium shot, Kid, on the right of the frame, raises a bottle of beer to his lips and replies, 'No sweat.'

Cut to Arnold Rothstein, huge in the foreground of the left of the screen, dominating the space Kid did not occupy in the previous shot. His out-of-focus plush surroundings contrast with the busy space centring on Kid, emphasising his isolation. A phone in his massive, foregrounded right hand, Rothstein lifts the earpiece and begins to talk. However, we do not hear his words, because the dressing room exchange continues in voice-over: Fullerton asks, 'What makes you so confident, Kid?' Kid replies, 'I think the boys are back on their form. They've got a look at…' – dissolve to a sombre-looking Monk Easton in a telephone booth, taking (it is implied) Rothstein's call – '…[Reds' manager] Moran's stuff and they'll be swinging free from this point on.' Dissolve to Sullivan sitting in a lobby, a money clip in his hand. He occupies the left foreground of the frame. Kid's voice-over continues: 'I tell you, class always comes through in the clinches. Eddie came to me this morning and he says, "Kid," he

Eight Men Out: lines of power and influence

says, "I can't miss." We got Lefty Williams rolling for us tomorrow…' Monk looms up in the right-hand side of the frame, squeezes Sullivan's shoulder and speaks into his ear. Sullivan's expression changes. Cut to the dressing room, Kid in medium close-up, more centrally positioned but still to the right of the frame, pontificates, gesticulates, '…one of the best pitchers I ever seen. He's due a big game, Lefty.' As the reporter in the boater scribbles down Kid's words, Weaver, wearing his shirt under his hat, sidles into the left background of the frame and tips the boater down over the reporter's eyes. Suddenly Ring Lardner starts to speak. The camera begins to move to the right, but almost immediately there is a cut to Lardner, standing tall in profile on the right of the frame. Erect, high-collared, he towers over the reporters to either side of him. 'How do you explain the way your boys lay down in the other games?' Cut back to Kid, now on the left of the frame, looking right. There is a change in his posture, as if this question and the incomplete camera movement have removed him from his seemingly secure position in the frame. A reporter's left shoulder fills the right-hand side of the frame, the reporter in the boater has turned to follow this fresh exchange, and Kid now seems surrounded once more: 'What d'ya mean, "lay down"?' Cut back to Lardner, the attention of the other reporters making him seem even more upright: 'Well, they didn't seem too enthusiastic about their jobs.' As Kid replies, there is a cut to Sullivan in a phone booth in a lobby. Shot from a low angle, the camera slowly rises as he speaks into the phone. Although the image has again changed to a different location, we stay with Kid's dialogue: 'Nobody did any lying down.' Then, in a more conciliatory tone: 'Might have been a little overconfident, maybe we didn't have the fine edge, but the boys've been putting out.' There is a cut from Sullivan, who was on the right of the screen, to the unknown man receiving the call. His head and shoulders fill the left half of the screen. The camera tracks away from him as he hangs up. A voice responds to Kid, 'The boys been put out more than they've been putting out', prompting laughter. The man strides across a hotel room. Fullerton asks, 'You really think you can take the series, Kid?' He replies, 'No sweat.' Fullerton: 'The odds are pretty steep.' The man stops, opens a suticase, the edge of its lid entering the bottom of the frame. Kid: 'My boys don't care about the odds…' – the camera continues to track around the man as he raises the lid higher – '…Anything can happen in this game…' – the man drops the lid, revealing a revolver – '…anything' – the man flips open the gun, examines it.

This sequence is full of ironies. Weaver messes about in the background, believing his team-mates have straightened out for good. It is the last time we will see him happy. The same dramatic irony frames Kid's pride in his team, who he describes as a reliable investment – but the term 'blue chip' originates in gambling (it is the highest value poker chip). Moreover, there is the unfolding irony of his words as the viewer begins to anticipate that Lefty will indeed face a 'big game', that anything is possible as the hired killer prepares to threaten his wife. Kid leaves his doubts about the team behind, and believes himself to be back at the centre of what is going on – only Lardner can dislodge him briefly from this position – but his public centrality is contrasted with the private centrality of Rothstein and Sullivan, both of whom occupy the edges of the frame.

This sequence also makes visible the lines of power and influence utilised by the wealthy, symbolised here by telephony and telegraphy. (Again, this is not a critique of technology *per se* or these technologies in particular, but of how technology can make available to capital new means of exercising power.) Just as the reporters surround Kid, so does a network of unseen forces, pulling strings to change the outcome of the game. In *Matewan*, exploitation happens at a distance, the mine owners remaining unseen. In *Eight Men Out*, we see the exploiters, although Comiskey rarely, and Rothstein never, occupies the same frame as the exploited players. Comiskey distances himself from them, courting reporters in the clubhouse and appearing as a prosecution witness, while Rothstein operates through interme-diaries. The telephone enables the gamblers and their henchmen to organise the fix, and the ticker tape, which enables a New York elite to enjoy a virtual reconstruc-tion of the games, carries the message to Rothstein that the fix is on. These basically private means of communication are contrasted with Bucky and PeeWee's crystal set, wireless telephony being not a point-to-point but a public broadcast medium. Although it is no more inherently democratic than telegraphy, it is contrasted with the telephone and ticker tape by being used neither for control nor for gambling but for the boys to listen to their team playing in another city. It here symbolises a positive use of technology to build community, even as professionalised baseball loses that capacity.

By following *Matewan* with a film set a year earlier but in major urban centres, Sayles effectively leaps ahead several iterations of the determinate class conflict. Although it remains central, there are a number of characters who occupy potentially ambiguous positions within the opposition between capital and labour. The broad contrasts of the opening sequence of *Eight Men Out* – Comiskey's luxurious existence, the players' impoverishment – become more complicated as the film proceeds, as complex interre-lations and actions arise from this dynamic dialectic. Whereas the unionised miners of *Matewan* found a collective response to their economic exploitation, *Eight Men Out*'s players merely translate their individual discontents into an exchange of bosses. *Mate-wan*'s Danny and *Eight Men Out*'s Weaver embody this contrast. Both young men are forced to grow up: one becomes a union man and spends his life fighting for workers' rights, the other becomes an ex-baseball player who until he died sought, unsuccess-fully, to clear his name.

Lenin argued that the proletariat could develop 'trade union consciousness' but class-consciousness had to be brought to them by professional revolutionary intellectuals. Rosa Luxemburg instead emphasised the role of experiencing exploitation and class struggle, arguing that even the errors that would be made were important in the development of class-consciousness. *Matewan* straddles these positions, with an intellectual coming from outside, but with an analysis informed by his own lengthy experience of class struggle, while *Eight Men Out* is an exemplary depiction of errors made in the development, and derailment, of class-consciousness. Central to this is the antagonism which sets the players at each others' throats. Except for Collins, who had negotiated a decent salary when he transferred to the Sox, they were the worst-paid major league team in America. Other players ridicule Collins' middle-class background, college education and teetotalism. When Williams stands up for Jackson, who is teased for his illiteracy, they are both mocked as Southerners. And so on. There is no Kenehan to argue the irrelevance of these differences and, instead of recognising their class position as a basis from which to respond to their shared exploitation, some of them develop a kind of trade union consciousness *manqué* and try to exploit the system that is exploiting them, even though this takes the form of subordinating themselves to another set of bosses who, like Comiskey, are more concerned about the profitability than the well-being of the players. Whether by Comiskey or the gamblers, the players are given enough to subsist, to reproduce their labour power – 'just enough to know [they are] hungry' – but that is all.

Lukács argues that:

> If the meaning of history is to be found in the process of history itself and not, as formerly, in a transcendental, mythological or ethical meaning foisted on to recalcitrant material, this presupposes a proletariat with a relatively advanced awareness of its own position, i.e. a relatively advanced proletariat, and, therefore, a long preceding period of evolution. The path taken by this evolution leads from utopia to the knowledge of reality; from transcendental goals fixed by the first great leaders of the worker's movement to the clear perception by the Commune of 1871 that the working-class has 'no ideals to realise', but wishes only 'to liberate the elements of the new society'. It is the path leading from the 'class opposed to capitalism' to the class 'for itself'. (1971: 22)

Like the miners, the players struggle to become opponents of capital. For the miners, playing baseball symbolises becoming a class for itself, but for the players it is the very site of their exploitation. Through its urban setting *Eight Men Out* represents capitalist modernity and class dialectics after several more turns of the historical screw. The sensitive dependence on initial conditions from which simple determinants give rise to complex social organisation becomes more complex away from the almost diagrammatic simplicity of *Matewan*'s contained hollow. In the big cities, a wider array of subject positions is available but that does not invalidate the fundamental distinction between 'them that work and them that don't'. Lukács argues that it was only with capitalism, 'with the abolition of the feudal estates and with the creation of a society with a *purely economic* articulation, [that] class-consciousness arrived at the point where *it could become conscious*. From then on social conflict was reflected in the ideological struggle for consciousness and for the veiling or the exposure of the class character of society' (1971: 59; emphasis in original). This process of coming-to-consciousness involves transcending 'the limitations of particular individuals caught up in their own narrow prejudices' while not overstepping 'the frontier fixed for them by the economic structure of society and establishing their position within it' (1971: 52). The principle obstacle is that proletarian class-consciousness 'is divided within itself', the 'most striking division ... and the one most fraught with consequences' being 'the separation of the economic struggle from the political one':

> The cause of this aberration is to be found in the dialectical separation of immediate objectives and ultimate goal and, hence, in the dialectical division within the proletarian revolution itself. ... The dialectical cleavage in the consciousness of the proletariat is a product of the same structure that makes the historical mission of the proletariat possible by pointing forward and beyond the existing social order. In the case of the other classes we found an antagonism between the class's self-interest and that of society, between individual deed and social consequences. This antagonism set an external limit to consciousness. Here, in the centre of proletarian class-consciousness we discover an antagonism between momentary interest and ultimate goal. The outward victory of the proletariat can only be achieved if this antagonism is inwardly overcome. (1971: 70, 73)

In *Matewan*, the miners begin to subordinate the momentary interest to the ultimate goal; in *Eight Men Out*, the ball players are in no position to do so. Lukács continues:

> *Only the consciousness of the proletariat can point to the way that leads out of the impasse of capitalism.* As long as this consciousness is lacking, the crisis remains permanent, it goes back to its starting-point, repeats the cycle until after infinite sufferings and terrible detours the school of history completes the education of the proletariat and confers upon it the leadership of mankind. But the proletariat is not given any choice. As Marx says, it must become a class not only 'as against capital' but also 'for itself'; that is to say, the class struggle must be raised from the level of economic necessity to the level of conscious aim and effective class-consciousness. (1971: 76; emphasis in original)

Matewan depicts this attempt to transcend mere opposition to capital (in order to secure subsistence) and to achieve effective class-consciousness. Ultimately, the attempt fails, sending the proletariat back into the school of history; but for several brief, conflicted moments, we are privileged to see – to feel – the hopeful texture of that emerging consciousness, figured in the baseball match, and in Danny's recognition of Doolin as a fellow worker. In contrast, and apart perhaps from their occasional on-field celebrations, the White Sox never leave the school of history.

City of Hope (1991)

There is a sequence in *Eight Men Out* which provides an image of the multiple interlockings of the various conspiracies and narrative strands. Gleason, suspecting match-fixing, strides down the stem of a T-shaped hotel corridor – passing Sullivan's henchman, Jimmy (Philip Murphy), who lurks furtively before going into Sullivan's room – to Comiskey's room at the juncture of the T. He knocks on the door and enters. Swede turns into the corridor, passes Comiskey's room and turns down the stem of the T to Gandil's room; Gandil admits him, and as the door closes, Gleason and Comiskey storm past, down the stem of the T, and turn out of sight at the far end. Burns and Maharg, who have just passed them, go into Attell's room. The bed is covered in cash, but Attell tells them he has no more money for the players because it is all out on bets; when Burns presses him, he gives them $10,000, saying, 'but that's the end of it'. As Burns and Maharg leave, Comiskey, Heydler and Gleason come charging back up the corridor and hammer on Ban Johnson's door. He admits Comiskey and Heydler, leaving Gleason in the corridor. Johnson dismisses his visitors with a cry of 'That's the whelp of a beaten cur!' Comiskey and Heydler return to their respective rooms, again leaving Gleason in the corridor. Jimmy emerges from Sullivan's room and scurries off. Risberg emerges from Gandil's room, mutters a greeting to Gleason, and disappears. Gleason wanders off.

Except for the scene in Attell's room, this sequence has just two shots. The carefully choreographed handing over of the action from one set of characters to another insists upon the shared social space of owners, gamblers and players as well as the links in the conspiracy which remained invisible until Asinof's account was published 45 years later. It also pioneers the 'trade' technique central to *City of Hope*'s complex interimplication of characters within a social sphere that tends to alienate them from one another. Set in fictional Hudson City, which is being asset-stripped by a declining Italian-American power bloc before control shifts to African- and Hispanic-Americans, its interrelated narratives are structured along the model provided by this sequence. The plot description that follows is deliberately detailed so as to capture some sense of just how complex these interrelations are.

The film opens with Nick Rinaldi (Vincent Spano) begging Yoyo (Stephen Mendillo) for some coke. They are both on the payroll of Nick's father, Joe (Tony Lo Bianco), although neither of them actually do anything on the construction site run by Riggs (Chris Cooper). Nick quits and leaves with his friends Bobby (Jace Alexander) and Zip (Tod Graff), while Joe argues with Councilman Wynn (Joe Morton) about employing some black workers from the local community he represents. Wynn visits the P Street Community Center, where he asks Levonne (Frankie Faison) and Malik (Tom Wright) to help him pack out a Council meeting, but both are sceptical of his involvement with the white political machine. Wynn's wife, Reesha (Angela Bassett), asks him to help find a job for her ex-con brother, Franklin (Daryl Edwards).

Outside Mad Anthony's electrical goods store, the deranged, homeless Asteroid (David Strathairn) imitates Mad Anthony's television advertisement. Connie (Maggie Renzi) and Joann (Marianne Leone) complain to two cops, Rizzo (Anthony John

Denison) and Bauer (S.J. Lang), about the deterioration of the neighbourhood. As the uninterested cops drive away, they run into O'Brien (Kevin Tighe), a detective Bauer dislikes for his relentless politicking. They drive past DeLillo's restaurant, where Rizzo's ex-wife Angie (Barbara Williams) waitresses. Nick sees her through the window. Inside, the District Attorney's assistant, Zimmer (Michael Mantell), discusses a property deal, clarifying the size of his bribe.

Wynn recommends Mad Anthony (Josh Mostel) hire Franklin as a security guard; Anthony assumes this is a favour he will be able to call in at a later date. Two bored-looking kids, Desmond (JoJo Smollett) and Tito (Edward Jay Townsend, Jr) wander around the store. At City Hall, Zimmer makes it clear that for the Galaxy Towers project to proceed on schedule, Mayor Baci (Louis Zorich) will have to get the L Street apartments torn down; they turn to Pauly Rinaldi (Joe Grifasi), whose brother Joe owns the slum buildings in question. That same afternoon, Bobby and Zip ask Nick to help them rob Mad Anthony's store, a job organised by auto-shop owner and small-time crook Carl (John Sayles). First, Nick stops off at his parents' home, where a party is in progress. Pauly tries to persuade Joe to evict the L Street tenants. Nick's mother refuses to pay his $2000 gambling debt to Carl, and his sister Laurie (Gina Gershon) – who is in the kitchen with their housekeeper, Mrs Ramirez (Miriam Colon) – can only give him a few dollars. Nick argues with his father about quitting work and about his older brother, Tony, who died in Vietnam. Nick decides to help with the robbery, even though Mad Anthony is a family friend.

En route to his new job, Franklin passes Desmond and Tito, who are picked on by two cops, Paddy (Jude Ciccolella) and Fuentes (Jaime Tirelli). The cops then spot Ramirez (Serafin Jovet) heading into a bar. Inside, Zip scores off Ramirez before joining Bobby on stage to play some pseudo-Springsteen rock. Carl reminds Nick of his debt. Nick runs into Angie, who used to go to the same school, and tries to make a date with her before leaving with Bobby and Zip.

Desmond and Tito walk through a park, grumbling about the police. Tito takes it out on the first white man they see, beating up Les (Bill Raymond), a college professor out jogging. The cops soon pick up the two boys. At a council meeting, Wynn's impassioned plea for a bond issue to raise money for local schools is defeated. Franklin catches Bobby and Zip when they try to rob Mad Anthony's, and Nick runs off. In the police station, Tito claims that Les tried to touch them. Levonne, who is there with Malik to report vandalism of the P Street Center, gets the boys a lawyer. Bobby and Zip are brought in; only then does Franklin reveal that his gun is a plastic replica.

Nick bumps into Angie and walks her home. She agrees to see him again. The next morning, the papers are full of the alleged sexual assault on the boys and the failed robbery attempt. Rizzo warns Nick to stay away from Angie, his ex-wife. Malik and Levonne challenge Wynn to stand up for the boys; Wynn says he will investigate the matter. O'Brien quizzes Bobby and Zip, but they refuse to name their driver, instead convincing Asteroid, who is in the same cell, to confess. O'Brien blackmails Carl into revealing Nick's identity, and passes the information to Zimmer, in exchange for a promotion to the D.A.'s office. When Wynn questions Desmond at home, he persists in lying about the assault.

At the construction site, to put pressure on Joe about L Street, the workers have been ordered to down tools. Pauly tells Joe that the police are after Nick; that the D.A. is after Joe's family to help his chances when he stands for Senator; and that L Street must be shut down. Nick goes to DeLillo's to see Angie. There, Yoyo warns him the cops are looking for him, while at another table Baci tries to bribe Wynn. Joe goes to see Kerrigan (Lawrence Tierney), the gangster from whom he borrowed the money for his current construction project; Kerrigan tells him he must do what Baci wants. At Madison State, where Angie is a student and where Reesha works, Les receives a less than sympathetic reception from his boss.

That night, Nick visits Angie and meets her autistic son, Jessie. Joe meets Carl, who has been given the job of making L Street uninhabitable through fire- and flood-damage. Les goes out running, determined his life will not be changed. Rizzo watches Angie's apartment; inside, Nick and Angie make love. Joe tells his wife about the trouble Nick is in, but that he has done what is necessary to sort it out. That night, the derelict side of L Street goes up in flames, killing Ramirez's girlfriend and baby. Paddy refuses to arrest Ramirez, who is comforting his mother, the Rinaldi's housekeeper. The next day, when Wynn is trying to help out the newly homeless at the P Street Center, the news comes out that Joe has sold L Street to property developers. Rizzo's partner tells him that Nick is wanted on suspicion of robbery. Joe secretly arranges to pay half the costs of the Ramirez funeral.

Because Malik and Levonne are bound to ask Wynn publically whether he believes Desmond and Tito, he visits Errol (Ray Aranha), the city's former black mayor, who tells him that he needs to make some good come of the situation. Joe confronts Baci about the L Street deaths and is told that, for a couple of years, until the blacks and Hispanics take over, the city will be one big yard sale. Nick tells Laurie that he wants to turn himself in but is worried his father is in trouble. Riggs, who served with Tony in Vietnam, finds Nick hiding out at the construction site and lets slip that it was Carl who squealed on him. Wynn persuades Les to drop the charges against Desmond and Tito.

Nick visits Carl, accuses and attacks him. Carl tells him that years ago, he and Tony stole a car while drunk; Tony ran over a pedestrian and left the injured Carl trapped in the car. Nick does not believe him. As Jeanette (Gloria Foster) takes Desmond to the public meeting, he admits to lying about Les, but before they arrive Wynn announces that he has got the charges against Desmond and Tito dropped; he then persuades the people to march on a nearby hotel where Baci is holding a campaign banquet. Nick shoots hoops with Franklin (who knew Tony and also served in Vietnam). Nick then runs into the drunk, off-duty Rizzo, who attempts to arrest him. They get into a fight, and as Nick flees Rizzo shoots him. Paddy and Fuentes arrive. They tell Rizzo that Nick is no longer wanted, and Fuentes refuses to help cover up what Rizzo has done. Les, on his way out jogging, runs into Desmond, who has come to apologise. Joe finds Nick at the construction site. He reveals that Carl's story was true, and that Joe pulled strings to get Tony the choice of 'the service or prison'. Realising that Nick is bleeding to death, Joe yells for help but the only person who hears is Asteroid, who repeats his words over and over again.

City of Hope's concern with the complex intertwinings of daily life in capitalist postmodernity demands lengthy synopsis. Where *Matewan* is concerned with articulating economic relations through a melodramatic plot and *Eight Men Out* focuses on the working-out of a less-than-watertight conspiracy which has always been treated as an exceptional event, *City of Hope* presents conspiracy, corruption, graft, bribery and blackmail as business as usual. It offers an image of capitalist postmodernity after further iterations, but probably its nearest equivalent is Dos Passos's modernist naturalism. Cecelia Tichi's description of *Manhattan Transfer* and the *U.S.A.* trilogy apply equally well to Sayles' films: 'These novels show Dos Passos's commitment, in narration, to a national consciousness, a sociocultural totality of America. That commitment found expression in a particularly modern form of narrative omniscience ... moving the world of the novel out of the protagonist's mind and into the material universe' (1987:197). Dos Passos himself said 'In a great city ... there is more going on than you can cram into one man's career. I wanted to find some way of making the narrative carry a large load' (quoted in Tichi 1987: 197). He offered cross-sections of metropolitan life, filling such novels with large numbers of characters, many of whose life stories are told and who are often connected to each other by that most tenuous of links: their transit through the city's social spaces. His characters

> coexist without kinship or home territory ... There is no familial or spatial rationale for their lives, which, by Victorian standards, makes theirs an arbitrary coexistence, one disturbing to some readers ... He needed a basis on which his novel[s] could govern a large cast of characters unconnected by class, caste, family or community origins, or even friendship or temperament or ideological commitment to a political, religious or artistic movement ... Dos Passos needed, in other words, a way to encompass an arbitrary aggregation of people and symbols even as he faithfully evoked a metropolitan style of life characterised by its fast pace and its disjunctions. (1987: 200–1)

Tichi describes Dos Passos's solution in terms of presenting his characters as 'human components integrated in a large-scale, dynamic system conceived on the model of the machine and structural technology', and central to this was his use of stock characters: 'in the era of the machine production of component parts, the stock character is but one standard figure interchangeable with countless others' (1987: 202).

The similarities with Sayles' films are obvious: the external view of characters in a material realm which gives the viewer little direct psychological insight; the attempt to develop a representative totality through an emphasis on structure, even as the stability of the whole is doubted; the increasingly large aggregates or networks of characters, most of whom are sufficiently rounded to carry their own narratives; and the frequently ingenious casting of distinct physical types so as to suggest stock characters who are also rounded individuals. There is however a major difference between Dos Passos and Sayles. The former's commitment to modernist experimentation – he was influenced by Marinetti and the Italian Futurists – encouraged a perspective on the modern metropolis characterised by technocratic enthusiasm and a disassociation of characters from traditional ties of kinship, class and ethnicity. Half a century later, Sayles depicts the failure of the modern either to rebuild the world as an efficient machine for living in or to eradicate those more traditional ties. *City of Hope*'s complex narrative is built on the structural principle that the lives of all the characters intermesh – as actors in Hudson City's dynamic ecology as well as components in the narrative machinery – so it is important not only to outline the plot but to indicate the connections, both fixed and fleeting, between characters. Space permits only an indicative rather than exhaustive account.

Let us begin with Mad Anthony: he is a friend of Joe Rinaldi and his wife, whose children are Nick, Laurie and the dead Tony; Nick works for Riggs, his father's foreman, who had served with Tony in Vietnam; Nick, with his friends Bobby and Zip try to burgle Mad Anthony's store for Carl, an old friend of Tony's; Nick starts dating Angie, the ex-wife of the cop Rizzo; Rizzo and his partner Bauer warn Ramirez's girlfriend and baby daughter to move out of the condemned half of L Street; Ramirez's mother is the Rinaldi's housekeeper; Ramirez is Zip's dealer; Zip and Bobby end up sharing a cell with Asteroid. Let us return to Mad Anthony: Wynn, at his wife Reesha's request, asks Mad Anthony to employ his brother-in-law Franklin as a security guard; as Reesha walks with Franklin to his first night at work (where he will capture Bobby and Zip), she is admired by Tito and Desmond (who we have already seen in Mad Anthony's store); Tito and Desmond are harassed by two cops, Paddy and Fuentes (who will later arrest Rizzo for shooting Nick); in retaliation, Tito and Desmond assault Les, and are taken to the same police station as Bobby and Zip, where Levonne and Malik are reporting the smashed Community Center window; Levonne knows Desmond's mother Jeanette and offers to help out; Les teaches in the same college as Reesha, where Angie is also a student and where Wynn previously taught; confronted by Levonne and Malik, Wynne visits Jeanette and Desmond at L Street to try to discover what actually happened; the L Street apartments are owned by Joe, who is blackmailed into letting Carl burn them down so as to get Nick out of trouble; Mayor Baci, for whom Joe's brother Pauly works, blackmails Joe so as to avoid being investigated by the D.A., whose assistant, Zimmer (whose wife used to date Carl), has made a deal (in DeLillo's, where Angie waitresses) to redevelop L Street in exchange for a large contribution to the D.A.'s Senatorial campaign.

While far from complete, the above indicates that relational chains can be drawn between any pair of characters. (The key exception is Asteroid, whose homelessness and mental illness – 'like autism crossed with Tourette's' (Sayles quoted in G. Smith 1998: 191) – prevent him from connecting directly with anyone. Like a parody of Dos Passos's metropolitan subject without 'kinship or home territory … familial or spatial rationale' (or, indeed, of Altman's disconnected characters), his random outbursts of things heard on television resemble the materials – headlines, journalistic fragments, advertisements, and so on – Dos Passos interpolated into novels like the *U.S.A.* trilogy and *Mid-Century*.) These interconnections and circulations are emphasised by the technique of 'trading' which draws diverse, often tenuously-related characters into the same frame. On nearly two dozen occasions, the camera's attention 'trades' from one set of characters to another as they cross the same space. The technique, Sayles notes, 'is hardly original … Orson Welles used it in the opening shot of *Touch of Evil* [1958], and Max Ophüls used it in such films as *La Ronde* [1950]', but its frequent use in *City of Hope* elaborates Sayles' interest in how 'the hero fits into his world' by 'pay[ing] attention to the background of the story as well as to what's up front' (quoted in Baron 1999: 134). In *City of Hope*, the use of trading ranges from the conventional – the camera follows two young men walking up the street before turning to Nick, Bobby and Zip; the camera prowls around among the firefighters and paramedics outside the L Street apartments – to self-consciously elaborate long takes: outside Mad Anthony's, Asteroid declaims the words spoken by Mad Anthony in an advert showing on a television in his store window; the camera pans past Asteroid and trades on to Wynn and tracks behind him down the street; the camera trades on to Connie and Joann walking in the opposite direction, complaining to Bauer and Rizzo about the deterioration of the neighbourhood, and stays with them until the cops get into their patrol car and in turn complain about the two women. By counterbalancing its use of conventional editing with this in-camera alternative, *City of Hope* emphasises the interconnective tissue that conventional continuity editing habitually severs.[63]

These complex connections between characters and locations (including the P Street Community Center, Mad Anthony's store, Carl's garage, DeLillo's and, most importantly, the L Street Apartments, a modern housing project which has become a machine unfit for living and which will be replaced by the Galaxy Towers mall and condominium complex) are not the only structures around which *City of Hope* is built. A temporal dimension, stretching beyond the couple of days in which the principal action occurs, underpins the events: the successive waves of ethnically-defined patriarchal hierarchies who have run the city. First, around the turn of the century, there were the Irish, departed now but for the cop Paddy and Kerrigan, the Irish godfather figure. Power currently resides with the Italians, headed by Mayor Baci, 'the second most indictable mayor in the state', but he can sense a shift going on around him: in one direction lies multinational capital, with which he is keen to ally himself; in the other, the black and Hispanic communities represented by Wynn. The film is also structured around a series of doublings. In a minor key, for example: Pauly is to Baci as Zimmer is to the D.A.; Bauer is to Rizzo as Fuentes is to Paddy; Tony is to Nick as Tito is to Desmond. But the doublings most central to the narrative are concerned with literal or figurative father-son/teacher-pupil relationships: Kerrigan is to Joe as Errol is to Wynn; Joe is to Nick as Les is to Desmond.

Significantly, before Joe sees Kerrigan or Wynn sees Errol, there is a scene in which Wynn meets with Baci, the patriarch from a different hierarchy. Baci espouses trickle-down economics to justify mere greed: by enabling property developers to profit from L Street's destruction and the construction of Galaxy Towers, they will provide jobs, and 'with jobs people can afford higher rents'.[64] Wynn argues that the development, whether intentionally or not, will destroy the community he represents; moreover, from an earlier discussion with Joe, he knows that new jobs are unlikely to go to his constituents. Wynn, furious at being offered a bribe, states that he will 'make the L Street apartments a symbol for everything that's fucked up in this city'. Ominously, Baci replies, 'they can't be a symbol if they aren't there'.

This scene cuts to another visit to the patriarch of a different hierarchy. Joe's own construction project was funded by Kerrigan because Joe wanted an alternative to Baci, but when Joe protests that Baci is using his family against him, Kerrigan replies, 'You think he didn't check with us before he made a move?' He lectures Joe on 'the way our society works', evoking the kind of socio-economic hierarchy up which a giant alligator might eat its way: 'You got something good, first everybody on top of you gets a taste, then you share what's left with everybody below you. We're social animals. Human beings, not dogs.'

Paralleling these scenes are a pair in which Wynn and Joe visit the patriarchs of their own ethnic hierarchies. Errol, like Kerrigan, is found in a green suburban setting, and like his Irish-American counterpart he has retired from a direct grasp on the reins of power. After an unsatisfactory exchange about Wynn's 'nice little mess', Errol observes: 'You always try to gain some ground. No matter what the situation is, make some good come out of it.' He suggests that Wynn could say he believes Desmond and Tito, but Wynn insists, 'If we're going to take power we have to take responsibility, too.' The scene cuts to an old people's home where Joe confronts the gladhanding Baci. Joe is distraught at the deaths of Ramirez's girlfriend and child, but Baci's response is far from sympathetic: 'They were trespassing. Those are the kind of people accidents happen to ... Joe, things change fast. People get hurt. I'm sorry about that. It was an accident. Now if everybody stands up, like a good soldier, we can stay on top. Joe, the next couple of years this town is gonna be one big yard sale, and anyone with half a brain will make tracks and let the blacks and the Spanish duke it out over whatever's left.' As a concession, Baci removes Nick's name from police records and persuades Mad Anthony to drop the charges against Bobby and Zip, adding 'Ninety years ago the Irish ran this town. There were horses shitting on Jefferson Street. My grandfather got here off the boat, they gave him a scoop and a shovel; now, I run the place. America, huh?'

After a brief scene between Nick and Laurie, which starts ironically with school-children singing 'America, the Beautiful', the film returns to the golf course, where Errol explains to Wynn what happened when he became mayor:

> Lot of media pressure, a million people affected by my decisions, but there was no way I could turn my back on the people who put me in, so I brought some of them along with me. Some of them messed up. But they're only people, they're human. I let it go at first because I didn't believe it, and then because I didn't want to believe it, finally because we would lose more ground by cleaning house in public than by sweeping it under the carpet. It took twelve years for all that to catch up with me. That's a pretty nice run, the way things go nowadays ... There were three grand jury indictments hanging over my head. If I'd stood for another term a lot of people would have gone down, and I would have gone down with them ... This isn't the Old Testament, Wynn. People didn't vote you in so you can test your moral fibre. If you're going to be a leader, lead. Take it to the Man every chance you can ... You don't defend anything, you attack what's wrong. That's what a leader is.

Wynn is surprised by Errol's ruthlessly pragmatic regard for the very flawed system of the city – should he really just hope for twelve effective years? what if it isn't about white prejudice? – but begins to balance his principles against attainable goals.

These scenes – between Wynn and Baci, Joe and Kerrigan, Wynn and Errol, Joe and Baci, Laurie and Nick – are important in several ways. Baci's attempt to bribe Wynn and Baci's deferral to Kerrigan suggest that regardless of the importance afforded to ethnicity it is not necessarily the pre-eminent consideration in the operation of power; but as Errol makes clear, to successfully attack what is wrong frequently requires recourse to ethnicity as a motivating and unifying category (a point reinforced by Malik's discreet approval when Wynn seizes control of the public meeting and – literally – takes it to 'the Man'). Whether Errol is correct is a moot point: his advice to Wynn centres on his own experience of endemic corruption and the need to work within the system as it actually exists. This is the lesson that the men who grow up in *City of Hope* – primarily Nick and Wynn – must learn, just as their literal (Joe) and figurative (Errol) fathers did. Like the players of *Eight Men Out*, they trade the ultimate goal for short-term interests – as Marx wrote, people 'make their own history, but … they do not make it under circumstances chosen by themselves, but under circumstances directly encountered, given and transmitted from the past' (1979: 103).

Among these scenes, the exchange between Nick and Laurie, in which she asks what happened to the 'us against the world' deal they made after Tony's death and why she is always helping him but getting nothing in return, might seem out of place. However, the interpolation of this private scene between ones about public life, enables *City of Hope*'s anatomisation of power to emphasise not only the role played in public life by affective relationships but also the tendency even in affective relationships to make deals, to come to instrumentalist arrangements and understandings, and for the distribution of power in such relationships to be unequal. This raises a question which will form an essential part of the dynamic of *Passion Fish*: in a capitalist society, to what extent do calculative public relationships follow a pattern established by affective private relationships, and to what extent do affective private relationships follow the pattern established by calculative public relationships?

Sayles claims that *City of Hope*'s 'title is not only ironic' (in Crowdus & Quart 1999: 155). Perhaps its clearest moment of hope is the nascent relationship between Les and Desmond, although it too is not without its ironic dimension. Following a series of scenes in which various plot strands achieve partial closure – Wynn takes 'concerned citizens' to confront Baci; Nick shoots hoops with Franklin; Fuentes refuses to cover for Rizzo – and preceding the partial resolution of the conflict between Nick and Joey, Desmond apologises to Les:

Desmond: Sorry we fucked you up.
Les: Little late for sorry.
Desmond: I know you're not a faggot.
Les: (exhales) We got a long way to go, don't we? Look, I gotta run.
Desmond: You mind if I hang with you for a minute?
Les: It's a free country.

Desmond:	Where d'you hear that one?
Les:	(laughs)
Desmond:	You're a teacher, huh?
Les:	Yeah.
Desmond:	What d'you teach?
Les:	Urban relations.
Desmond:	Yeah? What's that?

Les recognises Desmond's experiential truth about the lack of freedom (Desmond is repeating a line delivered by Paddy when he and Fuentes accosted Desmond and Tito); Desmond is curious about 'urban relations', a discipline one senses Les has only recently come to experience first hand. Although it is problematic to conclude this plot strand with the start of an educative relationship between a middle-class white man and a working-class black teen, this ambiguous balancing of hope and irony, of their respective experience of city life, moderates such criticism. Hope resides in each learning from the other.

This core of hope also marks the final scene, in which Nick and Joey reconcile even as Nick bleeds to death. The irony of Asteroid taking up Joey's cries for help – no one will respond to him – is also hopeful. Throughout, Asteroid has picked up on whatever is 'in the air'. Consequently his repeated 'help we need help' – which we have heard him utter before – can be understood as the generalised appeal of the city; and a city which cries for help is, however bleak its situation, a city with hope.

Passion Fish (1992)

Engels describes historical materialism as 'the view of the course of history which seeks the ultimate cause and the great moving power of all important historic events in the economic development of society, in the changes in the mode of production and exchange, in the consequent division of society into distinct classes, and in the struggles of these classes against one another' (1990: 289). *Matewan* offers, through its isolated setting, an almost abstract account of the dialectical conflict between capital and labour, shaping historical material so as to reveal this division without reducing the proletariat to the dehumanised ciphers which populate, for example, *Metropolis*'s underworld. Yet even in the West Virginia hills, there are characters who occupy ambiguous class positions, such as the agents and guards whose only means of subsistence is to sell their labour but who nonetheless side with the capitalists rather than their fellow proletarians. Such ambiguous positions are multiplied in *Eight Men Out*, whose urban setting effectively locates it in *Matewan*'s future. Regardless of the players' ethics, it is clear that they were punished for selling their labour to more than one capitalist at the same time and thus threatening profitability. By the time of *City of Hope*, the dynamic Engels describes has gone through further iterations: the growth of Fordism; the 'postwar consensus' in which American labour favoured institutionalised bargaining over industrial action, strengthening American capital's hegemony while enabling mass production of affordable commodities and general improvements in living standards; the growth of middle-class managerial and technological sectors; the 1970s crisis of overaccumulation (the oversaturation of consumer durables prompting a collapse of demand), exacerbated by the OPEC oil embargo; the ensuing collapse of the postwar consensus, increased industrial action and spiralling inflation; and dein-dustrialisation and capital flight as American capital internationalised production so as to reduce labour costs.[65] *City of Hope*'s many complicated interrelations demonstrates the complex structures which can derive from 'the mode of production and exchange' and 'the consequent division of society into distinct classes, and in the struggles of these classes against one another'.

If the dialectic of class conflict dominates these three films, becoming increasingly ubiquitous but also more difficult to discern in terms of class-based action (the march Wynn leads *is* class opposition but mediated through race), *Passion Fish* traces a microcosmic dialectical process, best understood through Hegel's Master/Slave dialectic (also known as the lord-bondsman dialectic), which models class conflict and the possibility of a hopeful resolution. Its simple premise returns to a more intimate scale, following the relationship that develops between May-Alice (Mary McDonnell), a crippled ex-soap opera star, and her nurse, Chantelle (Alfre Woodard).

Hegel argues that the self-conscious subject 'exists in and for itself when, and by the fact that, it so exists for another; that is, it exists only in being acknowledged' (1977: 111), and describes the confrontation between one self-consciousness and another. In coming '*out of itself* … it has lost itself, for it finds itself as an *other* being' and 'in doing so it has superseded the other, for it does not see the other as an essential being, but in the other sees its own self' (ibid.; emphasis in original). By superseding 'the *other* independent being' it becomes 'certain of *itself* as the essential being' and 'in so doing it proceeds to supersede its *own* self, for this other is itself'; and 'by superseding *its* otherness, it again becomes equal to itself' (ibid.; emphasis in original). This is complicated by the fact that while one self-consciousness is doing this, so is the other: 'Each is for the other the middle term, through which each mediates itself with itself and unites with itself; and each is for itself, and for the other, an immediate being on its own account, which at the same time is such only through this mediation. They *recognise* themselves as *mutually recognising* one another' (1977: 112; emphasis in original). However, this mutual recognition is asymmetrical: one self-consciousness recognises while the other is recognised. Although each is 'certain of its own self' it is uncertain of the other's self, 'and therefore its own self-certainty still has no truth' (1977: 113). A struggle ensues between these self-consciousnesses, resulting in the tragic compromise of one-sided recognition, of a Master/Slave relationship, as one self-conscious seeks to make the other 'thing-like and dependent, the self-consciousness of a bondsman as opposed to that of a lord' (1977: 521), thus concealing their fundamental similarity as self-consciousnesses. Recognising this similarity does not erect identity at the expense of difference: as Robert R. Williams explains, 'Mutual-reciprocal recognition is possible only if coercion is renounced. The authentic "cancellation" of other-being means that the other is not eliminated but allowed to go free and affirmed. But if the other is allowed to go free, this means that it is affirmed, not simply in its identity, but also in its difference' (1997: 56).

As self-consciousnesses, the lord exists in relation to the bondsman in that the bondsman, in serving him, mediates between him and the objects of his existence, and in that the lord holds power over the bondsman. In this asymmetrical relationship, the bondsman has renounced his being-for-self, his existence now revolving around the lord, to whom he is just another object of existence; but 'the lord cannot get the reciprocal recognition that his self-consciousness demands from a consciousness so degraded and distorted ... The lord therefore paradoxically depends for his lordship on the bondsman's self-consciousness, and entirely fails of the fully realised independence of status which his self-consciousness demands' (Hegel 1977: 522). As Williams puts it, 'The master's goal was to gain recognition, that is, independent confirmation and legitimation of his freedom. But in spite of his victory over the slave, the master remains uncertain of his own truth, precisely because the slave's recognition is coerced ... Although the slave can and does "recognise" the master, his recognition, as a slave, is deficient because it is coerced, and thus provides the master an unreliable, distorted recognition' (1997: 63). Paradoxically, the lord, who seemed possessed of self-consciousness cannot actually possess it because there is no self-consciousness to acknowledge it, while the bondsman's consciousness, 'forced back into itself', has 'transformed into a truly dependent consciousness' (Hegel 1977: 117). Seemingly lacking self-consciousness, he has become the self-consciousness he perceived in his lord, and because he has laboured, interacted directly with objects of his existence rather than having another mediate them for him, he is able to attain 'a more genuine self-consciousness' (1977: 522).

Passion Fish opens with May-Alice waking in hospital in a scene which emphasises her eyes, her entrapment and the differences between her and Scarlet, her character in the daytime soap playing on television – when asked if she remembers who she is, she points to the television and says, 'She's the one with amnesia.' Despite this, May-Alice does not remember the accident or the surgery she has undergone. The emphasis on her eyes has already suggested that she is trapped in a dysfunctional body, a sense reinforced by clumsy hand movements, shots through the bars around her bed and a camera which tracks in and down on her motionless form. The story that follows is concerned with her learning to see the world again and moving towards a sense of reintegration with a body she has started to hate. A long take of her staring direct-to-camera is an early clue to her confrontational attitude. Based in a rejection of other people as self-consciousnesses, it predates her accident.

Malcolm Bull suggests that the Master/Slave dialectic can be interpreted as being intrapersonal, that a single person can possess two self-consciousnesses.[66] One of the several ironies surrounding the soap opera is May-Alice's transformation of herself into someone like the character she plays, with Scarlet functioning as her other self-consciousness, the medium through which she interacts with material reality. While she insists that Scarlet is the amnesiac, the interrelation of actress and character is evident in May-Alice's own memory loss. Later, the fans who ask for May-Alice's autograph obviously regard her as a soap character, capable of a miraculous comeback, rather than a person. There are repeated confusions about Scarlet between May-Alice and Nina (Nancy Mette), who replaced her in the role: when Nina announces she is pregnant, May-Alice does not at first realise that she means that Scarlet is; when May-Alice recalls she had a hysterectomy, Nina assumes she means herself rather than Scarlet.

The opening scene is followed by a montage in which May-Alice rejects the assistance of three physical therapists and a psychologist. These figures barely exist on the screen: the first therapist is shown briefly in profile; the second therapist and the psychologist are heard, not seen; the third therapist is reduced to out-of-focus legs and torso in the background. Although we see more of Louise (Maggie Renzi), May-Alice's Louisiana physical therapist, and of the succession of agency nurses, her attitude towards them is no better. Confronted by these other self-consciousnesses, she reduces them to the object-like status of bondsmen, exercising the power over them she derives from being their employer. The first agency nurse, Drushka (Marianne Muellerleile), attempts to exercise the power her mobility and strength gives her, to make May-Alice thing-like and dependent through closely regulating her day-to-day existence. Neither self-consciousness is willing to renounce coercion – Drushka holds the television remote control hostage against May-Alice eating her breakfast; May-Alice flicks a forkful of scrambled eggs at the walls Drushka has patiently scrubbed clean. Unable to achieve mutual-reciprocal recognition, Drushka leaves.

The scenes with the agency nurses establish a pattern which haunts May-Alice's relationship with Chantelle. The conflict between these two self-consciousnesses is immediately evident:

> *Chantelle*: I'm Chantelle.
> *May-Alice*: Didn't think they'd send another one.
> *Chantelle*: How long have you been without somebody?
> *May-Alice*: I dropped the remote. I think it's behind the couch.
> *Chantelle*: You really ought to have a ramp out there.

May-Alice ignores Chantelle's name, reducing her to the thing-like 'another one', while Chantelle asserts her identity, insisting that she is 'somebody'. May-Alice responds by ignoring the question, casting Chantelle as a mediator between her and the objects of her existence. Chantelle responds in kind, ignoring the implicit order, recommending instead that May-Alice improve the quality of her life through the use of an actual object rather than treating her as an object. (The presence of the scrambled egg on the wall suggests May-Alice has not been particularly successful in dominating Drushka's replacements.)

May-Alice realises that she has soiled herself and Chantelle offers to help her wash. Having extracted this co-operation, she again attempts to reduce Chantelle to an object, calling her 'Sharelle' and telling her to keep any personal problems to herself. Chantelle quietly insists on her name. Self-assertions continue in the next scene:

> *May-Alice*: You been doing this long?
> *Chantelle*: No. You?
> *May-Alice*: You are a nurse aren't you?

Chantelle: Yeah. I just haven't done this caretaker thing before. I mean, staying over at somebody's house.

May-Alice defines Chantelle by her function, and Chantelle responds in exactly the same way – 'somebody' could easily be just 'some body'. May-Alice gets Chantelle's name wrong again – and is again corrected – and reduces her to a kind of prosthetic extension: 'All the things I can't do, you do 'em for me. These days that's just about everything. Can't go anywhere by myself. I can't cook any more. I can't work any more. I can't shit without a suppository. I can't have sex I can feel – unless I really get into blow jobs. Sorry. You're probably a big Christian, right, and I just put my foot in my mouth?' Chantelle, deadpan, replies, 'It's none of my business what you put in your mouth, Miss Culhane', imitating the position of the bondsman. Having rejected May-Alice's interpellation of her into this subject position, she adopts it ironically so as to assert her personhood (like the Zombies in *Alligator*). Then, as the Master/Slave dialectic suggests, Chantelle also defines May-Alice, a wealthy, T-10 paraplegic 'bitch on wheels',[67] as an object to be managed and the financial mediator of her existence. Later conversations demonstrate this ongoing conflict between self-consciousnesses. For example, when Chantelle returns late from her first shopping trip:

> *Chantelle*: I'm really sorry I'm so late.
> *May-Alice*: I need a glass of wine.
> *Chantelle*: Car broke down. Didn't have any gas in it.
> *May-Alice*: With ice.
> *Chantelle*: I had a really terrible day.
> *May-Alice*: Mine was a scream. If you'd just bring the bottle over I can pour
>   my own.
> *Chantelle*: I'm not your waitress.
> *May-Alice*: What are you then?
> *Chantelle*: I'm going to get the rest of the groceries. If you want a drink, I'll
>   be in the kitchen.

In the Hegelian dialectic, the Master achieves independent self-consciousness through subordinating the Slave, by making him a dependent consciousness. Although the relative positions of May-Alice and Chantelle as employer and employee, white and black, might imply that May-Alice is the Master and Chantelle the Slave, such exchanges indicate that their relationship is far more complex. Sayles says of the origins of *Passion Fish*:

> I worked as an orderly in hospitals and nursing homes … and I had a lot of
> nurse friends who would moonlight as home-care companions. I got fasci-
> nated by the relationships between people who spend eight, 10, 20 hours at
> a time together, and yet don't necessarily have anything in common. They're
> stuck together; one needs the job and the other needs the care. Often, it's a
> power relationship – one has the power to hire and fire and the one has the

power of being physically able to get up and leave the room. And that balance of power might switch during the day. (Quoted in Ebert 1999: 162)

May-Alice fears Chantelle's power to leave whereas Chantelle fears May-Alice's power to fire her. Their mutual dependence becomes clear, even as they attempt to assert themselves over each other. Chantelle tries to make May-Alice exercise her upper body because 'I'm not taking you to the potty every four hours, wipin' your butt, and pretty soon you're gonna be too weak to do it for yourself'. May-Alice refuses, so Chantelle leaves her outside. When Chantelle returns, she occupies the dependent position of bondsman by accepting the role of just one more in a succession of nurses, but by doing so succeeds in exercising Mastery:

> *Chantelle*: Are you going to do something to get stronger?
> *May-Alice*: And why do you think I need to be stronger?
> *Chantelle*: Because the next one might not be so nice as me.
> *May-Alice*: Right. And you're Florence fucking Nightingale.
> *Chantelle*: You got a telephone any time you want to get rid of my ass. But if I'm going to stay I have to be able to do my job. Are you going to try it?
> *May-Alice*: Don't leave me places.

While abandoned beside the lake, May-Alice begins to see the world afresh (like Lianna, like the Brother). Shortly after, she takes up photography. Rather than being an image, she becomes the producer of images. This is a turning point for her internal dialectic. She starts to master the person, inextricably linked with Scarlet, who she became when she left Louisiana. This culminates in her rejection of the offer to return to the soap as Scarlet, crippled and blinded in a car accident that cured her amnesia. She cannot give up her new sightedness. Chantelle's internal dialectic takes two forms. There is the self-consciousness which wrestles with her drug addiction, and there is the double-consciousness W. E. B. Du Bois ascribed to African-Americans.[68] The latter is especially evident when May-Alice's friends mistake her for 'coloured help' or a 'family retainer', and when her visiting father mistakes her work for domestic service. May-Alice becomes increasingly uncomfortable with such ambiguities, even as Chantelle makes assumptions about how May-Alice sees her.

> *May-Alice*: Chantelle, do you have to wear that uniform all the time?
> *Chantelle*: I thought you wanted it on.
> *May-Alice*: It's so – nursey.
> *Chantelle*: I am a nurse. Not an assistant.
> *May-Alice*: Well, I didn't know what else to call you. You're not my servant…
> *Chantelle*: Thank you.
> *May-Alice*: …you're not my babysitter or my housekeeper.
> *Chantelle*: I'm not your friend.
> *May-Alice*: (pause) You know you can go out at night if you want.

Chantelle: I'm … I'm fine out here.

May-Alice: It must be so boring for you.

Chantelle: It's a job, it's supposed to be boring.

May-Alice: Oh no, Miss Culhane, it's never boring working for you.

Chantelle: If you want me to be that way, I'll try.

May-Alice: No! You have to be totally straight with me, okay? Whatever you
got on your mind, I want to hear it.

Chantelle: Yeah?

May-Alice: Yeah.

Chantelle: You drink too much.

May-Alice: No. I don't.

The Master treats the Slave as an object rather than as an equal self-consciousness, but to be sure of his being-for-self he requires an equal self-consciousness to recognise him. Although the Slave recognises the Master, his dependent consciousness makes this recognition inadequate. May-Alice and Chantelle acknowledge that a relationship of power holds them together, with Chantelle offering a further, ironic subordination. May-Alice wants an equal's recognition, but does not want to permit Chantelle this status. Later, when she asks Chantelle to call her May-Alice, Chantelle replies, 'Whatever you want', reasserting their relative positions by recasting this seeming equalisation as an act of obedience.

The crisis point comes after May-Alice, who has taken up the challenge not to drink for a day, discovers that Chantelle is a recovering addict. When the 24 hours are up, May-Alice demands a drink but Chantelle has poured all the alcohol in the house away. She refuses to buy any more, telling May-Alice that if she wants it she can get it herself.

May-Alice: I can't drive.

Chantelle: That's something to work towards, isn't it?

May-Alice: Don't hand me that condescending bullshit. Just go in and get me
some fucking wine.

Chantelle: Listen to you.

May-Alice: No, you listen to me. I hired you and I want you to do what I tell
you.

Chantelle: Dream on, girl.

May-Alice: Who made you the fucking warden?

Chantelle: Who made you queen of the whole damn world? You sit around
feeling sorry for yourself, you miserable old TV-watching dried
up old witch. You can't even go for more than one day without a
drink, and you're not even a drunk yet. You're just fucking spoiled.
Most mornings I wake up I want to get high so bad I can't even
breathe.

May-Alice: Cocaine is different.

Chantelle: Bullshit! What do you know about it?

Passion Fish: hope floats

> *May-Alice*: Where are you going?
> *Chantelle*: I am going away from you. I don't want to be around your shit no
> more – you understand that? – away from you.

The Master – whether it is May-Alice or Chantelle – can no longer regard the other as the Slave. The threat of separation removes even the consolation of being recognised by a dependent consciousness. The only hope that either has is to fully recognise the other's self-consciousness. Because Chantelle has laboured, directly interacting with the material world, she has attained the more genuine self-consciousness denied May-Alice; and because May-Alice begins to labour – she apologises to Chantelle by cooking her a meal – she too begins to develop such a consciousness.

The dialectic, however, is restless and without an endpoint. This is the why the dénouement occurs on the lake, a body of water, full of twists and turns, that reaches all the way to the ocean. Although it seems placid beneath the glorious sunset, it is not: it is fluid, constantly changing beneath them. Chantelle's internal dialectic is still evident as she bemoans having to play the role of the dutiful daughter so as to regain custody of her own daughter from her father, and May-Alice is still caught between independence and dependence. Although they have achieved a temporary resolution, there is a clear sense of irresolution, not least because theirs remains an economic relationship. They are 'stuck with each other'. May-Alice still needs a nurse and Chantelle still needs a job. This economic nexus is re-emphasised in the film's final line in which May-Alice, albeit half-jokingly, tells Chantelle, 'You are going to have to learn how to cook.'

Another film about history, class and community, about those who stay, those who leave and those who return, *Passion Fish* overtly embraces melodrama. Allusions to *Gone With the Wind* (1939), *Imitation of Life* (1959) and *What Ever Happened to Baby Jane?* (1962) acknowledge this American film tradition, and the treatment of soap operas recognises the power of the genre to compel (even as the uses to which it is put in *Passion Fish* recall the use of sentimental novels in William Dean Howells' *The Rise of Silas Lapham* (1885) and Theodore Dreiser's *Sister Carrie* as debased forms against which the authors can distinguish their own fiction and disavow certain of its elements). One of the strengths of *Passion Fish*'s critique of overly-mediated, and thus alienated, experience (in contrast to the shared history and being of a local culture and community) lies in its preparedness to acknowledge the convolutions of daily life: the four major characters – May-Alice and Chantelle begin tentative relationships with, respectively, Rennie Boudreau (David Strathairn) and Sugar LeDoux (Vondie Curtis-Hall) – have back stories as complex as those found in soaps, and each of them is left in an unresolved situation. Less fatalistic than the preceding three films, *Passion Fish* articulates the politics of relationships around those of class, race and employment, and suggests a limited and utopian solution in the irresolution of constant dialectical renegotiation. Its pastoral evasion of urban modernity evokes hope in the potential benevolence of the private world as figure of utopia:

> Utopia is to be found in the Not-yet, or the Not-Yet-being, or the in-Front-of-Us, or simply the Front, as Bloch variously designates it. Utopia can never be fixed in the perspective of the present, because it exists, to a considerable, degree, in the dimension of futurity; not, however, in the future as the latter is imagined by mere chronological forecasting, or in the mechanistic and philistine notions of bourgeois 'progress', but rather as the future is the object of *hope*, of our deepest and most radical longings. These are longings that can never be satisfied by the fulfillment of any individual wish (say, for personal wealth) but that demand, rather, a revolutionary reconfiguration of the world as a totality. Utopian hope or longing, in other words, possesses an inherently collective character and at bottom has nothing in common with individualist impulses like greed. (Freedman 2000: 64)

However faulty, embattled or stalled the varied collectivisms depicted in *Matewan*, *Eight Men Out* and *City of Hope* might be, they betoken hope, as does the dyad with which *Passion Fish* ends. Despite the cash nexus between them, May-Alice and Chantelle are in the process of forming an atom of community. They cannot reconfigure the world, because, in Freedman's words, utopia is 'in one sense … always *elsewhere*, always escaping our actual horizons', but in 'another and no less important sense [it is] inscribed in the innermost core of our being' (ibid.; emphasis in original). May-Alice and Chantelle's struggle against coercion and for mutual reciprocal recognition, and the consequent affirmation not only of identity but also of difference, however precariously it is poised, reveals the inner inscription of utopia, of hope.

CHAPTER FIVE

Telling Stories: *The Secret of Roan Inish, Lone Star, Men with Guns/Hombres armados* and *Limbo*

This chapter considers the significance of storytelling in Sayles' films. *The Secret of Roan Inish* and *Lone Star*, in rather different ways, address the roles played by stories in the building and maintenance of communities. In the former, the past is remembered through the act of storytelling, offering a utopian image which can be projected into a more homely future; its emphasis on the fantastic is precisely a way to keep open possibilities threatened by the enclosures of capitalist imperialism. A similar process can be observed in the latter, in which the nature of the present and the future is determined by the stories told about the past. This is evident in both the single scene about school history books upon which my analysis concentrates, and in the decision by Sam (Chris Cooper) and Pilar (Elizabeth Peña) to continue their relationship even though they have discovered they are half-brother and half-sister, projecting a future which, not unproblematically, promises both sexual and familial fulfilment. *Lone Star* and *Men with Guns* provide an opportunity to explore in some detail – and in the context of the films' liberal postcolonial position – the nature of the disavowed authorial privilege of the naturalist artist. *Men with Guns* and *Limbo* further develop the critique of capitalism and neo-colonialism found across Sayles' oeuvre, while also returning to the nature and possibilities of storytelling. *Limbo*'s self-conscious refusal of a resolution emphasises the difference between stories and reality, opening up again the possibility of different futures to the one scripted by capital.

The Secret of Roan Inish (1994)

Sayles' films often include isolated moments which celebrate the pastoral as a utopian site of romantic or collective connection, a shelter from the modern and the urban, a home to be saved. They typically evoke the problematic nature of refusing the social realm and modern world, of extracting oneself from history: these utopian pastoral moments exist only as contained instances of respite, reminders and anticipations of fullness. In contrast, *The Secret of Roan Inish*, a children's fantasy, situates the pastoral at its very core. It celebrates the need for, and the power of, the desire for a more harmonious existence, while nonetheless recognising that mere nostalgia cannot successfully divert or overcome capitalist-imperialist expansion and domination.[69]

Set some time after World War Two in Eire's western isles, *The Secret of Roan Inish* tells of the return of Fiona Coneelly (Jeni Courtney) from the city to live with her grandparents, Hugh (Mick Lally) and Tess (Eileen Colgan), on the west coast, and of their subsequent return to Roan Inish, an island they had earlier evacuated when the younger families relocated to the mainland. When they left Roan Inish, Fiona's infant brother Jamie (Cillian Byrne) was swept out to sea and lost. Taken and raised by the selkies, he is held hostage against the family's return. Guided by seals and gulls, Fiona finds her brother, and with the aid of her cousin, Eamon (Richard Sheridan), repairs the homes they left behind. As a powerful storm breaks, the children and their grandparents return to Roan Inish and Jamie is restored to his family.

'They say the east is our future and the west is our past,' Tess notes on Fiona's return from the city. *The Secret of Roan Inish* is elaborated across a series of contrasts between the west/past (traditional skills, ties to the land and sea, shared language and lore) and the east/future (modernity, speed, industrial pollution, the erosion of community, the imposed language of a colonial power), but the film validates Fiona's trajectory into the west. Her movement against the grain of progress resonates with the myth of American development, in which the direction of progress is to the west; *The Secret of Roan Inish* reverses this, identifying the future with eastern industrial cities. However, this was, contradictorily, also the case with America. The western frontier not only promised expansion but also a place to which one could flee in order to escape industrial modernity and live a simpler life, subsisting in isolated harmony with nature – a peculiar ideological fantasy which naturalised westward expansion in order to disguise its genocidal, exploitative reality. A similar set of contradictions underpins the Celtic mythological framework of *The Secret of Roan Inish*, offering a consolation to both characters and audience which is nonetheless juxtaposed with the carefully enunciated economic mechanism which also drives the family's return to Roan Inish: the grandparents' landlord has served notice on their tenancy because he can make a greater profit by renting out the house in which they live to a wealthy family (if not English and Protestant, then certainly members of the urban bourgeoisie) who want it as a summer residence. The meanings of east/west, past/future, and the array of connotations each of these terms and pairings evoke, are far from fixed. They are not the certainties 'they say' they are.

This twin mythological and economic motivation for the return to Roan Inish underlies the epistemological and ontological challenges posed by the four films this chapter will discuss. Arguing that modernist fiction is predominantly interested in epistemological questions and postmodernist fiction in ontological ones, Brian McHale outlines the kinds of questions these are. Epistemological fiction asks: 'How can I interpret this world of which I am a part? And what am I in it? … What is there to be known?; Who knows it? How do they know it, and with what degree of certainty?; How is knowledge transmitted from one knower to another, and with what degree of reliability?; How does the object of knowledge change as it passes from knower to knower? What are the limits of the knowable?' (1989: 9). Ontological fiction asks, 'Which world is this? What is to be done in it? Which of my selves is to do it? … What is a world? What kinds of world are there, how are they constituted, and how do they differ?; What happens when different kinds of world are placed in confrontation, or when boundaries between worlds are violated?; What is the mode of existence of a text, and what is the mode of existence of the world (or worlds) it projects? How is a projected world structured?' (1989: 10). The epistemological and ontological are not discrete realms, but instead often shade over into each other: 'Intractable epistemological uncertainty becomes at a certain point ontological plurality or instability: push epistemological questions far enough and they "tip over" into ontological questions. By the same token, push ontological questions far enough and they tip over into epistemological questions – the sequence is not linear and unidirectional, but bidirectional and reversible' (1989: 11).[70] Postmodernist-ontological fiction has not replaced but sublated modernist-epistemological fiction (just as the postmodern sublates the modern), and so while it is of course impossible to be a modernist in a postmodern age, Sayles' filiations to modernist naturalism are still evident in the films discussed in this chapter, all of which emphasise the act and meaning of storytelling. They elaborate upon and together constitute an extended self-reflexive engagement with narrative and the construction of worlds.

In his DVD commentary for *The Secret of Roan Inish*, Sayles says that 'in a children's story, you're always playing … between what would people actually do and how does the imagination see it'. He lists 'various strategies … for storytelling' in the film – 'sometimes you just hear a person tell a story, sometimes they start telling it and then their voice fades out and you see it illustrated, sometimes the voice keeps going through the illustration scenes, the flashbacks' – which enable him to pose the questions: 'how would this little girl imagine it? … How tall a story is it? How apocryphal is it? How realistic do we want to be?' These seemingly straightforward epistemological questions, concerned with the nature, limits, transmission and reliability of knowledge tip over into ontological questions because the stories being told hint at or contain fantastic elements which seem to be confirmed by the film's conclusion, in which it is revealed that Jamie has survived alone among the islands for three years, apparently nurtured by the selkies.[71] That these questions might ultimately prove irresolvable is suggested by the ambiguity of an exchange between Fiona and Eamon. He tells her that one day every year the seals gather to choose their new king and 'whichever of the island girls he fancies most is taken below to live as his queen'. She protests, 'That's just stories', to which he replies, 'Some stories is true, though.'

Near the end of the film Fiona's grandparents tell her how her parents met. Brigid 'came from Balleybofey, back in the mainland,' Tess begins, 'travelling the hills' with her day-labourer father 'in search of a meal and a place to sleep'. When she was 16 – a 'beautiful, strong, Christian girl; sun or stars never shone on a better one' – she was in Donegal for the Saint Brigid's day pilgrimage. Jimmy, Tess's 'youngest and the dearest of [her] heart ... but ... an airy boy', was in town because, as Hugh explains, 'We'd a brilliant run on the mackerel that year. Great patch of them shoaling up behind the island, and our men were barely able to dip their nets in the water fast enough.' Selling the surplus on the mainland, Jimmy saw Brigid 'leaving the church, and he was struck speechless with the sight of her ... So there he is, making honey in his heart of her good looks, and meanwhile she's just as struck, with him a big, handsome, powerful lad, with eyes that melted all the girls. And she's in a hundred pieces, wondering what she could do to meet him.'

'Did he speak to her?' Fiona asks. 'What did he say?'

Laughing, Hugh replies, '"Would you like to buy some fish, miss?"'

Tess continues: 'And she said she'd love to as she'd never tasted fish from the salty ocean in all her life, but she hadn't a shilling to her name to buy it with. They fell into talking, then, great with each other immediately, as happens with the young.'

Hugh reminisces about 'the day she came, sitting in the back of the curragh, and I says to Tess, "Will you look at the prize Matt Margonn's brought back from Donegal?" "No," she says, "for look at how Matt's got his eyes straight ahead at the island. It's our Jimmy is rowing so's he won't let her out of his sight." From that day, Jim had the name of a steady husband and a hard worker. As fine as any that ever broke bread.'

This seems to be the end of the story, but Tess adds, 'She grew to love the island, our Brigid. She was the last one to marry onto Roan Inish. And the last one to die on it.' Hugh concludes, 'He always blamed himself for bringing her into the life of the sea. But life can be hard on the mainland, too.'

Although this story contains no fantastic elements, it does tell of the meeting of and transition between different worlds – islands and mainland, subsistence agriculture and wage labour, sacred (church) and profane (market), men and women, youth and adulthood, life and death – as memory becomes story and particular events become generic ones (and vice versa). These transformations are especially evident at those moments when the story Hugh and Tess weave together falls into colloquial expression (such as 'sun or stars never shone on a better one' and 'an airy boy') or familiar story tropes (such as the poor girl wandering the hills and the bounteous catch of mackerel). Despite seeming oft-told, Jimmy's first words to Brigid simultaneously have the ring of authenticity. Hugh attempts to end the account with an almost ritualistic closure – Jimmy matures into Jim, as good a husband and worker 'as any that ever broke bread' – but Tess fluctuates between story and account, reintroducing Brigid's death as a more permanent closure, not only to the story but also to the family's habitation of their home. Recounted while Eamon and Hugh mend fishing nets and lobster pots and while Fiona helps Tess with the washing, this transformation of events into story is part of the fabric of the characters' lives, both a story and true. Just as Jimmy and Brigid's meeting is a meeting of language-worlds, so the telling of their story lies on

The Secret of Roan Inish: telling stories, making lives

the border between Hugh and Tess as they weave it together, and between them and Fiona as they retell it for her, drawing her into the life into which she was born but departed when young. Simultaneously, the telling plays out along the line between fact and fiction, actuality and story – between 'wide-awake and dreaming', as Hugh says of Tadhg Coneelly (John Lynch), between 'earth and water', as Tess adds.

Shortly after Fiona first arrives at her grandparents' house, Hugh tells her the story of his great-grandfather, Sean Michael (Fergal McElherron), back when 'the English were still a force in the country'. When Sean Michael was not much older than Fiona, he attended a school run by the English and, as in many other colonial situations, 'it was their language and their ways you had to learn there, or else'. As these words are spoken, the image dissolves from Hugh, smoking his pipe, to the schoolroom many years previously. The sepia tone of the children at their desks emphasises the much darker garb of the new schoolmaster, 'as stiff as a cat's whiskers', in the foreground. A close-up shows Sean Michael whispering – we do not hear the words – in a friend's ear, and as the camera tracks back he is seized by the schoolmaster who puts the cingulum, a kind of halter, around his neck as a punishment for speaking in his own language. Other children taunt him as an 'idjit' until he can take it no longer, flings down the cingulum and attacks the schoolmaster, cursing him in his native tongue. His words remain untranslated, but the film cuts back to the present day, where Tess chastises Hugh, before he ascertains that Fiona does not 'have any Irish' and thus cannot understand.

Hugh picks up the story. Sean Michael's father wished him to learn the English language and laws and 'grow to be a leader for his people', but he refused to return to school and instead joined his father in a life of 'black rocks' and 'wild waves' beneath a 'hard sky'. On his first trip to sea, though, a storm capsizes their fishing boats. His father, brothers, uncles and cousins all drown, but Sean Michael fights to stay afloat. Here the image cuts from a close-up of Hugh to Sean Michael's viewpoint, tossed by a dark sea. His struggle is so fierce that 'the sea grew to hate him and refused to swallow him up'. A day later, women gathering mussels find him, 'more dead than alive'. He is nursed back to consciousness, warmed between two cows and watched over by the women. Cut back to Hugh as he explains Sean Michael believed he had died and gone to heaven, or at least to Tech Duin, the islands where 'the souls of all Ireland's dead were held to rest', and swore that a seal had saved him, bringing him through the storm and to the shore. Cut from Sean Michael's viewpoint, clinging to the neck of a seal, back to the present. Hugh ends his story with the fact that with all his male relatives dead it fell to Sean Michael 'to keep the Coneellys alive in these islands'. Fiona adds, 'And he was saved by a seal?', to which Hugh replies, 'And two cows.' 'And,' Tess notes, 'a woman as had her wits about her.'

Fiona concludes it is a 'wonderful story', but Hugh is not so certain: 'Some say you should never save a drowning man. What the sea will take, the sea must have.' Tess chides such foolishness, but Hugh insists that 'It's said that some that are saved turn wicked afterwards', adding with some pride that Sean Michael died in jail aged fifty, imprisoned by the English for smuggling arms to the Fenians.

Flashbacks are normally taken to confirm the words of the speaker, although in fact they might bring them into question, not least because the informational density of the image often overwhelms or contradicts the more limited voice-over narration (see Britton 1992). In this instance, the relatively simple images seem to anchor Hugh's words quite securely, but they are also images of problematic provenance. The flashback does not illustrate Hugh's memories but represents his version of a story he has been told, his memory of his great-grandfather's memories, which had been reshaped in the telling and are reshaped yet again in this telling. Fiona's presence introduces a further complication. Seated at her grandfather's feet, looking up with a light in her eyes, she eagerly devours the story he tells. Are the flashbacks, then, not flashbacks but what she imagines as she listens to Hugh? The interpretive problems posed by this sequence mirror the epistemological problems raised by storytelling within the film. History is always story, but at what point does story pass into legend?

Whatever meaning Hugh wishes to give the story, it does contain traces of a moral that might have been ascribed to it when 'the English were still a force in the land' and a moral that Hugh is trying to learn as he tells it. Describing the drowning men, Hugh notes that, 'Out as far as they were, in a northern storm, an experienced fisherman will swallow his draught of water and swim to the bottom. For to fight the cold sea is only to prolong your suffering.' In the context of the English occupation, this might be taken as a counsel to conform, to accept the fate of a colonised people; and in the context of this telling, it suggests that Hugh might recognise the 'wisdom' of abandoning the old ways and accepting modernity. However, he is proud of Sean Michael fighting to survive because he knew no better, just as he is proud of his role in the anti-colonialist republican struggle.

The story of Sean Michael reaches back into the past, but it also extends into the future, foreshadowing Fiona and Eamon's return to Roan Inish. It brings other worlds into play, too: coloniser and colonised, men and women, land and sea, human and nature – and the mundane and the fantastic: was the seal that saved Sean Michael really just a seal?

The fantastic seems not so much to erupt into the real as constitute part of its fabric when, one morning soon after, Hugh, who is recaulking his curraugh, tells

Fiona, who he has enlisted to stir the tar, of the day Jamie disappeared. It 'was a strange day', the air 'very still, like it is sometimes before a storm': 'It was like a dream that day, a slow, terrible dream that you watch but you can't stop it.' Hugh sets the scene – all the islanders apart from Jimmy and his brother, and Jamie in his cradle at the water's edge, are already aboard the evacuation ship – and then, as he pauses to drink his tea, his medium close-up dissolves to Jamie's cradle, waves lapping a couple of feet from it. The camera tracks around and in so as to show Jamie in it. Cut to a close-up of a man's legs splashing through water, the image slowing as he vaults into the boat carrying belongings out to the ship, and then cut again to show the boat further out to sea. Two men carry a mattress out of a cottage. There is a close-up of one of them – it is Jimmy (Dave Duffy) – as he turns to survey the shore on which the last bits of furniture and livestock are waiting to be transported. Cut to open water, a seal's head bobbing in the middle of the frame. Cut to Jamie in his cradle as the waves begin to reach it – he is crossed by a shadow, and a grey gull squawks, flaps, lands on the cradle. Jimmy, in close-up, looks into the sky; behind him, his brother does the same. Gulls gather overhead. The montage accelerates as the gulls swoop at the men, a sequence composed almost entirely of close-ups which deny us an immediate view of what is happening on the shore while the brothers are distracted. Then the grey gull takes to the air as the water finally reaches the cradle, which begins to drift out to sea. The seal bobs back underwater. The attacking gulls fly away. This sequence begins not in silence but with an eerie quietness, the gentle lapping of a calm sea, accompanied by the faint slow cadence of a bodhran which quickens and becomes louder as the gulls attack, joined by a haunting pipe, the music then fading as the cradle drifts far out to sea. Jimmy and his brother notice the cradle, already impossibly far out to sea. They race to the beach, and as Jimmy runs across the sand the image again briefly slows. By the time he reaches the water, Jamie has drifted out much further than seems possible. Jimmy's calls for help are distorted, slowed down. A boat picks him up and they row after the cradle, while the islanders on the ship react, again in slow motion, their voices distorted. A dark cloud passes in front of the sun. The ship raises anchor. The pursuit continues, never seeming to gain on the cradle. A squall breaks and visibility drops. Jimmy's cries of his son's name are slowed down. And as he loses sight of the cradle, so the viewpoint pulls away from the boat, leaving him standing, lost. The beat of the bodhran, which picked up again during the pursuit, fades away. Cut back to the present, the tar bubbling as Hugh ends the story, still puzzled about how the cradle 'could have made up so much speed', convinced that the sea took Jamie because 'it was angry with us for leaving Roan Inish'.

This sequence again highlights the intertwining of memory and narration. Hugh recalls just two men on the shore, the flashback shows three. He describes Jamie asleep in his cradle, the flashback shows him awake. These two small contradictions problematise the nature of the flashback by introducing information which exceeds or counters Hugh's words. The possibility that the flashback is actually how Fiona imaginatively 'sees' Hugh's story is closed down by these details which she has no reason for introducing. Is Hugh remembering accurately but choosing to discard certain information, reorganising what he recalls so as to create a more effective story? Does the shot of Jamie awake operate to reveal the way assumptions construct memory, story and history even when they are wrong? Are the contradictions intended to convey that the images show the reality of what happened, regardless of Hugh's attempt to turn it into a story?

These uncertainties are part of a much greater field of ambiguity. The recollected stillness of the air and dreamlike nature of the day set the stage for a fantastic occurrence. The soundtrack selects and emphasises ambient sounds connected to the sea and wildlife. The music, played on traditional instruments as the islanders are in the process of abandoning tradition for modernity, signifies the approach of something ominous. The strangeness of that day is further generated by a predominance of close-ups, which separate individuals from the totality of the scene and the world, and which gently push at the bounds of conventional continuity editing, unbalancing the safe space it typically creates. This separation of the world into different spaces is accompanied by a separation into different temporal realms. Although its advance is never depicted, the sea comes in much too quickly. The cradle, which is only ever seen gently bobbing along, outstrips its pursuers, travelling much too far between shots, while the actions and voices of the islanders are slowed down, distorted. On the one hand, this is an effective depiction of the subjective experience of crisis, when things seem simultaneously to happen too quickly to control and so slowly that details become crystal clear. On the other hand, it represents a world imbued with the fantastic. Similar ambiguities occur throughout the sequence, most importantly in the two shots of the seal, in the middle of the frame, bobbing in the water. The implication that it is watching the shore is merely shot/reverse-shot convention; the location of the two shots in the sequence, one before the gull attack and one after the cradle has started to float out to sea, implies that it is co-ordinating or at least observing events – but only if the viewer is prepared to interpret the image in excess of what it actually shows, to entertain the possibility that the seal is more than just a seal. Such ambiguities – Todorovian hesitations between rational and fantastical motivations – foreground narrative construction: is the seal there because Hugh includes it in his description of that day? If so, does he include it as part of the scene-setting or as a supernatural agency? Or does it only take on the role of the latter in Fiona's hearing of the story?

The film's only apparently incontrovertibly fantastic moment comes when Tadhg, one of the dark ones the Coneellys produce every generation, tells Fiona the story of Liam (Gerald Rooney) and Nuala (Susan Lynch). Gutting fish, Tadhg recalls a time when only Irish was spoken in the islands, when the seals and the birds moved aside to make room for the Coneellys to settle in Roan Inish. As he describes his young ancestor, the film cuts to Liam, walking on a beach. In the distance, he spies a seal, basking on a rock, transforming into a woman. Liam sneaks up on the selkie and steals her skin, forcing her to stay in human form. He brings her – Nuala – home as his bride. Cut back to Tahdg telling the story, and then back to Nuala, striding in slow motion into the sea. She asked for a cradle for her firstborn, to be made from driftwood and covered in shells, but without rockers as it will float on the sea (it is the cradle in which Jamie is later swept away). Cut to Tadhg telling of their marriage and their children, and then back to Nuala, haunted by sadness. One of her daughters asks, 'Why does father hide a leather coat in the roof?' Nuala hands her baby to her daughter and races to the house: 'Later that evening, as Liam was rowing home, he was followed by a solitary seal. It seemed joyous in its movements. It rolled and dived in the waves, joyous in the sleekness of its body. Its eyes, as with all its kind, held a sadness as deep as the soul.' Liam, fearing the worst, hastens home, to find his children alone on the shore: 'For once a selkie finds its skin again, neither chains of steel nor chains of love can keep her from the sea.' Cut back to Tadhg and Fiona once more, as he says, 'From that day on it was forbidden to harm a seal on the island. And man and beast lived side by side, sharing the wealth of the sea. And sometimes the Coneellys would see her out in the waves, basking in the sun on Trabeg, watching them, watching her children. And the cradle was passed on through the years, with each new infant of the Coneellys rocked upon the waves within it. And every so often, there'd be one born with the dark hair and the black eyes that the selkie had left in their blood. And these dark ones were most at home at sea. Great sailors and fisherfolk, every one of them.'

This sequence differs from the others described not only in its inclusion of the overtly fantastic – Nuala's transformation from seal to woman, depicted with a remarkable material tangibility – but in the fact that no dialogue is spoken in the flashback footage. Tadhg alone tells the story, reporting speech or, more accurately, attributing words to the characters he creates in his telling of this past which lingers on the threshold of history and legend, charting a world between these worlds. The centrality afforded to his voice emphasises the narrative construction not only of history and identity but also of the ontologies we inhabit, raising epistemological and ontological uncertainties even as he speaks with a certainty which enables the generic verisimilitude of fantasy (the fantastic exists) to overcome cultural verisimilitude (the fantastic does not exist).[72] This tension between verisimilitudes maps onto the variety of fantastic hesitation between supernatural and rational explanations for events inconsistent with empirical reality. What is fascinating about *The Secret of Roan Inish* is that it establishes a world in which the possibility of the fantastic remains credible (for both characters and viewers) without ever straightforwardly depicting it. It is as if the world itself is imbued with the fantastic, and because the world that is presented is so bound up with storytelling, with real events being crafted from shared memory into public narratives, ontologies never come into collision so much as invest each other. The political significance of this cannot be underestimated, as Sean Michael's story demonstrates. Colonisers typically work to eradicate the language and customs, lore and history, knowledge and identity of the colonised, as well as the symbolic and cultural significance of landscapes and environments. Capital works to similar ends, expanding across levels and dimensions, rationalising and reifying, stripping out histories and identities and replacing them with commodified forms. Just as Sean Michael's refusal of English schooling is concerned with keeping a pre-colonial world alive, so the return to Roan Inish is concerned with forestalling, or evading, the rapid acceleration of capitalist modernity. As China Miéville argues, the ubiquity of commodity fetishism renders '"Real" life under capitalism … *a fantasy*' and therefore '"realism", narrowly defined, is … a "realistic" depiction of "an absurdity which is true"' (2002: 42, quoting Geras 1971: 76;

emphasis in original).[73] The displaced islanders' storytelling keeps alive a relation to the world before colonial incursion, a relation that has struggled to exist even as capital has radically transformed social reality, and refused to cede the fantastic to its rationalised function – commodity fetishisation – within capital's mechanisms of equivalisation. If taken literally as an uncomplicated advocacy of tradition over modernity, this is a problematic strategy with which to attempt to resist capitalist modernity's structural depredations. But this is not what the film is doing. Rather, just as the storytelling within it retains the fantastical, the utopian and the *heimlich* rather than relinquishing them to capital, so *The Secret of Roan Inish* itself is an act of storytelling which recovers and preserves their value from the way in which the market would, of its own inner necessity, colonise and articulate them. While figured in terms of a return to a mythical past, this resistance articulates a desire for fullness and harmony which could only exist in a radically 'other' future.

According to Jack Zipes, Freud argues that 'the word *heimlich* means that which is familiar and agreeable *and* also that which is concealed and kept out of sight', concluding 'that *heimlich* is a word the meaning of which develops in the direction of ambivalence, until it finally coincides with its opposite, *unheimlich* or uncanny' (1983: 173; emphasis in original). Freud describes the uncanny as 'something which is familiar and old-established in the mind and which has become alienated from it only through the process of repression' (1955: 241). Roan Inish, and the way of life it represents, is both homely yet hidden, familiar yet something from which the Coneellys have become alienated: it is both a past that has been lost and a future which has yet to come; it is utopia.

In *The Principle of Hope*, Ernst Bloch differentiates between 'abstract' and 'concrete' utopias. The former are historically-specific compensatory fantasies, in which the world is repaired rather than radically reconstructed; the latter foreshadow the radically different – and hence ultimately unrepresentable – future. *The Secret of Roan Inish* imagines a repaired world in which some immemorial 'natural' balance is restored. This harmony-that-never-existed is a trace of hope (Bloch's *Hoffnung*), anticipating a future beyond capital and colonialism when a richer, fuller existence might be attained. In Zipes' words, Bloch argued that 'even when a dream appears to indicate conservative nostalgia, we must pay attention to its forward-looking gestus that offers *more* than the simple desire to stay at home. Home is always more than a return to the past' (1997: 10; emphasis in original). Anton Kaes explains that *Heimat* does not merely mean 'home' or 'homeland' but almost breaks under the intensity of its 'emotional connotations': it is 'the site of one's lost childhood, of family, of identity', it 'stands for the possibility of secure human relations, unalienated, precapitalist labour, and the romantic harmony between the country dweller and nature', and it 'refers to everything that is not distant and foreign' (1989: 165). For Bloch it means even more than that, as Jamie Owen Daniel notes: 'an *anticipated* state of reconciliation with conditions of possibility that do not as yet exist, and indeed *will not* exist until present conditions have been radically reconceptualized so that they can be transformed into something as yet impossible to define' (1997: 59; emphasis in original). In the diegesis of *The Secret of Roan Inish*, the imagination of the future is caught up with the modern east.

The Coneellys cannot see a solution which negates that future, but their retreat into a fantastic enclave, into the past their stories tell and which they tell in their stories, signals a yearning for a future in which such a negation has occurred and suggests part of what living in that future might *feel* like. Similarly, in our world, in which a vision of a post-capitalist, postcolonial future often proves difficult to discern – particularly when 'the historic alternatives to capitalism [seem to] have been proven unviable and impossible, and … no other socio-economic system [seems] conceivable, let alone practically available' (Jameson 2005a: xii) – *The Secret of Roan Inish*'s closing sense of restored balance not only offers a *feeling* of closure and fullness, but also demonstrates 'our constitutional inability to imagine Utopia itself', not because of 'any individual failure of imagination but as the result of the systemic, cultural and ideological closure of which we are all in one way or another prisoners' (Jameson 2005b: 289). Both within and without the film, then, the future utopian possibility is to be found in the past: 'What is most desired is missing in the often uncontrollable present but can be present in a controllable, if, in varying degrees, mythic, past. Harmony, warmth, and belonging can live in the supposed golden days of long ago … The future … is not a return to the past but draws sustenance from this past. Memory is the means in the present to ground the future in the past' (Geoghegan 1997: 17; 31). This relationship of past, present and future, and the importance of storytelling to its maintenance is why Fiona's politically imperative last words, addressed to Jamie, are 'I'll teach you to talk and I'll tell you stories'.

For Brecht, realism was not a window on the world but an argument about it; likewise for Sayles, despite his eschewal of Brechtian devices, and this is why a fantasy film is so central to a naturalist oeuvre. The generic shift which enables storytelling within the film to open up the possibility of the fantastic draws attention – just as surely as Godard's cutting of the soundtrack in *Bande à part* (1964) and his lateral tracking shots in *Tout va bien* – not only to the fact that all stories are constructed but also to the ways in which this happens, which encompasses questions of what is included and excluded, who gets to tell the story and where from. To say that we shape the world through narrative is not to deny its materiality. As Alain Badiou (2002; 2006) argues, historical 'situations' only become 'events' retrospectively, when stories, which embody interpretations, are told, considered, debated and circulated until such time as they either achieve consensus or are rejected.[74] This is not to claim an absolute idealist relativism in which there is only language and discourse and subjectivity in play, but a contingent and constantly becoming struggle between discursive and other material agents about the meanings possible within the historical situation. But beyond such arguments about the capacity of the fantastic to draw our attention to the constructed and variously told nature of our social realities, *The Secret of Roan Inish* has something else to offer realism. Commenting on Bloch's contention that 'Where the prospective horizon is omitted, reality only appears as become, as dead, and it is the dead, namely the naturalists and the empiricists, who are burying their dead here' (1986: 223), Phillip E. Wegner explains that for Bloch, 'any model of the real that fails to take into account the category of becoming represented by the utopian surplus, and which thereby denies the always already "unfinished" nature of any world, society, or culture, falls prey to the mystification of an ideology that posits a full self-presence of the present' (2002: 18). By including the fantastic, or rather by constructing a fabric of story which utilises the expressive and hopeful powers of the fantastic, Sayles infects the real – and the realistic – with a trace of the fullness that it could become.

Lone Star (1996)

The political significance of storytelling, of constructing narratives and identities, is central to *Lone Star*. In the desert outside the small town of Frontera, on the Texas side of the border with Mexico, two soldiers from Fort McKenzie discover a human skeleton. Sheriff Sam Deeds identifies it as that of Charley Wade (Kris Kristofferson), a brutal and corrupt sheriff who disappeared in 1957. Most people believe he was run off by his deputy, Sam's father Buddy Deeds (Matthew McConaughey), who one night stood up to him and told him to leave Rio County or risk being shot or jailed. Subsequently, Buddy became sheriff and ran Frontera for nearly thirty years. Just as Buddy, who died some years earlier, is being honoured by having the town courthouse named after him, Sam's investigation begins to reveal that not only was his father every bit as corrupt as Wade but may also be Wade's murderer. Simultaneously, Sam begins a relationship with his old high school sweetheart, Pilar Cruz, only for his investigation to reveal that she is his half-sister (which is why their parents so forcibly separated them in their teens). In a parallel and interwoven story, Colonel Delmore Payne (Joe Morton) takes command of nearby Fort McKenzie, returning to the town in which he was born and raised. His experience there enables him to start relating to his son, Chet (Eddie Robinson), and to reconcile with his estranged father, Otis Payne (Ron Canada), the unofficial 'mayor of darktown' and the owner of Big O's, the county's only black bar. Sam's investigation finally brings him to Big O's, where he learns the truth about Wade's death from Otis and Mayor Hollis Pogue (Clifton James).

As a young man, Hollis (Jeff Monahan) was Wade's deputy along with Buddy. Generally prepared to go along with Wade's corruption, he was badly shaken when Wade murdered Eladio Cruz (Gilbert R. Cuellar, Jr) for smuggling Mexican immigrants into the country without letting him in on the deal. Similarly, the young Otis (Gabriel Casseus) was running a card game out of the roadhouse (which later became Big O's) without giving Wade a cut. After the stand-off with Buddy, Wade and Hollis went to the roadhouse where, realising that Wade intends to kill Otis, Hollis shot Wade. Otis, Buddy and Hollis buried Wade's body in the desert. To make it look like Wade fled town, Buddy stole $10,000 of county money, which he then gave to Eladio's widow, Mercedes (Miriam Colon) to start a restaurant. Later, they became lovers.

Sam decides to let people believe that Buddy killed Wade because he is 'a goddam legend – he can handle it'. The film ends with Sam and Pilar deciding to continue their relationship: 'Everything that went before, all that stuff, all that history,' she says, 'the hell with it, right? Forget the Alamo.'

With its emphasis on fathers and sons, on patriarchal authority and incest taboos, it is tempting to read *Lone Star* through a Freudian lens, a perspective which, for example, Susan Felleman (2006) extends, through Harold's Bloom's work on the anxiety of influence, to consider the film's relationship to its various intertexts, among which one would find such key American films as *Citizen Kane*, *Red River* (1948), *The Searchers* (1956), *Giant* (1956), *Touch of Evil*, *The Man Who Shot Liberty Valance* (1962) and *Chinatown* (1974). However, recalling the dialectical tension Mikhail Bakhtin described in language between centripetal, homogenising authority and centrifugal, heteroglossic dispersal, both of these critical moves, while not without their rewards, favour centration over proliferation. In its crudest application, and many of its commonest ones, the Oedipal complex strips texts of their particularity and diversity, flensing them of detail so that they conform to the structure of myth, a unificatory tendency completely at odds with *Lone Star*'s politics. Similarly, placing *Lone Star* at the centre of an intertextual web not only subordinates these other films to it, reducing them to its image, but also – simultaneously, contradictorily – reduces it to the image of its illustrious fathers, imposing a reductive Oedipal relationship between these texts. Instead, then, I will focus on precisely this centripetal/centrifugal dynamic, which is evident across all levels of the film. This fractal structuring is clearest in the intercatenation of public and private worlds, an infolding which questions any distinction between them. (This is succinctly demonstrated when Delmore visits his estranged father. Ostensibly there to determine whether or not to place Big O's off-limits to his troops, Delmore is not entirely certain how to respond to Otis asking to meet his family. As Delmore leaves, he says, 'You'll get official notification when I make my decision', a line which, because of his character and manner, could be taken as a statement about either issue or both.) Furthermore, the investigation narrative – which deems certain details relevant and others not – poses the question of where, and on what level, one should begin to analyse a film, and the wrong conclusions that Sam reaches demonstrate precisely the dangers of a centripetal drawing-in. And while the narrative selects a certain trajectory through the community it depicts, that depiction itself is produced by the self-same trajectory.

In order to elaborate upon these complexities, I will focus almost entirely upon a single scene: the school meeting in which teachers' departures from the approved history textbook are called into question. The scene starts with an Anglo mother (Dee Macaluso), hair fixed firmly in place, sat in the centre of the screen. Behind her, covering the blackboard, is a map of Texas whose key obscures the bordering portion of Mexico. The camera tracks in and pans slightly towards her as she speaks, her head positioned just inside the Texan side of the border visible on the map: 'Tearin' everything down! Tearin' down our heritage, tearin' down the memory of people who fought and died for this land…'. The camera pans past half a dozen other parents to focus on a Chicano father (Luis Cobo) who interrupts her. On the blackboard behind him is a picture of American Indians in a ritual dance around a fire. He points out, 'We fought and died for this land, too. We fought the US Army, the Texas Rangers…'. He is interrupted by an Anglo father (Marco Perella): 'Yeah, and you lost, buddy.' The camera pans to find him. The wall behind him is decorated with older maps and a picture of a cowboy leading a wagon train. 'Winners get the bragging rights, that's just the way it goes.' Seated in front of him, the Chicano journalist Danny (Jesse Borrego), disbelieving and dismayed, grins.

Lone Star: cultures coming together

'People, people,' the Anglo Principal (Don Phillips) interjects, and the film cuts to him in medium close-up, more formally dressed than the parents. 'I think it would be best if we don't view this thing in terms of winners and losers.'

Cut back to the Anglo mother, increasingly irate, who points at the offscreen Pilar, saying, 'Well, the way she's teachin' it's' – cut briefly to a medium close-up of the Anglo teacher, Molly (Eleese Lester), dressed in white and Pilar dressed in dark blue, her head obscuring much of Texas on the map on the blackboard behind her; and then back to the mother – 'got everything switched around. I was on the textbook committee and her version is not…'.

'We think of the textbook,' the Principal interrupts as we cut to his medium close-up, 'as a guide, not as an absolute…'.

There is a cut back to the mother: '…it is not what we set as the standard!' She draws a breath, calming herself before addressing the Chicano parents. 'Now you people can believe whatever you want to, but when it comes to teaching our children…'.

'They're our children, too,' a Chicana mother (Mary Jane R. Hernandez) interrupts, the camera panning to find her. Behind her are more pictures of American Indians, and a soldier in imperial finery. She jabs her finger downwards to emphasise her point: 'And as the majority in this community we have the right…'. The Anglo father speaks out again, and the pan reveals him with his arm raised, pointing into the air. 'Oh, yeah, well, the men who founded this state have the right, the right to have their story told the way it happened, not the way someone wanted it to have happened.'

In the foreground, Danny has had enough. 'Hey, the men who founded this state broke from Mexico because they needed slavery to be legal to make a fortune in the cotton business!' Pilar at last speaks up, the film cutting back to her as she gestures in a placatory manner and gently shakes her head: 'I think that's a bit of an oversimplification.'

There is a cut back to the previous shot. The Anglo father challenges Danny. 'Are you reporting this meeting, Danny, or are you running it now?'

'Just adding a little historical perspective.'

'Oh, yeah, well you call it history,' says the father rising to his feet and throwing his arms wide, 'I call it propaganda.' The camera tracks in on him, making him seem more threatening. 'Now I'm sure they've got their own account of the Alamo on the other side, but we're not on the other side…'.

We cut back to Pilar as she, too, rises to her feet: 'There's no reason to be so threatened by this.' Cut back to the father, who has continued, voice raised, as she speaks: '…and we're not about to have our schools taught that way'.

The film cuts back to Pilar, defending herself at last from the accusations: 'Excuse me. I've only been trying to get across part of the complexity of our situation down here.' More calmly, making eye contact around the room with offscreen figures, she sits down, saying, 'Cultures coming together in both negative and positive ways…' before a cut back to the Anglo mother, who responds, 'If you're talking about food and music and all, I have no problem with that. But when you start changing who did what to who…'.

Pilar's daughter, Paloma (Corina Martinez), enters the room and whispers something to her mother, as Molly interjects, 'We're not changing anything, we're just trying to present a more complete picture.'

'And that's what's got to stop!'

As Pilar gathers her things and leaves with Paloma, Molly tries to soothe the situation: 'Look, there's enough ignorance in the world without us encouraging it in the classroom.' The Anglo mother bristles: 'Now who are you calling ignorant?'

Sayles' inspiration for this scene arose from 'a particular situation in Texas. Because the people who publish textbooks don't want to make a different version … for every state, states with a market the size of Texas have a stranglehold on which textbooks are used across the United States. In Texas there was an extremely conservative husband and wife team[Mel and Norma Gabler, who run Educational Research Analysts] who had the power to shape what history textbooks were used across the nation. Had they been from Rhode Island they wouldn't have had the power; they could have had the same opinions but they wouldn't have had the clout' (in Neff 2002: 26). As Gina Neff explains, the Gablers' criteria for judging the suitability of social studies textbooks, for example, includes privileging Christianity, derogating the New Deal and using spurious data to champion Reaganomics (2002: 38). Their blatantly ideological criteria attempt to impose a conservative limitation on the types of meaning available to students not only in their own state but, because of the market, throughout the US. This is mirrored in all the positions held in the scene from *Lone Star*, not merely that of the Anglos, although their stance is presented through various means as the most problematic. The scene starts *in media res*, with the Anglo mother midway through a tirade. By denying us any sense of what has led to this point, she is made to seem both the cause of the ensuing argument and an overbearing presence whose natural condition is an always-roused defence of white privilege. Her position in relation to the map behind her makes it seem as if she is shouting into Mexico. Her antagonism is reiterated through the patronising tone she adopts when addressing the Chicano parents collectively and her aggressive gesticulations in Pilar's direction. Her thin frame, tidy appearance and motionless hair suggest a rigidity of outlook reaching far beyond her insistence on the textbook. And her final line is set up so that it does not require an answer. The Anglo father is likewise thin, his haircut and short-sleeved blue shirt giving him an anachronistic air, as if he really belongs in the parts of the film set in the 1950s. As with the mother, the camera's framing and reframing makes him a dominant presence in the room, enabling him to occupy space with confidence as his gestures become more expansive and his voice louder.

In contrast, the Chicano parents seem less at ease, with the mother speaking from a position seated behind other characters and the father placed at the back of the room. Their argument is more ambiguous than that of the Anglos. While the father could be arguing for a version of history from a Chicano viewpoint every bit as mythic and uncomplicated as that preferred by the Anglos, he could also be merely supporting Pilar and Molly's 'more complete picture'. So, too, could the mother's insistence on the rights of a community to have a representative voice in how their story is told. Moreover, she does not appeal to some version of history but to a vague notion of the 'rights' of citizens. Casting rounder, less angular, physical types in these roles reinforces a sense of their willingness to compromise. Unlike the Anglos, they never directly address or challenge the teachers, so this compromise might equally be a sense of subordination to authority figures. Danny is a different case, there to report but clearly unable to maintain the supposed objectivity of a journalist because the story involves his community, and the education which enabled him to become a journalist also enabled him to learn more about the 'complete picture'. His claim to offer 'a little historical perspective', though, is really concerned with countering an Anglocentric organisation of history with one centred on Chicano identity.

This debate is structured by the absence of representatives from the school's other ethnic groups, the African-Americans and the Kickapoo Indians. The absence of the former, and by extension the latter, can perhaps best be explained in the words of Otis: 'There's not enough of us to run anything in this town.' Equally significant in the construction of this scene is the presence of the Principal and his two history teachers. The pans between parents which suggest the possibility of a genuine exchange between them are disrupted by the spatial organisation of the scene and the editing. The potentially circular camera movement is reduced to movement around an arc as the occupants of the room are not sat in a circle, which might imply equality, but in a semi-circle around the three members of staff, which positions the parents if not as children then at least as less powerful. This is emphasised in two ways: firstly, the parents talk to the authority figures at the front of the room as often as they do to each other; second, when the Principal or teachers speak, the longer, unedited takes with a mobile camera are replaced by a shot/reverse-shot pattern and generally static camera which separates the space of the parents from that of the teachers and drives the discussion into confrontations between individuals. This is not to say that the longer takes depict anything like a genuine discussion– the characters merely state and, if they are Anglo, restate their positions – but it has a greater potential to, despite the multiple power relationships always already in play. Furthermore, the spatial and formal divisions of this scene not only inscribe a hierarchical relationship between staff and parents but also between the male Principal, who never shares the frame with anyone else, and his two female teachers. The Principal adopts a quiet authority that has the appearance of neutrality. Molly is softly-spoken, her tone conciliatory if her words are not always well-chosen, while Pilar allows herself a moment of indignation before returning to her calmer voice and reseating herself so as to seem less threatening while also making eye-contact with those she addresses. Together, they seem to represent the voice of decency and reason – but things are not that clear-cut, as their gender and ethnic stereotyping indicates.

Slavoj Žižek argues that multiculturalism, the cultural logic of multinational capital, treats '*each* local culture the way the colonizer treats colonized people – as "natives" whose mores are to be carefully studied and "respected"' (1997: 44; emphasis in original). Therefore, multiculturalism is

> a disavowed, inverted, self-referential form of racism, a 'racism with a distance' – it 'respects' the Other's identity, conceiving the Other as a self-enclosed 'authentic' community towards which he, the multiculturalist, maintains a distance rendered possible by his privileged universal position. Multiculturalism is a racism which empties its own position of all positive content (the multiculturalist is not a direct racist, he doesn't oppose to the Other the *particular values* of his own culture), but nonetheless retains this position as the privileged *empty point of universality* from which one is able to appreciate (and depreciate) properly other particular cultures – the multiculturalist respect for the Other's specificity is the very form of asserting one's own superiority. (Ibid.; emphasis in original)

This multiculturalist perspective informs the position taken by the Principal and teachers. The Principal seems to want to arrive at a consensus version of history which offends no one. By permitting *supplements* to the approved textbook he privileges it even as he admits that its account might be inadequate. Thus, while appearing to speak from a position without its own specific content and which seems to rise above such petty disputes, he nonetheless tacitly supports one view of history as being predominantly correct and only in need of tinkering or rounding out. This is also the case with Molly and Pilar. Seated alongside each other in a two-shot, Anglo Molly dressed in white, Chicana Pilar dressed in dark colours, as if to emphasise their ethnicities, they seem to fulfil the image of multiculturalism: made distinct from each other in terms of their appearance, and thus of their ethnicities, they share a space of equality. However, this image is contradictory. While their two-shots are of a shared continuous space, the gap between them might equally render this a discontiguous space. While Molly might be taken as speaking in support of Pilar, thus inverting a typical ethnic hierarchy, this relationship can be read differently, with Pilar as the fiery, outspoken Chicana and Molly as the calm, reasonable and conciliatory Anglo.

Pilar's argument that all they are trying to do is give a fuller picture of history is likewise ambiguous. Does she identify with the Principal's multiculturalist perspective which would strip politics and conflict from accounts of history by euphemistically treating all such things as merely cultures coming together in different ways? If so, she is party to a whitewashing of history that excuses the dominant Anglo version, and by failing to refute it offers it support. Or is she promoting a subaltern history from below which she is forced to describe euphemistically? It is certainly unclear whether she disagrees with Danny or just realises how impolitic it would be for her to openly agree in this situation, but her call not to oversimplify reinforces a multiculturalist agenda which in its proliferation of perspectives shies away from actively challenging the dominant Anglo mythology. The indeterminacy of Pilar's position can be seen to stem from her own, often self-conscious, embedding in a complex community, most evident in scenes she shares with her children and her mother. For example, in the scene in which Pilar is driving her children, their bickering is articulated through ethnic stereotyping conflated with social class. Amado (Gonzalo Castillo) calls his sister 'Little Miss Honor Roll' and accuses her of pretending she came over on the Mayflower, while Paloma mocks his friendship with a 'bunch of *pachuco* wannabes'. Paloma seems to be positioned as being like her mother – they sit in the front of the car, Paloma is a good student – while Amado, seated in the back, is more like his dead father. Paloma and Pilar seem to aspire to a middle-class (Anglo) identity, while Amado is attached to a working-class (Chicano) identity and what Pilar describes as a 'big Tejano roots thing'. Pilar and Paloma are what Pilar's mother would call Spanish, while Amado is what she would call Mexican, 'a *chulo* with grease under his nails'. This affiliation between Pilar and Paloma is, however, recast in the same scene. Paloma ridicules a 14 year-old girl who claims to be 'desperately in love' with one of Amado's friends. To her surprise, Pilar, who has just seen Sam through the windscreen, defends the girl, arguing that being in love at 14 is not only possible but has nothing to do with whether or not one is smart. Her defence of emotion feminises her just as her defence of passion Latinises her, moving her to a position closer to Amado's in terms of an ethnic stereotyping which rejects Paloma's commitment to middle-class respectability. As in the textbook debate, it is unclear whether Pilar occupies a complex position or whether her middle-class Anglo aspiration and identity is really a façade over a deep-rooted (and stereotypical) ethnic identity which cannot help but erupt at moments of emotional intensity.

The ambiguities of Pilar's character are, on the one hand, the product of a naturalist narrative method, which, as Lukács argues, tends to present social problems as social facts, and which in this instance risks presenting her complexity as arising from a fixed inner being rather than from the complex social and intersubjective webs she occupies. Related to this, and indicated by the positioning of the Principal and teachers, is the problem which arises from the multiculturalist perspective of Sayles' films. Typically positioned as observing from outside the community it depicts, a Sayles film is, of course, a pseudo-observer, the creator and stager of these communities, and while its generally distanced camera attempts to depict the real, to construct fictional ontologies based on close observation of actual locales and communities, it in fact stands in a specific relationship to the real and to the image of the real it creates. It offers up for our inspection 'authentic', self-enclosed communities, and Sayles' often-criticised lack of a distinctive visual style (or rather his underplayed style, typically unburdened by overt stylisations) helps to create the illusion that it occupies a universal and empty position. I will return to the similarity between the teachers' and Sayles' positions in relation to *Lone Star*'s most obvious stylistic flourishes, but first there are three final elements of the schoolroom scene I wish to comment upon in relation to the rest of the film.

Firstly, the desire of various groups and individuals to fix down the meaning of history, which is reiterated throughout the film, particularly in relation to the declining Anglo power bloc. Their most public display is the dedication of the Buddy Deeds courthouse, but even this civic event reveals a centrifugal tendency. The plaque in Buddy's honour is positioned beneath a bas-relief of Buddy, in uniform, with his hand on the shoulder of a Chicano boy. This whitewashed, mythicised depiction of Buddy as a friend to all signals how patronising this image is to the Chicano community. It reduces them to a child in need of support *and* guidance and seems completely unproblematic to the Anglo community and those of the Chicano community most closely allied to them, like Mercedes Cruz, who voted for the court-house to be named in Buddy's honour. The resistance of signification to centripetal fixity is also evoked by Fenton's (Tony Frank) aside that it looks like Buddy is 'gonna run that Mexican kid in for loitering'. Sam also experiences this resistance when he gears his investigation of Wade's murder towards proving Buddy was the murderer, only to find that the signifiers – the clues – actually tell a different story. Likewise, Delmore has a fixed notion of why people join the army, which is deflated when Athena (Chandra Wilson), one of the black troops under his command, explains that she enlisted not out of a sense of duty or service but to escape the chaos of the world outside and because 'It's their country. This is one of the best deals they offer.' From this perspective, Delmore's whole career and his rank suggest he is no different from Mercedes, who strongly identifies with Anglo culture, calling the border patrol when she spots some illegal immigrants and despising other Chicanos as Mexican rather than Spanish; or from Jorge Guerra (Richard Reyes), Frontera's next mayor, and Ray (Tony Plana), Sam's deputy and probable replacement, both of whom are being groomed by the Anglo power bloc so as to enable them to retain not only standing and authority but also the ability to make a profit by building a new and utterly superfluous jail. (This corrupt deal echoes one from thirty years earlier in which hundreds of Chicanos were dispossessed and their shanty town, which had stood for over a century, flooded to make a lake, enriching Buddy and Hollis in the process – a story which Guerra helps to quash.) And finally it is worth considering Sam's ex-wife, Bunny (Frances McDormand), who in the single scene in which she appears offers a cautionary image of monadic bourgeois subjectivity, cut off from material history and social being, her 'tightly wound' centripetality stalled in fixed inward patterns of neurosis.

Secondly, just as the Kickapoo and black parents are missing from the classroom, so are images of blacks missing from its walls, while the depictions of American Indians seem to be of the most stereotypical sort. This is indicative of the Anglo version of history which still dominates the 'more complete picture', relegating certain historical agents to the room out the back of Big O's bar where Otis has pieced together an exhibition devoted to the black Seminoles. When Pilar asks Sam about the lack of pictures on the walls of his house, he explains that the past they would represent is 'nothing that I want to look back on'. Whether or not this private scene provides a protocol for reading the schoolroom's omission of certain images, such as those which would reinforce Danny's argument that the Texas Republic seceded from Mexico to join a nation where slavery was legal, this is certainly part of the history of Texas's founding that the Anglos deny. In contrast, the history of the black Seminoles is precisely something Otis wants to look back on, not treating John Horse, Wild Cat, Osceola and their people as uncomplicated heroes of mythic proportions – although the root of their appeal lies in their resistance to slavery and the American state – but as marginalised ancestors who were caught in a complex, hostile world but managed to carve out a place of sorts for themselves.

Thirdly, the classroom scene also draws attention to borders: their arbitrariness, their invisibility, the fluid relations that they conceal. There is, for example, a contradiction in the shot in which the Anglo mother seems to be shouting into Mexico while the people she is actually talking to are in the same American schoolroom as her. This conflation of the US with whiteness is echoed in the words of the Anglo father, who champions Yankee bragging while derogating alternative views as propaganda, and who implies that on each side of the border there are unitary views of the meaning of the Alamo even though the people who disagree with the version he prefers live on the same side of the border as him.

In *We Have Never Been Modern*, Bruno Latour identifies modernity with two contradictory and interrelated impulses, one which separates and purifies and one which creates hybrids. Intriguingly, it is only the action of the first, the attempt to impose a grid of meaning on the world, that enables the latter to occur. Without first dividing the world into separate phenomena with unique identities, one cannot produce or identify hybrids. This dynamic process – which can be seen as describing something similar to Bakhtin's centripetal/centrifugal dialectic – is useful in considering the contradictions between borders, which assume fixed and stable identities, and the world onto which they are imposed. The arguments of the Anglo mother and father are predicated on a belief in the reality of borders and stable identities, a position from which it is possible to see the Chicanos as either disturbing hybrids or as subjects misplaced on the wrong side of a border (especially when the mother invokes her rights as an American citizen to challenge Anglo history and identity).

Latour also offers a way of thinking about those sequences in which the action moves from the 1990s to the 1950s, or back again, without conventional cutting or dissolving. These transitions are often achieved by a camera movement which emphasises spatial continuity between past and present while also implying that the past is effectively located in the present as something still active in the world. Rather than thinking of time as linear, as having clear boundaries between past, present and future, Latour suggests regrouping

contemporary elements along a spiral rather than a line. We do have a future and a past, but the future takes the form of a circle expanding in all directions, and the past is not surpassed but revisited, repeated, surrounded, protected, recombined, reinterpreted and reshuffled. Elements that appear remote if we follow the spiral may turn out to be quite nearby if we compare loops. Conversely, elements that are quite contemporary, if we judge by the line, become quite remote if we traverse a spoke. Such a temporality does not oblige us to use the labels 'archaic' or 'advanced', since every cohort of contemporary elements may bring together elements from all times. (1993: 75)

Sayles' reworking of *City of Hope*'s trading technique, so that it passes between times and often between the same person in different times, brings to the fore the complex temporality of social being, just as *City of Hope* charted its complex spatiality. And just as Dos Passos's introduction of newspaper headlines and autobiographical passages into his novels signalled the inadequacy of earlier naturalist techniques to capture a complex, overdetermined reality, so these transitions, however smoothly they convey the viewer between different times, reveal the limitations of the conventional linearity of narrative film and of the conventional editing between different times which typically separate out the past from the present. In *Lone Star*'s particular exploration of intersubjective being it becomes clear that time 'is not a general framework but a provisional result of the connection between entities' (Latour 1993: 74).

However, the apparent omniscience of the filmic narration which brings all these elements together announces itself as occupying a position divorced from the world it depicts. Like the Principal and the teachers, it respects the enclosed community of the film and displays it, warts and all, from a position which does not overtly condone or condemn. By arguing for the need for a more complete picture and demonstrating the complexities which underlie both personal and public history, this multiculturalist perspective risks relativising all experience and promoting a 'plurality of struggles' which are 'strictly correlative to the silent abandonment of the analysis of capitalism as a global economic system and to the acceptance of capitalist economic relations as the unquestionable framework' (Žižek 1997: 47). While Sayles' films always recognise economic determinants and reveal the costs of capitalism, the avoidance of political commitment that a liberal multiculturalism enables becomes far more problematic in *Men with Guns*.

Men with Guns/Hombres armados (1997)

Like *The Secret of Roan Inish*, *Men with Guns* travels from the modern city to the utopian possibility – always just out of reach – of premodern tradition. Recently widowed, Dr Humberto Fuentes (Federico Luppi) decides to journey into the rural interior of his unnamed, generically Latin-American country to visit the young doctors he trained a few years earlier as part of a project to aid the indigenous population. Before he leaves, he discovers one of his former pupils running a black market business in the poor suburb of Los Perdidos who tells him that the project failed. Puzzled, Fuentes proceeds with his trip and discovers, one by one, that the doctors were murdered by 'men with guns' – it is never clear whether by soldiers, guerrillas or criminals. En route, he gathers fellow travellers: Conejo (Dan Rivera González), a boy whose mother rejected him because she became pregnant with him when raped; Domingo (Damián Delgado), a deserter turned thief; Padre Portillo (Damián Alcázar), a Catholic priest who, fearing for his life, abandoned his station; and Graciela (Tania Cruz), a young woman who

Men with Guns: Cerca del Cielo, but still not there

has not spoken since she was raped by soldiers two years earlier. Fuentes' journey takes him across the plains and into the mountains, searching for Cerca del Cielo, a village said to exist among the trees, so well hidden that the men with guns cannot find it, and where the last of his students is rumoured to live. Stripped of his possessions and of his ignorance about the state of his country, Fuentes and his remaining companions find Cerca del Cielo, which is no paradise. There is no doctor there, and Fuentes, acknowledging that his supposed legacy was just a dream, quietly dies. Domingo, who was an Army medic, reluctantly picks up Fuentes' medical bag and takes on his mantle. Graciela looks out through an opening in the jungle and sees other, higher mountains rising in the distance, further on.

This final shot of pristine jungled peaks echoes a shot near the start of the film of two anonymous glass-faced office buildings rising above the streets of the capital city, bookending the journey but also blurring the distinction between modern and premodern, culture and nature. Both mountains and buildings are imbued with a desire for transcendence, for a utopian separation from the confusions and conflicts of history and circumstance, for enclave and sanctuary. Despite very obvious differences, that these two views share this desire suggests that the modern/premodern and culture/nature should not be seen as binary opposites but as terms within a more complex dialectic. Fuentes' journey, like Fiona's in *The Secret of Roan Inish*, is not into the past but into the present, into Latour's spiral-time, in which city and country, modern and premodern, produce a complex, contingent *now*. The dialectic of city and country is common to both the pastoral tradition – which in the full, rich sense described by Raymond Williams is primarily about the ownership and reconstruction of land for the benefit of a minority class – and utopian fiction – in which the flight from the city is typically redemptive, although the bucolic redemption is also often ironised. The history of the city and the country in England extends far beyond national boundaries, and is, in fact,

> a history of the extension of a dominant model of capitalist development to include other regions of the world. And this was not, as it is now sometimes seen, a case of 'development' here, 'failure to develop' elsewhere. What was happening in the 'city', the 'metropolitan' economy, determined and

was determined by what was made to happen in the 'country'; first the local hinterlands and then the vast regions beyond it, in other people's lands. What happened in England has since been happening ever more widely, in new dependent relationships between all the industrialised nations and all the other 'undeveloped' but economically important lands. Thus one of the last models of 'city and country' is the system we know as imperialism. (Williams 1973: 279)

This suggests that those things in *Men with Guns* which appear to belong either to modernity or premodernity are interrelated through the operations of capital. As Fuentes' journey takes him further from the city, he encounters the salt people, the sugar people, the coffee people, the banana people, the gum people and the corn people. Each group names itself after the crop they harvest, and because it is left unexplained this can seem like a traditional division of regions and agricultures rather than the consequences of transformations wrought by the demands of international capital.[75] Consequently, the agricultural land through which Fuentes passes and which could be taken for a rural premodernity is in reality deeply bound up in the processes of capitalism's modernising drive.

David McNally argues that the idealist linguistics erected on Ferdinand de Saussure's foundations are 'constituted by a radical attempt to banish the real human body – the sensate, biocultural, labouring body – from the sphere of language and social life' and consequently 'reproduce a central feature of commodified society: the abstraction of social products and practices from the labouring bodies that generate them' (2001: 1). Marx notes that, for the capitalist, the surplus-value (profit) produced by labour in the portion of the working day in which labour creates value over and above that of the cost of wages, 'has all the charms of a creation out of nothing' – and such surplus-value should really be conceived as a 'congelation of surplus-labour time, as nothing but materialised surplus-labour' (1996: 226). Capitalism, however, effaces this reality, perpetuating instead the related notions that capital creates wealth and that capital is something other than accumulated surplus-labour. Just as commodity fetishism imbues the commodity with values and properties which occlude the real source of its value in the labour which produced it, thus enabling the supercession of use-value by exchange-value, so capital separates itself from its own materiality and constructs itself as something immaterial. In its information-age form, capital has restructured societies '*around a bipolar opposition between Net and the self* (Castells 2000a: 3; emphasis in original), with the Net standing in for the global flows of capital-as-information, circulating, apparently weightless and friction-free. This fantasy that capital exists outside of human space and time, while the self remains in the human rhythms of movement and duration, has profound material consequences. Manuel Castells describes a world in which 'capital is global, and core production networks are increasingly globalized, [but] the bulk of labor is local', with 'only an elite specialty labor force, of great strategic importance ... truly globalized' (2000a: 131). While neoliberal deregulation allows capital to flow with relative freedom, 'labor is still highly constrained, and will be for the foreseeable future, by institutions, culture, borders, police, and xenophobia' (2000a: 247).[76] The continuities with the imperialism Williams describes are self-evident.

The twin corporate towers which rise imperiously into the air above the capital, and whose reflective surfaces refuse the surrounding city in the manner Fredric Jameson ascribed to the Westin Bonaventure Hotel's mirrored facades (see 1991: 42), are physical manifestations of capital's fantasy of separation and immateriality. Their physicality is deeply ideological: beyond the power they symbolise, they seem like a discontiguous alien presence, but are also utterly familiar, as if they could be inserted into any major city's skyline. They are an interface between global capital and local labour. Fuentes, for all his education, wealth and status, does not quite belong to the globalised professional class that Castells describes. As his emotional investment in the Ambassadors of Health programme suggests, he is more modern than postmodern, a believer in gradual, ameliorative progress, although his Mercedes and Wagoneer four-wheel drive jeep do simultaneously place him in Alan N. Shapiro's globalised consumer class. While his medical practice does not free him from embodiment as such – we first encounter him sticking his finger up a General's rectum – he is nonetheless separated from the material realities of his country. All of his patients are rich and powerful – one woman complains that her kidneys bother her whenever she drinks red wine; the more expensive the wine, the sharper the pain – and not one of them is indigenous. Despite the daily contradictions he encounters, like the General's insistence that the guerrillas are merely a rumour but that his men 'spend half their time chasing [them] in those fucking mountains', Fuentes cultivates the 'careless, willful ignorance' of a 'man who subconsciously does not want to know' (Sayles 1998a: vii). In this refusal, he rises above material reality, transcending aspects of local intersubjective being, separating himself from the producers of the wealth that enable his lifestyle. This separation is eloquently evoked several times as he drives through the countryside. For much of his journey, he struggles to make the territory in which he finds himself conform to his roadmap's conventional abstraction of the land. Early on, he stops in the middle of a vast plain, and asks an Indian selling salt beside the road what town he is from. He replies, 'From here ... We're salt people. This is where we live.' Fuentes insists that there is nothing there, to which the Indian replies, 'You can't see anything from a car.' The enclosed elevation afforded by his jeep raises Fuentes up above the land, enabling him to see further but preventing him from seeing what is around him. This is emphasised later when Conejo, riding in the jeep for the first time as it cruises down a country road, speaks in an indigenous dialect to Domingo. Asked by Fuentes to translate, Domingo replies, 'He says he's never been in an airplane before.' For all that Conejo was raised in a relatively isolated village, he is able to translate his experience into that of Castells' globalised specialty labour force whose international travel aspires to the condition of capital-circulation. Soon after, there is a 25-second shot of a two-lane road, gently curving around a hill. The jeep appears in the distance, while nearer to the camera a heavily-laden peasant trudges patiently along. The jeep passes him but rather than cut, the camera stays focused on the peasant for a full eight seconds, again creating the sense that Fuentes is passing through a world to which he is not connected. His recurring encounters with the battered truck carrying Kokal – a bottled soda whose logo says not 'Always' but 'Inevitable' – demonstrates not only the infiltration of capital throughout the country but also, as Fuentes comes to learn, that the fantasy of immaterial disconnection is precisely a fantasy.

Also passing through this landscape are a middle-aged American tourist couple, Andrew (Mandy Patinkin) and Harriet (Kathryn Grody), separated from Fuentes by language and nationality but joined to him by social class. Like him, they repeatedly attempt to match the territory to pre-existing maps, a tendency succinctly captured when Andrew, who speaks no Spanish, asks Harriet, 'What's the word for "fajitas"?' When Fuentes first meets them, Andrew is examining a map of ancient paths through the country, pointing out that 'it was a hub here, like Chicago or Atlanta'. Their experience of the country is dominated by texts rather than places. While concerned about encountering atrocities of the sort described in New York newspapers, Andrew is immersed in history book knowledge, typically describing the ruins they visit in terms of what he has read. Fascinated by ancient stories of sacrifice and bloodshed, by the myth and legend the landscape signifies to the imperialist and tourist gaze, he is oblivious to the current inhabitants other than as obstacles to his right to be there. Caught up in this fantasy of history, Andrew dismisses Fuentes' explanation – that if human sacrifice had happened it was the doing of 'other tribes, attacking from the north' – because it is not 'what it says in the book', while all of them miss the parallel implied with the US role in present-day atrocities. Like the multiculturalist, Andrew is not overtly racist. He merely occupies a divorced position which normalises and naturalises the apparently neutral terms of his own cultural specificity, as when he semi-seriously suggests that mass human sacrifice was really just a way of dealing with a labour surplus. However, his touristic preference for Latin America as a place of legend at the very least risks complicity with a more obviously racist perspective, which constructs and utilises a history of bloodthirsty savagery to suggest that the violence of the current situation is just 'natural' to 'their' culture rather than the material conse-quence of a long, ongoing history of colonisation and exploitation.

This multiculturalist 'racism with a distance' extends to the film itself, which constructs as its setting a non-specific Latin-American country – the only thing we learn about it is that it is not Mexico (although it was filmed in Mexico City, Vera Cruz and Chiapas) and probably not Venezuela or Colombia (as Pico de Aguila does not seem to refer to the mountains of that name in those countries). This reordering of Mexican geography to create a composite Latin-American country, which could also be Guatemala but is not, is mirrored by Mason Daring's score, which incorporates music from across the continent (in his DVD commentary, Sayles says 'we used a lot of songs from many, many places … from all over Latin America'). Sayles' films are typically fastidious about specificity of locale, and even their fictional towns and cities are continuous with the real world (Frontera is in Texas and Sam does make a trip to San Antonio). In contrast, *Men with Guns* eschews this degree of particularity and embeddedness in order to treat 'a dynamic as old as human society – men who have weapons and are willing to use them have power over those who don't' (Sayles 1998a: ix) as a generalised condition, pertaining throughout the world and specifically in the so-called 'developing' nations. (This non-specificity might also be about respecting and refusing directly to commodify the suffering of specific peoples.) However, while the film succeeds in capturing some sense of the experience of living in constant fear of men with guns, the decision not to tell a story in relation to a particular named locale is problematic. For example, while telling the story of one specific community or atrocity would perhaps make it seem exceptional rather than part of a total fabric, in the way My Lai or Fallujah have been represented as anomalies, to present a totalised dynamic as old as human society reaches too far in the other direction, prompting such mystificatory notions as original sin or the human condition,[77] especially when unanchored in the world. By evading the material history of a specific place, by producing an image of 'Latin America' rather than representing a particular Latin-American country and culture, by refusing to name names or map social, economic and political determinants, *Men with Guns* speaks from a position akin to that of *Lone Star*'s Principal, respecting the Other while producing an anodyne, uncritical version of history.

In one sense, this is again the naturalist shortcoming of presenting social problems as social facts rather than as contingent, overdetermined circumstances. However, like *The Secret of Roan Inish*, *Men with Guns* puts naturalism under pressure, introducing a narrator who verges on the fantastic but is better understood in terms of Sayles' occasional metaleptic violation of the text's ontological levels (a tendency evident, as we saw, as early as *Return of the Secaucus Seven*). The film opens with an indigenous woman (Iguandili López) and her daughter (Nandi Luna Ramírez) kindling a fire. The mother is in the middle of telling a story about a doctor from the city who sometimes has problems breathing. As she explains that city people 'speak a different language, they wear different clothes, they don't look like us', there is a dissolve to Fuentes' office where he is conducting the General's rectal examination. We return to the mother and daughter some time later, after Conejo has taken up with Fuentes. While her daughter tries to make a tortilla, the mother explains why it is that Conejo's mother rejected him and describes his life as being like that of a dog: 'He takes the scraps that real people leave ... Dogs can't be bad or good. They're just dogs.' They reappear again as Fuentes and his companions finally reach Cerca del Cielo, the narrators of his tale at last – and impossibly – turning up in it. The tortillas are cooking. The girl offers to get the doctor for her mother, whose leg is infected from a landmine fragment buried in it. The mother tells her, 'There's no hurry. He's come to stay.' After Fuentes' death, she will become Domingo's first patient.

This narrator introduces a certain tension into the film. Sayles describes Fuentes as being 'drawn further and further into the dark heart of his own society's violence' (1998a: vii), and even though the film's sympathies typically lie with the subaltern it remains, like Joseph Conrad's *Heart of Darkness* (1899), the story of a representative of the white ruling class. The narrator – who apparently occupies a different temporality to that of Fuentes and perhaps possesses supernatural powers which give her knowledge she could not otherwise possess – signals an anxiety about this. Her words turn Fuentes into a character within an indigenous woman's story. However, the weight of the film's preoccupation with his journey ultimately turns her into a minor character in his story, of little more significance than the heavily-laden peasant. Her marginalisation, along with the deflation of the utopian Cerca del Cielo, signifies a defeat: no dialogue is possible between these worlds which barely brush against each other. In contrast to the woman, who cannot walk because of her injured leg, Fuentes climbs a mountain and completes his quest, which Sayles describes as 'a kind of Pilgrim's Progress' (1998a: viii), and finally rises above material circumstances as, stripped of his illusions, he slips into a peaceful death.

Sayles' reference to John Bunyan is unsurprising as the film often teeters on the brink of allegory. Fuentes encounters people with generic rather than specific names (salt people, coffee people, and so on) and visits towns and villages whose names seem pregnant with significance: Los Perdidos (The Lost), Rio Seca (Dry River), Tierra Quemada (Burnt Earth), Caras Sucias (Dirty Faces), Les Martîres (The Martyrs), Pico de Aguila (Eagle's Peak), Los Sueños (The Dreams) and Tres Cruces (Three Crosses). Cerca del Cielo is particularly instructive in terms of the problem presented by allegory. Traditionally, this form creates narratives with two distinct but directly related layers of meaning, one manifest and mundane, the other latent and divine. However, the latter meaning, disengaged and immaterial, is the privileged one, not hidden but in plain sight: Cerca del Cielo means 'close to heaven', in the sense of being close both to the sky and to God. This emphasis on the 'spiritual' meaning of mundane events is at the very least homologous to idealistic linguistics' abstraction of language from materiality, of capital's abstraction of surplus-labour time as surplus-value, and of the commodity's abstracted and fetishised exchange-value over its material use-value. Furthermore, by risking the allegorical form, *Men with Guns* falls into the role of the multiculturalist who occupies a 'privileged universal position … as the privileged *empty point of universality* from which to appreciate (and depreciate) properly other particular cultures' (Žižek 1997: 44) – a position from which the film is able to construct the 'true' meaning of the countries and cultures it is not actually depicting.

This problem is especially apparent in the film's use of multiple languages, which in turn problematises Bakhtin's notion of welcoming into the text the words of others 'that are already populated with the social intentions of others' (1981: 299–300); and arguably this is true of all Sayles' films, not just those which use 'foreign' languages and subtitling. Shot primarily in Spanish, which Sayles speaks, and four indigenous languages (Nahuatl, Tzotzil, Maya and Kuna), which he does not, the screenplay for *Men with Guns* was written, as Sayles explains, not just in English but in 'subtitle format … no more than thirty-six characters and spaces per line and no more than two lines per screen' (1998a: x). Moreover, the Spanish spoken in the film was deliberately stripped of local and regional idiom so as to prevent those familiar with the language's national variations from identifying the setting of the film as a particular country. The assumptions underlying this process gesture towards Shapiro's dystopian prospect in which 'a cybernetic language, devised in a technical project, [will] come to replace human language, which was too entangled in history and living discourse' (2004: 139). Like the Federation's universal translator, the restrictions of subtitling (which are directly economic in terms of marketing the film to a primary Anglophone audience and of the parameters established for the subtitling technology) postulate 'a universal cybernetic grid to which all languages are programmable or convertible' and assume 'that it is possible and desirable to commute the grammars and signifying terms of all languages into each other', absorbing 'the meaning (or dispersed "non-meaning") of the alien's message into the self-fulfilling prophecy or tautological circuitry of the translation model' (2004: 136). This is the case in Sayles' method of writing the subtitles in English before the words are even uttered in the other languages; and for the majority of the film's audience everything spoken in the Mayan languages 'which is singular and unreconcilable with other languages' (ibid.) is lost, untranslated. Although on the film's official website Sayles says that 'If everyone was speaking English, it wouldn't make as much sense', they are all, in effect, speaking English. Sayles' 'honour system', in which he trusted those delivering dialogue in languages he did not speak to admit to any errors in their delivery, could not of course control or delimit the excess of meaning those words generate for the native speaker; but for the Anglophone viewer that excess fails even to register. As Shapiro notes of the alien language heard through the universal translator's cybernetic communications protocols, 'It all comes out as our – projected universal – language' (ibid.). The notion that it is possible to produce a 'neutral' Spanish stripped of idiomatic specificity similarly eradicates difference and establishes a particular position as a supposedly universal position empty of all specific content.

In their 1969 manifesto, 'Towards a Third Cinema', Fernando Solanas and Octavio Getino wrote:

> In a world where the unreal rules, artistic expression is shoved along the channels of fantasy, fiction, language in code, sign language, and messages whispered between the lines. Art is cut off from the concrete facts – which, from the neo-colonialist standpoint, are accusatory testimonies – to turn back on itself, strutting about in a world of abstractions and phantoms, where it becomes 'time-less' and history-less. Vietnam can be mentioned, but only far from Vietnam; Latin America can be mentioned, but only far enough away from the continent to be ineffective, *in places where it is depoliticized* and where it does not lead to action. (2000: 276; emphasis in original)

My treatment of *Men with Guns* emphasises some of the problems arising from its adoption of forms and strategies which tend precisely to depoliticise it in this way. However, it is also a film in which expression – artistic, political, critical, hopeful – can be discerned between the lines as centrifugal heteroglossia works against the centripetality associated with the overtly commodified English-in-subtitles. One such moment, which depends upon the problematic logic of translation but which simultaneously opens up the possibility of communication across languages and between subjects, comes when Fuentes dissuades Graciela from suicide, describing Cerca del Cielo to her by recalling, and translating, a passage from a tourist brochure describing a resort near Bali which he overheard a tourist (Maggie Renzi) read aloud – 'a very special place, where the air is like a caress, where gentle waters flow, where wings of peace lift the burdens from your shoulders. A place where you can forget. A place where each day is a gift and each person is reborn.' For a fleeting moment, Fuentes succeeds in taking back both language and the utopian impulse which capital has colonised and turned into fetishised commodity forms. He liberates these words from their alienated context and along the permeable boundary between Fuentes and Graciela, despite being more or less the same words, they mean something completely different. For a moment, they enter into history and hint at the possibility of fullness.[78]

Limbo (1999)

In Port Henry, an Alaskan coastal town, Joe Gastineau (David Strathairn), a former fisherman and pulp-mill worker, now employed as a general-purpose handyman by Frankie (Kathryn Grody) and Lou (Rita Taggart), a middle-aged lesbian couple from Seattle who have moved there to run a tourist lodge and trekking business, meets and becomes involved with Donna De Angelo (Mary Elizabeth Mastrantonio). Donna, a single mother, is a singer who has managed to make a living over the years, having performed in '36 states and the territory of Puerto Rico', but who is probably now too old to ever make the big time. Her teenage daughter, Noelle (Vanessa Martinez), who has a history of eating disorders and has begun to self-harm, feels perpetually alienated. Her part-time work at the lodge has brought her into contact with Joe, upon whom she had a crush before her mother met him. As Joe and Donna's relationship stutters into being, his stepbrother Bobby (Casey Siemaszko) returns to town in need of a favour. He persuades Joe to crew his boat on a trip up the coast but lies about the reason. Joe invites Donna and Noelle along. After a squall forces them to anchor in a remote channel, Bobby admits he is there to meet drug dealers who think he has double-crossed them. Soon after, two men board the boat and shoot Bobby. Joe, Donna and Noelle escape to an island and hide until their pursuers leave. They find a derelict house and shelter there for ten days, gathering whatever food they can. Eventually, a small seaplane spots their signal fire and lands. The pilot, Smilin' Jack Johannson (Kris Kristofferson), who has long blamed Joe for his younger brother's accidental death years earlier, claims his radio is broken and his fuel low, but will fly out ahead of the storm to try to get help; privately, he admits to Joe that two men hired him to look for them. Some days later, after the storm, another, larger seaplane comes in to land. Has Jack come to rescue them or has he brought the drug dealers to kill them? The film ends before the plane lands.

I will return to *Limbo*'s deliberate irresolution, but first I want to consider several instances of storytelling in the film. After the titles, which play over footage of salmon moving around relentlessly underwater, it cuts to an old-fashioned promotional film – actually a kinescope of specially-shot videotape – praising Alaska as a tourist destination, beginning with an aerial view of mountains rising up out of thick fog. The narrator intones:

> Welcome to America's last frontier. Where the final lumbering remnants of the Ice Age, the massive and awe-inspiring glaciers, calve cathedral-sized icebergs into the sea, where nature's bounty unfolds in a panoply of flora and fauna, the like of which is seen nowhere else on the planet. From the ocean depths, plumbed by ageless cetaceans, to azure skies, where the mighty eagle soars, this

land abounds with creatures great and small, strange and majestic. It is a land steeped in tradition, its mists redolent of the hearty souls of men who have gone to sea: Tlingit and Haida, Inuit and Aleut, Russian and Norwegian, their languages and deeds lingering on in the names of our countless islands and passageways. A land that for centuries has lifted its siren call to the bold and adventurous, to men and women willing to risk their lives for the promise of untold fortune, be it from fur or fin, from the heaven-pointing spires of old-growth spruce or from the buried treasures of yellow gold or black, energy-rich petroleum. A land visited each year by the relentless and mysterious salmon, each river and stream welcoming home the king and sockeye…

The images accompanying these words blend together footage one could still imagine being used in a promotional film, other footage one could imagine was once used in such films but which to current sensibilities reveals the normalised assumptions and ideological blindnesses of an earlier conjuncture and still other footage in which the comic juxtaposition with the voice-over comes to the fore. Shots of huge cruise liners harboured beneath massive white apartment blocks might convey either a sense of utopian promise (the ships are as modern as the apartments, like homes which move, conveying their inhabitants to wonderful places) or of dystopian inescapability (the ships are as unhomely as modern apartment buildings). Accompanying the line about glaciers calving cathedral-sized icebergs, these images could be a commentary on either human achievement or the temporal and physical insignificance of human endeavours in relation to geological time and scale. As a promotional film, it is presumably intended to convey utopian, positive connotations, yet the implied age of the film stock opens up the contrary possibilities. Talk of wildlife is mainly matched to still images, mostly of cuddly toys, pelts, furs and trophies, while other footage shows a cannery production line and a man in a polar bear costume posing for photos with tourists. Likewise, talk of tradition is matched to images of a totem pole, indigenous-style graffiti and Eskimo dolls, and talk of adventure to elderly tourists boarding a seaplane.

Central to the deflation of this promotional pitch is the footage of both economic decline (the word 'tradition' plays over a shot of a shop window, on which is painted '50% Off') and labour. In addition to the cannery – which might conceivably appear in a film geared more to attracting business than tourists, demonstrating the existence of modern, automated production in Alaska – the line about the hearty souls of various seafaring peoples accompanies shots of relocated Mexican workers making the Eskimo dolls, which are then shown on sale in a giftshop window. Just as in *Men with Guns* the touristic gaze does not recognise its actual local conjunctural situatedness, so the promotional film generically should not admit to the social or economic conditions of the tourist destination, but offer the safe distance and fantasy of detachment or disembodiment that the cruise liners' architecture and mobility promise – as local ex-fisherman Harmon King (Leo Burmester) describes it, 'I'll be out on the water, in my boat, and every time I make a set, there'll be one of those floating nursing homes with 500 sons of bitches and their cameras capturing the moment.'

Limbo cuts from the promotional film's footage of an automated production line mechanically removing the heads of the salmon to the film's diegetic and rather less-automated production line in which this is done by hand. The change in the image-quality emphasises this transition to a reality which seems, in contrast, almost hyperreal in its colour and clarity. Harmon, who is working there, picks up the narration:

> ...the coho and dog, pink or humpback, which is smashed into cans and quick-cooked to give the colourful local folks something to do other than play cards and scratch their nuts all day. A land where that nice old lady from Fort Lauderdale who had the stroke three cabins down was probably parked next to the thawed-out halibut you're eating onboard tonight while your floating hotel chugs through the Hecate Strait to deliver its precious load of geriatrics to the hungry Visa card-accepting denizens of our northern-most and most mosquito-infested state ... Soon as they close this place down, they'll turn it into a tourist attraction. They'll disinfect the joint and you can get a job in one of those, er, cases, like in a museum, one of those, er, displays ... dioramas. In that diorama, they'll hang fake fish guts all over you, put a label underneath says 'Typical Filipino Cannery Worker'.

This narration continues to deflate the advertising image of Alaska (although not without its own stereotypes). Significantly, though, Harmon's is not a disembodied 'voice of God' narration. It is not separated from the world depicted in the images over which it speaks, nor is it so certain of imposing its meaning upon them that it can be indifferent to what they actually show. And unlike the tourists with their 'floating hotel' and electronic currency, it is not detached from the physical and intersubjective realities of the place and situation. Rather, Harmon's is the voice of a subject inhabiting that world, who stumbles over his words and who does not shy away from the material realities of social being.

Even as Harmon imagines a future in which his co-workers' labour will be reduced to the spectacular simulation of labour, he fantasises a future for himself in which he can return to more 'manly' labour by recovering his boat from Frankie and Lou – he used it as collateral and then defaulted on a deal with them – and becoming a fisherman once more, living in the reality of 'the moment' that the tourists cannot experience directly. His recovery of masculinity (predicated on a feminisation of the tourists and his Filipino co-worker, as well as his antagonism to the lesbian couple from the big, bourgeois city) is nothing more than a fantasy. It is undermined both by his inability to escape capitalism outside of the factory (he cannot afford to get his boat back and even if he could, his catch would be restricted by the regulations governing the industry and threatened by factory vessels, and his livelihood would in any case be dependent upon the market) and more comically by the scene in which he catches a fish and has to shoot it with a handgun.[79]

This vision of a simulacral future is further developed in the next scene, in which Albright (Michael Laskin), a major figure in the tourist industry,[80] challenges the logging industry's logic in clear-cutting the trees – but for economic rather than ecological reasons:

> Look, our people cruise by an island … what do we show them? We show them a little Indian fish camp, some totem poles maybe. We show them a black bear foraging for breakfast in the early morning mist. We do not show them deforested hillsides and logging equipment … Heavy machinery they can see in New Jersey … We all have to make our living. I'm not arguing that. Cut the trees in the interior. Turn it into a parking lot. Just quit with the chainsaws when you get to where people can see. We're trying to develop themes for each area up here: The Whales' Causeway, Island of the Raven People, Kingdom of the Salmon, Lumberland.

This latter, he explains, is not the denuded landscape that industrialised logging creates, but 'a turn-of-the-century sawmill with a water-powered generator and a gift shop. That's history, Phil, not industry. History is our future here, not our past.' Albright's Baudrillardian argument has much older roots than postmodern theory might allow. It is an extension and perpetuation of the reorganisation of the landscape Raymond Williams analysed:

> Working country is hardly ever a landscape. The very idea of a landscape implies separation and observation … The clearing of parks as 'Arcadian' prospects depended on the completed system of exploitation of the agricul-tural and genuinely pastoral lands beyond the park boundaries. There, too, an order was being imposed: social and economic but also physical. The mathematical grids of the enclosure awards, with their straight hedges and straight roads, are contemporary with the natural curves and scatterings of park scenery. And yet they are related parts of the same process – superficially opposed in taste but only because in the one case land is being organised for production, where the tenants and labourers will work, while in the other case it is being organised for consumption – the view, the ordered proprietary repose, the prospect. (1973: 120; 124)

As in a theme park, or country estate, the labour which enables the landscape to exist as a prospect must as far as possible be removed from sight. Logging operations should move inland. Consumers should perceive only the fetishised commodity: Eskimo dolls rather than displaced Mexican labour; the factory as museum and history rather than industry – indeed, the cannery is going out of business because consumers everywhere have begun to prefer fresh to canned salmon, perhaps because the latter's industrial processing has become too obvious. Albright's vision extends beyond that, though. He wants to go beyond merely arranging prospects for his passengers to consume visu-ally from the liners, or pseudo-authentic locations for them to visit. We later see him telling potential investors that rather than give people 'bigger and better facsimiles of nature' they should be marketing 'nature itself … Alaska as one big theme park'. This argument, made from a position which resonates surprisingly with Sayles' decision in *Men with Guns* to reproduce a generic Latin America rather than a specific location, unflinchingly promotes the supercession of use-value by exchange-value. Like the multiculturalist, Albright's empty universal position actually represents an utter normalisation and naturalisation of the commodifying logic that drives capital. To survive in such a world, Harmon might do better to hire himself out to perform 'the moment' of 'real' and 'masculine' endeavour for those cruise ship passengers – as the scene in the Golden Nugget bar in which tourists are guided through it, heedless of the locals actually drinking there, suggests, he is already part of the colourful local scenery exposed to the consuming touristic gaze anyway.

The transition from the voice-over narration of the *faux*-promotional film to Harmon's deflationary continuation is another example of the Bakhtinian dialectic between the centripetal, unifying, disembodied linguistic tendency and the centrifugal resistance it finds in everyday, idiomatic, embodied speech – a tension already evident in the disjunctions between the voice-over and the images whose contrary and excessive meanings it tries to corral. It must, however, be noted that the dialectical totality is more complex than a straightforward polar opposition. Harmon's diatribe counters the thematisation of Alaska with his own nostalgic centralisation of the white male subject, both at one with and wrestling nature. This fantasy of premodern existence is profoundly modern, and the supposed superiority of Harmon's position – from which he gives his Filipino co-worker Ricky (Hermínio Ramos) a dictionary-style definition of 'redolent' – is also resisted: he has to rely on the indigenous Audrey (Dawn McInturff) to remind him of the word 'diorama'. She also reminds him that he does not actually own a boat any more.

Harmon fantasises that there is a recuperable distinction between the past he imagines and the future he dreads. Dismissing the claim that modernity has lost an earlier balanced and 'rich mixture of social and technical culture' and has become dominated by 'a technology devoid of ties with the social order', Bruno Latour argues that the real difference is that a modern collective 'translates, crosses over, enrolls, and mobilizes more elements which are more intimately connected, with a more finely woven social fabric' (1999: 195). This means that 'attributing "objectivity" and "efficiency" to modern technology and "humanity" to low-tech poesis' is a mistake – the 'adjective modern does not describe an *increased distance* between society and technology or their alienation, but a deepened *intimacy*, a more intricate mesh, between the two' (1999: 196; emphasis in original). It is this intricate meshing which produces, for example, the ambiguity of the images of cruise liners, and which becomes apparent by its relative absence when Joe, Donna and Noelle are torn from it and stranded on the island, which is where the second example of storytelling I wish to consider occurs.

In the derelict house, Noelle finds an old diary wrapped in an oilskin. It belonged to Anne Marie Hoak, who many years earlier had moved there with her parents to breed foxes. Each night Noelle reads a few pages aloud. The story she tells bears striking, if ambiguous, parallels to their situation and it gradually becomes clear that she is actually improvising it, although Joe and Donna do not realise this until just before she 'reads' the last entry. Her virtuosity is unsurprising as we have already seen her read out her story, 'The Water Baby', in class. Her performance on that occasion was less self-assured, but the story itself, which tells of the delivery of a human baby born with gills, captures her sense of alienation and builds on the film's piscine imagery as well as its metaphors of suffocation and drowning while expressing ambivalent feelings towards her mother and estranged father through a reworked primal scene fantasy full of anger and loss. As if to confirm such an interpretation, the film cuts from a close-up of Noelle reading it to a shot of her walking, isolated and alone, down a crowded school corridor. The film is slowed down, distorting diegetic sound. Everyone is absolutely oblivious to her, and she frowns as if she does not understand any of the activity going on around her.

In the story Noelle tells on the island, Anne Marie's life is one of hardship. Papa, a former logger who suffers from blackouts, is frustrated at not being able to provide for his family, and her unsympathetic Mother, disturbed by their isolation and poverty, succumbs to religious mania and madness. Anne Marie feels a kind of enchantment with the island, feasting on blueberries that stain her fingers, learning the 'manly' skills Papa teaches her, fantasising that she is 'possessed by the soul of some long-dead Indian girl or perhaps the spirit of a she-wolf'. She is critical of Mother, and spies on Papa, wondering if she 'can learn to become invisible'. When the vixens start to birth, one of them eats her own litter. As winter descends, conditions – and Mother's mental state – deteriorate: 'Papa calls it limbo, because it sure isn't heaven and it's too cold to be hell. Mother wondered about purgatory, but he said no, purgatory has an end to it. "Don't torture me so," said Mother.' Mother will have nothing more to do with the foxes and grows increasingly silent except for singing hymns: 'She asks me to join her but we don't harmonise well.' Anne Marie dreams about a young man called Fox: 'His skin and hair are dark but his eyes are ice blue. "All the others here are paired," he says, Papa and Mother, the sires and the vixens, but I am alone and he can't let that continue. Sometimes in the dream he stays with us but usually he picks me up and carries me to his own island.' Mother becomes violent. One morning Anne Marie discovers all the foxes have been slaughtered: 'I dreamed that Fox came and was angry for what we'd let happen, that he held me down on the snow and I felt his hot breath on my face, felt it bitter in my throat, and felt his ice eyes cutting into me. I wish, I wish he would come soon. Mother sleeps with me now, and it is cramped and tense. You would think that another body under the covers would bring warmth but I awake feeling drained, like she has pulled all the heat from me.' The axe has gone missing so they cannot cut the wood properly for the stove. 'Maybe,' she muses, 'I am the soul not of a she-wolf but of a soaring bird that flies south every winter and my heart is so sick because I am not supposed to be here in this cold, this dark, this wet. Maybe I am like the air in this house, the air that does not move when Papa and Mother pass in silence.'

The last entry tells of Mother's suicide: 'Later, we found the note and she told how the animals were Satan's handmaidens and how their sharp little eyes would not give her peace so she killed them and then threw the axe in the woods. "We have looked into ourselves," she wrote, "and what is there condemns us."' Donna pretends still not to know that Noelle is inventing the story and sympathises with Anne Marie because 'her mother didn't love her enough to stick around ... she left her daughter. I would never do that, no matter what.'

In allegory, 'the literal frame of reference ... is missing and must be supplied by the reader' (McHale 1989: 141), but whereas traditional allegories, like *Pilgrim's Progress* (1678), are fairly unequivocal, in the second half of the twentieth century they have, like the post-sacred, secular melodrama, become rather more elusive. Just as the place names in *Men with Guns* invite allegorical interpretation but mostly resist indicating any precise allegorical content, so Noelle's gothic expression of her own situation signals her complex feelings towards both her mother and Joe but their translation into a fiction presented as someone else's diary overdetermines the story she tells. As McHale notes, an overdetermined allegory has '*too many* interpretations, more than can possibly be integrated into a univocal reading' (1989: 142; emphasis in original). While a psychoanalytic reading would find much of note in Noelle's story – the Oedipal division of Joe into Papa and Fox, father and lover; the desire to see without being seen; the resentment of a maternal body which is at once forbidden or distant and too close, that gives birth and devours; fruit that leaves a tell-tale stain; a stolen axe – the story exceeds and resists this centripetal reduction. Noelle is an accomplished storyteller and so it is unclear, despite her increasingly emotional telling, how much of the story, and this kind of interpretation, she intends – the framing of it as Anne Marie's diary produces a distance from materials that her later tears do not necessarily close down. Like her anorexia and self-harming, her telling is an exercise in control.

Bryan S. Turner (1992) argues that anorexia can be read through a phenomenology of the mouth, that absence of appetite is like absence of speech, and that anorexia can be understood as a way for those who have no social voice to speak. Angela Failler almost seems to be describing Noelle (who has constructed an elaborate fantasy about her absent father, been hospitalised for an eating disorder, begun self-harming and has feelings for Joe that no longer seem appropriate now that her mother is dating him) when she writes:

> Anorexia ... may be an attempt to compensate for a loss or disappointment that has affected the subject so deeply as to leave him or her with a fear of dependency on others, and a resistance in making connections with others for fear of a repeated loss. This unconscious fear manifests as a refusal of food or, more specifically, as a refusal of appetite. In anorexia, appetite reminds one that they desire, and desire reminds one of neediness, and neediness of dependency, and dependency of relationship. Thus, to make a desireless, 'pure' self by refusing appetite is to keep buried a recognition of neediness, a recognition of the other, and a recognition that one's neediness was once traumatically let down, rejected, or violated by some ideal or some other that mattered. (2006: 104)

Stranded on the island, and in desperate circumstances, Noelle begins to improvise Anne Marie's story as the protest of one without a social voice, but her storytelling becomes something else. Her eating disorders, self-harming and silence can be seen as

Limbo: defying closure

strategies for 'psychic survival' and as symptoms 'adopted to stave off ... the prospect of living in recognition of traumatic loss and vulnerability and the daunting task of re-establishing dependence and trust' (2006: 106). By telling stories and learning to speak, Noelle begins to move from an isolated, alienated self into a fuller, intersubjective being. Her telling opens her to, and deflects, possible trauma. It exposes her being and language-world to her mother and Joe, but in an indirect and transmuted form which simultaneously speaks and remains silent. Like the Hegelian self-consciousness, she requires a recognition she cannot directly solicit. This is matched by Donna's response. Unable directly to admit to knowing that the story is about her, Donna's grasping after its meaning signals a competing self-consciousness attempting to conform Noelle to itself and, at the same time, recognising her as a distinct self-consciousness.

Indeed, Donna's response foreshadows the film's inconclusion. On one level, there is the rewarding sentimentality of this potential and apparent reconciliation between mother and daughter; but at the same time it is deeply undercut by the contrast between Noelle's intense, elaborate, gothic reworking of their situation and the brevity and banality of Donna's interpretation of it. Similarly, at the end of the film, as the seaplane bringing either rescuers or killers circles overhead, the three gather on the beach. Donna refuses to hide in the bushes, as if her act of faith will resolve reality in that direction. Joe joins her, and then Noelle, and the three stand together as a family. Their names even suggest those of the Holy Family. Are we to take this allegorical possibility as indicative of their survival? Or does it suggest the gulf between religious/ideological myths about the family and the realities of living in families?

Just as the allegory is overdetermined, so too is diegetic and actual reality. The film's refusal of closure is simultaneously a formal, if not exactly Brechtian, revelation of the fiction's constructedness, and its most profoundly realist gesture (much the same can be argued about the abruptness of the change of direction the film takes in its second half). Just as Albright's proposed thematisation of Alaska is about the 'illusion of risk' so too is a narrative that ends in a clear resolution. And just as Noelle's eating disorder, self-harming and storytelling manifest a desire for control over the traumatic contingency of the world, so too does the desire for narrative closure, as has already been demonstrated by Donna's shutting-down of the possible meanings of Noelle's story. And so *Limbo* ends in limbo, suspended in the present moment, open to contingency and unresolved – because anything else would just be a fiction, and because without closure hope can persist.

CHAPTER SIX

Living the Dream: *Sunshine State, Casa de los Babys* and *Silver City*

This chapter discusses the ways in which the critique of postmodern capitalism and its drive to the simulacral, found in Sayles' films as far back as *Return of the Secaucus Seven*, is developed through the irrealities of nonetheless real worlds in *Sunshine State* and *Silver City*. Central to this analysis are the possibilities opened up by the refusal of language to be fixed in place or shorn of its excesses of meaning. Despite everything, it remains heteroglossic, exposing the tensions and gaps in the centripetal monological project to contain and control. This is not to locate resistance to capital in some idealist linguistic realm, but rather to situate language within the material realm as both a site of resistance and as a metaphor for other material resistances. Capital is not uniform, as the *deus ex machina* ending of *Sunshine State* and the lessons of hydraulic pressure in *Silver City* demonstrate, but full of snags and cracks upon which resistance can gain purchase. *Casa de los Babys*, set in another composite and non-specific Latin-American country, opens up such contradictions by foregrounding the combined and uneven development of the capitalist world market. While its six protagonists illustrate the ways in which capital has made consumers of us all on a profound, psychic level,[81] and its refusal to acknowledge its own position defaults into presenting the situation as an unchangeable, if complicated, reality, it nonetheless identifies an affective level from which class-consciousness might emerge and upon which community might be built. While the bond between the adoptive mother Eileen (Susan Lynch) and the hotel maid Asunción (Vanessa Martínez) is tenuous, it is a grain of hope –

just like, if rather less ironic than, the dead fish which float to the surface of *Silver City*'s Arapaho Lake.

Sunshine State (2002)

In Delrona Beach, on Plantation Island, off Florida's Atlantic coast, it is Buccaneer Days week. Marly Temple (Edie Falco), who manages her father's motel and restaurant, is approached by the representative of an unnamed corporation who want to buy up seafront property and develop the area as a tourist resort. Having just broken up with her younger boyfriend, Scotty Duval (Mark Blucas), a failed professional golfer who is rejoining the PGA tour, she becomes involved with Jack Meadows (Timothy Hutton), a landscape architect working for the Exley Corporation property developers. Meanwhile, Lincoln Beach, a neighbouring black community, is also under threat from Exley Corporation, who have already bought a third of the original tract, including the cemetery. Moves are afoot to incorporate or, as Dr Lloyd (Bill Cobbs) puts it, 'expropriate' this now-valuable beachfront into Delrona Beach. Local hero and former college football star Leotis 'Flash' Phillips (Tom Wright), secretly fronting for Exley, is trying to persuade locals to sell their property before new town taxes drive them out of their homes. Desiree (Angela Bassett), invited by her mother, Eunice (Mary Alice), who might be dying, to visit her in Lincoln Beach, brings her new husband, Reggie (James McDaniel), with her. Apart from her father's funeral, this is her first trip back since, 15-years-old and pregnant by Flash, she was shipped off to an aunt (the baby was stillborn, and Desiree moved to New York to become an actress). She now presents promotional and industrial videos. Eunice is raising Terrell (Alex Lewis), the troubled teenage son of her dead nephew. A third narrative strand concerns the efforts of Francine Pinckney (Mary Steenburgen) to stage Buccaneer Days' public events. Her husband, Earl (Gordon Clapp), has a gambling problem and accepts bribes from the property developers, but is sufficiently guilt-racked to attempt, if repeatedly fail, to commit suicide. The film ends when, over the protests of Lincoln Beach residents, the Exley Corporation breaks ground on a new development – only to find an Indian burial site. As the developers withdraw, Jack moves onto his next job, leaving Marly behind. Desiree is reconciled with Eunice and Reggie becomes a surrogate father figure for Terrell. Francine and Earl have somehow survived the week.

In many ways, *Sunshine State* is a summation of all of Sayles' previous films: a character returns home to find herself both separated from and connected to her past; a black man finds himself in a strange land; faceless, emasculating corporations, who play on racial differences, supplant traditional white male labour; the dreams of an actress or two and a musician never quite work out; the histories of peoples and communities disappear under thematisation; subjects-for-themselves and their affective relationships are distorted by the capital's demand that they be subjects-for-capital; disconnected figures travel through landscapes and communities; political systems and the mass media tend to serve the interests of capital; people tell stories about their pasts, figuring the possibility of a utopian future through the hopes and possibilities they have already lost. *Sunshine State* creates a complex community through which characters and both public and private histories interweave. This is neatly captured in the few seconds of screentime shared by its two main characters, Marly and Desiree. Arriving in Delrona Beach, Desiree asks Marly's permission to use the bathroom in the Treasure Chest restaurant, and Marly points her to it. In terms of private history, it later emerges that Desiree used to be taught drama by Marly's mother, Miss Delia (Jane Alexander). In terms of public history, Marly's father, Furman (Ralph Waite), later tells how the restaurant was whites-only before integration, but now there is nothing remarkable about white people serving black customers. However, as Dr Lloyd makes clear to Reggie, such 'progress' has not been entirely for the good, because while civil rights programmes tackled certain social problems and attitudes they did nothing to address the nature of capital:

> Forties, fifties, Lincoln Beach was it. Only oceanfront in three counties we were allowed to step onto. Black folks ... got together and bought this land, built the houses. You'd drive through a couple hundred miles of redneck sheriffs, park your ride on the boardwalk, step out and just *breathe* ... [Then] civil rights happened. Progress. Used to be you were black, you'd *buy* black. Jim Crow days, you needed a shoeshine, you wanted a ride in a taxi to the train station, you wanted some ribs, a fish sandwich, chances are a black man owned the place you got it in. Now the drive-thrus serve anybody. But who owns them? Not us. All our people does wearing paper hats and dippin' out them fries. Only thing we got left are the funeral parlours, barbershops.

Reggie points out that 'now we can do anything'. Dr Lloyd replies, 'Them that can get over do fine. Them that can't are in a world of trouble.' Later, Reggie notes of the young Terrell, who is skilled with tools, that if this was 1925 he would have a future.

While Dr Lloyd's analysis, echoing arguments for black economic self-sufficiency familiar from throughout twentieth century African-American thought, recognises economic determinants, it articulates them primarily as a matter of race, through a specifically subjective experience of objective conditions. This results in a strong parallel between Dr Lloyd, who functions as a father figure in Lincoln Beach, and Marly's father, Furman, who argues that nowadays the most endangered species is the small businessman:

> In my day, life was simpler. You knew where you stood. A man was left to make his own way in the world. We didn't have any of these pressure groups, these advocate groups, special-interest groups handicapping the race. It went to the smartest and the strongest and the swiftest. Then if a man could carve out a little something for himself, he knew he'd earned it. No whooping crane or spotted owl, the Florida gator. The colored man, the white man, the Spanish, they all started out from scratch. If you couldn't survive the course, it was just tough titty. Nowadays, what they got, it ain't natural. They got us so zoned and regulated, politically corrected and environmentally sensitised to the point where it's only your multi-internationals with a dozen lawyers

sitting around like buzzards waiting for something to litigate that can afford to put one brick on top of another. The little guy, no matter how much grit or imagination he brings to it, ain't got a chance. They got him tied down so he can't hardly breathe … People used to come to Plantation Island, and ask where can I stay the night and where can I get a good meal? 'Furman Temple,' they'd tell them. 'Right down there on the beach. You go see Furman, he'll take care of you'.

Like Dr Lloyd, Furman recognises economic forces, but these he articulates through an overly-interventionist government which prevents individual initiative and favours wealthy corporations. Both men yearn for a past in which a different possible future existed, but neither sees capitalism itself as the problem, focusing instead on discontents with its current form. Significantly, both describe particular situations – Jim Crow oppression, the travails of the small businessman – in terms of asphyxiation, imagery already deployed in *Limbo*, and developed in *Sunshine State* to capture in physical terms the subjective experience of a circumscribed life. Such imagery depicts the lived social reality of late-capitalism as a universal system and its local manifestations as tending towards the production of alienated subjectivities like, in an extreme form, *Lone Star*'s tightly-wound Bunny. I will return to this imagery, but first it is necessary to outline *Sunshine State*'s critique of postmodern capitalism and the pressure under which it places Sayles' naturalist technique.

The commodity form, whose ubiquity *The Brother from Another Planet* indicated, reaches the point of supersaturation in Guy Debord's society of the spectacle, in which 'Everything that was directly lived has moved away into a representation' (1983: thesis 1), or in Jean Baudrillard's desert of the real, dominated by 'the generation by models of a real without origin or reality' and in which 'the territory no longer precedes the map … it is the map that precedes the territory' (1983: 2). Marx describes this tendency of capitalism in different terms: 'a definite social relation between men … assumes, in their eyes, the fantastic form of a relation between things … [in which] the productions of the human brain appear as independent beings endowed with life, and entering into relation both with one another and the human race' (1996: 83). Commenting on this passage, China Miéville writes:

> Our commodities control us, and our social relations are dictated by *their* relations and interactions. 'As soon as [a table, for example] emerges as a commodity, it changes into a thing which transcends sensuousness. It stands on its head, and evolves out of its wooden brain grotesque ideas.' Under capitalism, the social relations of the everyday – that 'fantastic form' – are the 'grotesque ideas', of the commodities that rule. (2002: 41–2, quoting Marx 1976: 163)

Miéville's presentation of Marx's argument is perhaps too rigidly determinist, but that does not invalidate his conclusion that '"Real" life under capitalism *is a fantasy*: "realism" … is therefore a "realistic" depiction of "an absurdity which is true", but no less absurd for that' (Miéville 2002: 41–2, quoting Geras 1971: 76; emphasis in original). This absurdity is the contemporary US that *Sunshine State* constructs and reveals beneath the bright Florida sunshine.

At the end of the opening scene, in which Terrell burns down the Buccaneer Days' pirate ship float, the camera tilts up from the flames and into the night sky. Over the black frame we hear Murray Silver (Alan King) proclaim, 'In the beginning there was nothing', before a dissolve to the golf course where he and three other white men are playing. 'Wilderness,' he continues. 'Endless raw acreage, the land infested with crocodiles … Alligators, crocodiles, if you're talking retirement bungalows, that's not a selling point. Mosquitoes that would strip you to the bone … Swampland they were asking ten cents an acre for, this was worse. The old name means in Seminole, "You shouldn't go there." … We bought it because we knew, we weren't selling land. I mean, what's land? A patch of dirt? A tree? Who cares?'

As Murray prepares to tee off, Silent Sam (Eliot Asinof), suggests that 'Farmers care'.

Murray drives. 'Farmers,' he says, as Sam plants his tee. 'Farmers are for TV ads. People with tractors, amber waves of grain. They shoot it all in Canada. I'm talking about certified public accountants from Toledo with a fixed pension and a little nest egg who don't want to spend their golden years trekking through slush. Dreams are what you sell. A concept. You sell sunshine. You sell orange groves. You sell gentle breezes wafting through the palm trees.'

'There were palm trees?' asks Jefferson Cash (Cullen Douglas). He is in his forties, easily twenty years younger than his golfing partners.

'In the brochures, there were palm trees,' explains Buster Bidwell (Clifton James).

'Stately ones,' says Silent Sam, preparing to tee off.

'And when they came down and saw it?'

'As long as the dredge stayed three lots ahead of the buyers, we were in like Flynn,' Murray says as Sam hits his drive. 'This was the end of the earth. This was a land populated by white people who ate *catfish*.' Looking into the sky and spreading his arms as if inspired by his own words, he continues, 'And almost overnight, out of the muck and the mangroves we created this.'

'Golf courses,' says Cash.

'Nature,' replies Murray, 'on a leash.' The camera tilts and pans up into the sky, and after an invisible dissolve it descends onto Delrona Beach as a truck drives by issuing, over a loudspeaker, the Chamber of Commerce's invitation to participate in the Buccaneer Days festivities.

This short scene reconnects postmodern hyperreality in two interrelated ways to the material history from which Baudrillard and others divorced it. Firstly, there is the history of expropriation, the capitalist-imperialist tendency to perceive the world as raw material, as being empty and devoid of identity and history until it is turned to productive purpose, and its human inhabitants as primitive – not fully human – until they too have been drawn into capitalist modernity. Murray's explication of how the contemporary Florida landscape of holiday resorts and retirement communities came into being – many of them constructed, as Jack later explains, with no attention to the existing environment – identifies this process with the expansion of capital, the long history of restructuring the land so as to enable the maximal extraction of surplus-value. Just as Raymond Williams described the dependence of the country house's prospect upon the rationalised agricultural land hidden from view, whether in Britain or overseas, so *Sunshine State* indicates that the landscaping of Florida is deeply impli-cated in the system which enables accountants from Toledo to accumulate nest eggs and their pension schemes to pay out regularly while also making a profit. Florida's golf courses and gated communities provide a similar separation from labour as that which Dr Fuentes experiences as he cruises through and above the land of indigenous peoples. Secondly, there is the history of material production concealed by commodity fetishism. Murray points to the way mediated representations stand in for the reali-ties of farming, while his suggestion that they are filmed in another country further removes any notion of productive labour from the Floridan prospect: not only does labour happen elsewhere, but that elsewhere is obscured by the image projected onto it. Similarly, Florida itself must be replaced by the 'Florida-concept' in order to be sold and bought. This fetishisation is extended to all of the US through the sly inclusion of lyrics from 'America the Beautiful' (1895) – those 'amber waves of grain'.

Having established its critique of the hyperreal as something both illusory *and* material – as Debord writes, 'The spectacle is not a collection of images, but a social relation among people, mediated by images … The spectacle subjugates living men to itself to the extent that the economy has totally subjugated them. It is no more than the economy developing for itself' (1983: theses 4 and 16) – *Sunshine State* is content to depict the forms of the hyperreal projected onto Plantation Island. The major example of this is Buccaneer Days, an annual tourist event supplanting a local history and identity to which its organisers cannot admit: there is the public, commodified image, of 'Indians, pirates, Spanish gold, all that plantation thing', and the reality of 'mass murder, rape, slavery' behind those more marketable clichés. The film adopts an ironic distance to the festivities, condemned by their own tawdry banality: they are poorly attended, some take place inside a shopping mall, the only Seminoles they celebrate are the local football team, and the increasingly dispirited Francine ends every announce-ment by acknowledging local businesses who have lent equipment or donated prizes.

There is, however, a parallel between the film and the chorus of golfers. Like them, it comments from a distance on something it is also responsible for creating. Delrona Beach, however based in observation, is nonetheless a construction, a model of a Floridan town whose ordinariness is heightened to the point of deadpan parody, as when Francine complains that people 'don't realise how difficult it is to invent a tradition'. The golfers, like the Indian mother in *Men with Guns*, occupy a liminal ontological position, simultaneously characters within the world of the film and commentators external to it. Sayles' DVD commentary compares them to Olympian gods looking down on the mortal realm and to those members of the capitalist class whose democratically-unaccountable decisions shape our daily lives. What is peculiar in *Sunshine State* is the extent to which other characters' dialogue is marked by a similar liminality.

Throughout the film, words convey multiple possible meanings. Sometimes the characters seem aware of this. For example, when Marly meets Jack, he is trying to imagine what the seafront would look like without the existing businesses on it. She describes this as 'mentally undressing it' and their conversation ends with her flirtatious enquiry as to how he thinks it might look 'without anything on it'. Later, her ex-husband, Steve (Richard Edson), dressed as a Union soldier, suggests that she pretend to be 'checking out the artillery'. More ambiguously, when Scotty explains to her his 'case of the yips' – 'Killer drive, beautiful approach shot, and I just couldn't get the damn thing in the hole' – her straightfaced response that it 'would seriously cut into your winnings' seems an almost conscious projection of her dissatisfaction with their relationship, and his lack of professional success, onto questions of his sexual potency. Dr Lloyd is clear on the very different meanings of 'incorporation' and 'expropriation', but it is unclear whether property developer Lester (Miguel Ferrer) recognises his euphemistic description of all those opposed to his corporate activities as 'anti-growth' as being part of a larger ideological battle between different language-communities. His grouping together of all opponents, his reduction of their centrifugal diversities to a value to which surely no right-minded individual could subscribe – how could anyone be opposed to something as natural as growth? – is an ideological sleight-of-hand in capital's drive to monologise reality for its own ends.

No one in *Sunshine State* advocates any kind of theorised or strategic response to this centripetalism, but many characters feel and resist its suffocating constrictions. Property developer Greg (Perry Lang) talks to Marly about the way 'you small business folks, you're being squeezed' by increased city taxes resulting from resort developments that have already happened, giving the whole process a sense of inevitability and trying to draw her into capitalism's cynical reasoning – regardless of whether Furman sells up, others, fearing more tax increases, will sell to the developers, driving up taxes even further, and so he might as well sell now when he can get the best price. Meanwhile, Flash makes a similar pitch to Desiree about Eunice's house, urging her to consider it, 'No big pressure.' When Dr Lloyd reminisces about Desiree's father, an upright 'race man' of substance and standing in Jacksonville, she recalls the pressure of living up to the expectations: 'It got to where I could hardly breathe when I was near him.' Eunice reminds Dr Lloyd that they did not build their lives and community from scratch, but that 'People fought their whole lives just to keep their heads above water. *We* got to start on dry land.' Such imagery is developed further in Marly's story. When she was younger, she became a Weeki Wachee Girl, part of an aquarium act in which, dressed as a mermaid, she performed underwater in a big display tank. Telling Jack about this, she competes with him to see who can hold their breath the longest. After winning, she removes his hand from her mouth to reveal a big fake smile: 'The important thing to do is to keep that smile on your face even if you snort some water down your nose', a line she soon reiterates with the variation 'even if you're drowning'. Such liminal dialogue is both fully of the world of the film – for Marly it describes being both a Weeki Wachee girl and a dutiful daughter – and a commentary on the demands made on all workers by late-capital's hyperreal illusionism which increasingly conceals the actual fact of labour and fetishises the commodity-image over material history.

The limitations of naturalist representation become more apparent when depicting the fantastic reality of late-capitalism because of the very particular dilemma posed by ubiquitous commodity fetishism: how is one to represent an irreal world which is nonetheless the reality we inhabit? *Sunshine State*'s solution – characters and dialogue which are simultaneously diegetic and exegetic – poses its own problems. For example, when Terrell admits his wariness of Lincoln Beach's undertow, the sightless Furman responds: 'There's always gonna be one of those. The trick is, you don't try to fight it. You swim parallel to the shore till the pressure eases up. You struggle with that whole wide ocean and you're a goner … No matter how strong you are, no matter how much grit you got, you try to take it head on, it, it'll pull you under.' How is one intended to understand these words, which seem to echo the lesson about the futility of resistance *The Secret of Roan Inish*'s Hugh uncertainly draws from Sean Michael's story? It is clear that Furman is talking about the current Terrell fears *and* about the social and economic pressures he himself feels; and as with one of the indigenous women from *Men with Guns*, there is a strong resonance with classical mythology's blind seers. But Furman, however amusing his curmudgeonliness, is not a particularly admirable character. And so how seriously are we intended to take his counsel?

However, perhaps more significant than the actual content of Furman's advice is its clear restatement of multivalent, heteroglossic reality. While others dread asphyxiation, Reggie is an anaesthesiologist, and Marly confides that when she was doing her solo mermaid number she hated to 'come up. It was like I was meant to live down there. You're soaring, you know? Weightless.' *Sunshine State* emphasises throughout the ambiguity, liminality[82] and frame-breaking capacities of language, and thus insists upon the contingency of capital's far-from-seamless fantastic reality. At such moments, 'the solidity and independence of the appearance-forms (what is their ghostly "object-ivity" as spectral things) is actually undermined' because 'the spectre suddenly acquires an *insubstantial* rather than independent quality' (Wayne 2003: 209; emphasis in original), making 'the present waver' so that 'the massiveness of the object world … now shimmers like a mirage' (Jameson 1999: 38). As Mike Wayne continues, 'This is no mere subjective loss of grip, but, on the contrary, something like the beginning of class-consciousness where the sceptical subject senses that the appearance-form of reality is not "as self-sufficient as it claims to be"' (2003: 209, quoting Jameson 1999: 38). Although lacking the clarity of *Matewan*'s vision of emergent class-consciousness, *Sunshine State* does offer moments of hopefulness. The arbitrary intervention of material reality which halts Exley's groundbreaking appears as a *deus ex machina*, but is not entirely unrealistic (and, moreover, reminds us that the ideological fiction of an empty and infinitely malleable land awaiting settlement, capital and productive use is precisely a fiction). Beyond allowing the Creek Indian Billy (Michael Greyeyes) to suggest that things do change, noting that nowadays 'they say the only *bad* Indian is a dead Indian', this scene demonstrates the possibilities for resistance arising from the chinks in capital's own armour. Rather than being unitary, different capitals compete with each other. The news team covering the event collude with the developers in not showing the protest, but the discovery of the Indian mass grave, possibly the result of a slaughter by Europeans, is too big a news story, and although Exley's representatives try to rush everyone off the site so that they can cover up

Sunshine State: not drowning but soaring

the discovery and proceed with clearing the land, they cannot keep a lid on the news. It is a victory, of sorts, and it emerges from faultlines within capital itself.

Beyond the various familial reconciliations, and the sense that Lincoln Beach might yet survive for a while, the other key image of hope is the slow-motion footage of Marly swimming underwater. She claims she gave up swimming when she quit as a Weeki Wachee girl and returned to help with her father's businesses, but in the closing minutes of the film, as she is working free from this obligation, she dives once more into the water and swims. What was once labour has become joyful: like the return to Roan Inish, it presages the possibility of unalienation.

Casa de los Babys (2003)

Based on one of Sayles' previously unpublished short stories, later collected in *Dillinger in Hollywood* (2004), *Casa de los Babys* is set in an unnamed Latin-American country which looks like Mexico but is not. It focuses on six women from the US – Gayle (Mary Steenburgen), Jennifer (Maggie Gyllenhaal), Leslie (Lili Taylor), Nan (Marcia Gay Harden), Skipper (Daryl Hannah) and Eileen, who is Irish but lives in Boston – as they wait at the hotel La Posada Santa Marta, known to locals as Casa de los Babys, for their adoption applications to be processed. Unlike the Secaucus Seven, they are strangers, but have come to know a little about each other during the weeks of waiting, and as in Sayles' first film the plot amounts to little more than their interactions over a day or so. We also glimpse fragments of the lives of various locals with whom they come into contact: Señora Muñoz (Rita Moreno) who runs the hotel and whose lawyer brother, Ernesto (Pedro Armendáriz), handles the adoptions and whose incompetent handyman son, Búho (Juan Carlos Vives), dreams of anti-imperialist revolution; Asunción, a maid, who is raising her younger siblings and who, four years earlier, gave up her infant daughter for adoption by an American woman; Diómedes (Bruno Bichir), a former student and construction worker struggling to support a young family; Tito (Ignacio de Anda), a street child; and Celia (Martha Higareda), the pregnant 15 year-old daughter of a well-off family whose mother (Tony Marcin) is forcing her to give up her baby for adoption.

Lunching with the other women, Leslie explains to Gayle, who asked for a 'cola' (which means 'tail') instead of a 'coke', that 'papaya' is a 'vaginal euphemism – beaver, clam'. Nan asks, 'Nobody here ordered clams, did they?' Skipper explains, 'The lower on the food chain you eat, the better the nutritional value, though the risk of toxicity increases.' This brief exchange introduces once more the concern with language common to Sayles' films. It exemplifies Bakhtin's sense that each utterance lives 'on the boundary between its own context and another, alien, context' (1981: 284), and occurs in terms both of national-linguistic textures, as Spanish words are shown to have meanings unintended by the Anglophone Gayle, and of what they reveal about each character: Gayle's well-intentioned struggle with Spanish; Leslie's sense of being experienced and knowledgeable; Nan's racism, typically expressed through assumptions about the locals' poor hygiene and her insistence on speaking English; and Skipper's aloofness, her constant monitoring of her body and food intake. This interplay of characters and tangential responses emphasises language's capacity for ambiguity and the material, intersubjective social being which produces specific and contingent meanings. Moreover, this dialogue also draws to the surface the fundamental dynamic shaping the film: the dilemma.

Skipper poses this dynamic in the bluntest of terms – nutritional value against risk of toxicity – but the scene as a whole (split into two by Jennifer's phone call to her husband, Henley) is replete with alternatives and dilemmas. What is the difference between grouper and snapper? Would anyone ever make a mojito with lemon rather than lime? Is it safe to drink unbottled water? How should one respond to Nan's racism? Does her authoritarianism (and her earlier approval of her mother's brutal discipline) mark her out as a potential abuser? Is Skipper merely keeping fit or is she obsessive? If Jennifer and Henley are having marital difficulties, should they really be adopting a child? Should the other potential mothers mention it to the agency? Should the people writing their references lie about the various women's suitability as parents? Should their desire to have children take priority over their suitability? Is the adoption process taking so long in order to ensure that the babies are placed with appropriate parents or because the longer it takes, the more money the potential mothers will spend?

The scene ends with Nan revealing perhaps more than she should of her own questionable suitability. Skipper's line about toxicity is apparently intended as merely a comment about food, an attempt to bridge between her alien context and the one(s) in which she finds herself. Leslie looks at her as if she were mad, and Nan sarcastically thanks her 'for sharing' before pursuing what initially sounds like a *non sequitur*: 'There is probably every disease known to man down here ... The thing for all of us to worry about are the infant syndromes, like, mm, er, where the mother is intoxicated ... And drugs. Crack, all that ... And then there's the genes ... You could adopt a ticking time-bomb and never know it ... [At least with] birth kids, you know both parents, you know family history.' However, what Nan has picked up on, if unconsciously, and interpreted through her understanding of the world, is the sense that Latin-American babies are further down the racial food chain and for all the affective value such a child might bring it is nonetheless more likely to be carrying some kind of racial toxicity:

'If you get dealt a weak hand, you can always train it out of them, but it's work ... If they are born with some kind of disability – racial, cultural, whatever – you make them aware of it. They've got some catching up to do and you stay on their case.' Just like the developers eyeing up Florida swamplands, she imagines the foreign-born child can have its material past edited out. None of the women challenge this racism, but they all try to move the conversation onto different grounds: Eileen argues that birth parents face the same time-bomb, that 'people assume that if they have kids, they'll inherit all their favourite qualities'; Jennifer reveals that some people in her family are born with six toes; Gayle argues that with children 'you just watch them and see who they are and encourage what's best in them'; Leslie responds sarcastically to the violence inherent in Nan's words but her joking invocation of the 'one-neurotic-per-family rule' implicitly concurs with Nan's sociobiological – Zolaesque, even – emphasis on nature over nurture. Meanwhile, Skipper just stares at Nan, quietly horrified.[83]

It is easy to demonise Nan. She is an outspoken, uncouth bigot, a liar (she tells Leslie and Gayle different things about her background) and a petty thief (she furtively lifts supplies from the maid's trolley). An embittered bully, she is envious of Jennifer's wealth. She is full of her own superiority, both towards the locals and the other women. She expects – whether because she is American or white or paying – to receive special treatment, and assumes the locals are corrupt and incompetent, deservedly possessed of a natural inferiority complex. Her casual everyday monstrousness makes her fascinating, if hardly an ideal mother – yet this is how she perceives herself: in an earlier scene, talking about the Jack Russells she breeds, she says that 'my George can get them fed on schedule and give them their shots, but they need their momma'.

However, Leslie's line, with which the scene ends – 'Ah, appetizers. Skipper, any damage this is gonna do to my wellness, I don't want to hear about it' – points to a much wider problem than Nan's apparent exceptionalism. In an early scene in the orphanage, Doña Mercedes (Angelina Peláez), walking up and down between the cots, comforting the baby in her arms, tells it, 'Easy, easy now. You're so lucky. You'll have a car with its own little house. You'll go to a pretty school with all the Yanqui kids. You'll have perfect teeth and a huge bedroom.' Such a consumerist utopia has shaped the six potential mothers – a point made evident when Diómedes, showing Jennifer and Skipper around an old Spanish fortress, talks of Philadelphia as 'the cradle of liberty', embarrassing them by thinking about their own country in a way they never do. Realising his faux pas, he immediately offers to show them something to do with a 'dangerous piracy' (he has, after all, learned English from movie subtitles, so he grasps the protocols of such exchanges) while Jennifer's only response is to worry whether he will be insulted if they pay him more than four dollars. Leslie's preference for appetite over wellness offers a key to understanding their relationship to both adoptive parenthood and the whole mechanism of international adoption by women whose own country does not consider them suitable parents.

Each of the women is concerned with appetite management. Nan, according to Marcia Gay Harden in 'The Making of *Casa de los Babys*', 'has some weight issues'. If she is telling the truth about raising dogs a dozen at a time, calling herself their 'momma' suggests an affective relationship with them as surrogate children; and if she is lying, the number of dogs she claims to raise at a time indicates a capacious appetite. Her lies about her education and husband's job suggest class or lifestyle aspirations, while her theft of shampoo sachets, soaps and pillow mints demonstrates acquisitiveness for its own sake, an uncontrolled appetite. Her disparagement of the locals focuses on their imagined abandonment to appetite – Foetal Alcohol Syndrome, drug addiction, a neglect of hygiene – while she advocates disciplinarian parenting and aggressive nurturing to overcome recalcitrant, 'non-white' nature. Leslie, who is actually able to have children, does not want to have to go through any of that messy stuff to do with either biology or relationships. Her rejection of her own body is perhaps indicated by her clothes – Nan questions her refusal to wear a bathing suit on the beach, 'like a normal person' – and by her pleasure in euphemisms. She also refuses to swim in the sea because 'fish urinate in it'. Jennifer is wealthy, with houses on Rhode Island and in D.C., but her phone conversation with Henley reveals a clear anxiety about the adoption being reduced to merely buying a baby: 'No, I don't think you should call the Korean people,' she tells him. 'This isn't the commodities market.' (This might also reflect her anxiety about becoming like her mother, married five times, always hoping 'the next one would turn out better' – a consumerist principle she does not want to apply either to husbands or babies.) And even Gayle, relentlessly generous of spirit, is an alcoholic.

Skipper is the most overt example of somatic self-surveillance and body discipline. Her attentiveness to and attempted subordination of her body seems to stem from her loss of three children. She carried her first pregnancy to term, even though they knew that Cody would be stillborn. Her second child, Joshua, born without fully-formed lungs, died after two days. Her third, Gabriel, born with heart defects, died after a week. Consequently, for all her attention to her body, she seems simultaneously to be punishing it and making it fit – in both senses – for motherhood. In the scene in which she reveals all this loss, Skipper is massaging Jennifer, which involves treating emotions as if they can take on physical form: she looks for 'hot spots'; she finds 'quite a knot … something emotional' in Jennifer's abdomen; she encourages Jennifer to visualise an emotional state and send it to one part of her body to be massaged out; and she notes from the feel of Jennifer's kidneys that she is not drinking enough water. Susan Bordo writes that images of unwanted bulges, flab and bloating function as 'a metaphor for anxiety about internal processes out of control' (1989: 89). By the end of the nineteenth century 'excess body weight came to be seen as reflecting moral or personal inadequacy, or lack of will' (1989: 94). Significantly, such discourses can only happen in a culture of abundance where dieting can become an option, and where Skipper's particular kind of slender and muscular body can signify achievement and discipline.

Bordo argues that 'the preoccupation with the "internal" management of the body (i.e., management of its desires) is produced by instabilities in the "macro-regulation" of desire within the system of the social body' (1989: 96) (this is hinted at in the same scene by Jennifer's revulsion at the notion of breast-feeding someone else's – that is, a foreign – baby). This macro-regulation produces a profound tension: 'On the one hand, as "producer-selves", we must be capable of sublimating, delaying, repressing desires for immediate gratification; we must cultivate the work ethic. On the other hand, as "consumer-selves" we serve the system through a boundless capacity to capitulate to desire and indulge in impulse; we must become creatures who hunger for constant and immediate satisfaction' (ibid.). These economic forces inscribe themselves on the subject, with bulimia emerging as 'a characteristic modern personality construction, precisely and explicitly expressing the extreme development of the hunger for unrestrained consumption (exhibited in the bulimic's uncontrollable food-binges) existing in unstable tension alongside the requirement that we sober up, "clean up our act", get back in some form of control on Monday morning (the necessity for purge – exhibited in the bulimic's vomiting, compulsive exercising, and laxative purges)' (1989: 97). Anorexia can therefore 'be seen as an extreme development of the capacity for self-denial and repression of desire (the work ethic in absolute "control")' and obesity as 'an extreme capacity to capitulate to desire (consumerism in control)' (1989: 99). Although none of the potential mothers are obviously bulimic, anorexic or obese, they can all be understood to nonetheless embody these tensions. For example, while none of them are seen to purge, Skipper practices 'compulsive exercising', building up her 'calorie deficit' before meals,[84] and while none of them are shown taking laxatives there are several discussions about the effects of local cuisine on the digestive system.

In a similar vein, Celia's mother complains she had not noticed her daughter's pregnancy because 'she never got fatter, which is a miracle with the crap kids eat these days'. Later, in the mall, Celia is isolated in the frame as she looks at clothes, her strict, unsympathetic mother out of shot, talking on the phone about the adoption arrangements as if it has nothing to do with her daughter. Celia, holding in her upset and uncertainty, tells the out-of-frame assistant, 'I need to buy jeans a size bigger, maybe two.' The final time we see her, she is standing in front of a mirror, stroking her stomach through her thin dress and holding up a magazine, comparing herself to the image of a model with a bare midriff. While Skipper is generally the least talkative of the potential mothers, Celia is typically depicted as incapable of speaking because of her powerlessness relative to her mother and Reynaldo (Guillermo Iván), the older boy who got her pregnant. Her mother completely dominates the interview with the social worker (ruling out abortion even though Celia's demeanour implies she might prefer it), describes Celia as being 'mute like always' and opines about the lack of fathers and role models while neglecting her own daughter's anguish. Celia's single scene with Reynaldo is shot with restless cameras which capture their mutual uncertainty as they fail to say anything which is not superficial and as Celia realises that there is no point in telling him.[85]

While Eileen is perhaps the most difficult of the women to consider in this light, she is nonetheless the one in whom appetite and economics are most closely intertwined. With her husband recently unemployed, she is supporting him and trying to adopt on just her clerical salary. She has to carefully manage her money – twice we see her counting her dwindling pile of banknotes – and struggles to make it last by missing meals. Of the three meals the women share, Eileen skips breakfast, orders tap water rather than a cocktail or a soda at lunch, and is treated to dinner because

Casa de los Babys: separated by the thin wall of language

Jennifer has guessed her financial situation. Despite this, she acts with spontaneous generosity towards Tito, the street child, giving him a book, not realising he cannot read and had intended to steal her purse. At the end of the film, she is one of the two women – along with Nan – to be given a baby. It is tempting to read this in terms of how different the babies' futures will be because one has a good mother and the other a bad one. But the situation is more complex than that. It is not, after all, as if Eileen is somehow free from living under capital. This becomes evident when she shares her fantasy of motherhood with the maid, Asunción.

Writing to her large family, she invites Asunción to work around her and, despite not speaking Spanish, tells her about her eight siblings; Asunción, who only under-stands the occasional English word, tells Eileen about her five siblings, two of whom are already dead. There is a certain tentative connection between these two women: both are Catholic and working class, both come from nations with a long history of colonial rule. Although they lack a common language – Sayles' DVD commentary describes language as a thin wall which separates them – Eileen starts to talk about her fantasy day: school has been cancelled because of snow, and so she lets her daughter sleep in; after a breakfast of cocoa with marshmallows, they go skating together and then for lunch, and then walk home through the snow. A curious blend of concrete detail and sentimental cliché, of desire for genuine human connection and an ordinary life, this fantasy is driven by a deeply-felt sense of lack or absence. While this might point to a conservative, psychoanalytical construction of femininity and motherhood, Eileen's final line, when she is snapped back to reality – 'This is ignoring the fact that I am supposed to be at work, right? I'm the one with the job' – at least positions this sense of unfulfilment within the context of capital. Like Lianna and Malvern from *The Brother from Another Planet*, her full human subjectivity is constrained and distorted by the requirement that she also be a subject-for-capital.

Part way through the story, Asunción stops making the bed, sits and listens, sensing that Eileen is telling her something very personal, exposing herself even though – or perhaps because – there is a linguistic barrier between them. Their alien language-worlds brush up against Bakhtin's 'thousands of living dialogic threads' (1981: 276), and resonate. For each, 'that which in their speech is untranslatable, that which in each language is singular and unreconcilable with other languages'

(Shapiro 2004: 136) is respected, the radical otherness and non-compatability of their languages is left intact – except for the monolingual audience, whose understanding is dominated by the subtitle translations.[86] Although Asunción only understands a few of Eileen's words, the wider material context in which they are uttered conveys something more of their meaning, and she responds accordingly with her own story, told in Spanish: four years earlier her daughter, Esmerelda, was adopted by an American woman and she knows nothing of Esmerelda's subsequent life; she was young and had siblings to care for and a living to earn, so the nuns persuaded her adoption was for the 'best'; sometimes when new prospective mothers arrive, she picks one, 'a good one', and imagines her daughter is with her, with someone like Eileen. Eileen explains that she did not understand Asunción, and as she tearfully leaves, Eileen murmurs, 'I'm sorry.'

While it is not entirely clear whether Eileen is apologising for her failure to understand or because adopting a baby means that its birth mother loses it, the scene does capture the way in which language both communicates and separates. Eileen decides to christen her adoptive daughter Esmerelda, demonstrating that she grasped at least some of what Asunción said. But this is at best an individual and sentimental solution to the broader problem of international adoption against which she has found herself suddenly cast by this conversation. However, whatever the extent of her sympathy for Asunción, she nonetheless accepts the baby offered to her. Her desire for a child is expressed as a potent fetishisation of an intimate mother/daughter relationship, perhaps of a kind she herself never experienced among her numerous siblings. And it is this 'human ability' to fetishise, 'to project value onto a material object, repress the fact that the projection has taken place, and then interpret the object as the autonomous source of that value' (Mulvey 1996: 127), that capital itself depends upon. Eileen's sentimental transcendence of her material circumstances – in terms of both her infertility and her economically-constrained life – is ultimately formally no different from the street children's paint-sniffing or Diómedes' forlorn purchase of a lottery ticket so as to win his airfare to the US (an emigration whose illegality is made all the more ironic by the fact that there are no such barriers for the adopted infants). Regardless of the fact that the prospective mothers are not literally buying their babies, their ability to adopt them does depend upon a range of economic exchanges between individuals, institutions, businesses and nations, situating the cash-nexus right at the centre of this human relationship. Although she expresses it crudely, and treats it as an unwarranted imposition foisted upon them by the greed, corruption and resentment of the locals, even Nan recognises this economic dimension, saying, 'They're gonna make us earn our babies – it's part of the balance of trade.'

This brings us to the dilemma at the core of the film: should these women be allowed to adopt the babies? Does the sanction of the state and the absence of a direct financial exchange make international adoption something other than trafficking in children? Or, in the film's own melodramatic terms, how do we – how should we – *feel* about it? The film does not presume to provide a direct answer, seeming instead content to present contingent circumstances as social facts. Moreover, it does make room for a critique of the systems and processes of international adoptions.

For example, having mentioned his country's economic crisis and political difficulties, Diómedes describes babies as 'our greatest exportations', while Ernesto, bullied by Nan, mutters to himself that 'here we don't accept American Express for our children'. The fullest critique comes from Búho. His mother's 'guests', he calls 'imperialists'; the 'service' she provides, 'selling babies'. Late in the film, he describes how the Americans have 'fucked' them 'economically, psychologically, politically', how the adoptions are 'just another form of cultural imperialism', with the babies as a 'raw material ... they refine': 'You think they'd let us bring their kids here?'[87]

However, this critique is undermined in several ways. Firstly, it is voiced by Búho, who has already been depicted as an idle, pot-smoking incompetent who is only able to stay out of jail because his mother has given him a job he is manifestly unsuited to perform. Moreover, this particular scene, set in a plaza where a Cuban song about Che Guevara can be heard in the background, features a drunken argument between Búho and two like-minded friends. The cameras circle around and around this stereotypical evocation of a romantic, Latin-American anti-capitalism, as if these men have had this same heated discussion, or ones like it, over and over again – going round in circles, achieving nothing, changing nothing. And, indeed, the only solution to capitalist-imperialism that Búho can propose is to 'imagine our lives if they [Americans] just disappeared'. Secondly, and most importantly, the film focuses overwhelmingly on the American women, on their personalities and interactions, tragedies and crises, on their childlessness and the suffering it produces in them. Just as the use of a generic rather than specific Latin-American country again delinks the situation the film depicts from global economic and political structures, removes it from material specificity, so this feminisation of imperialism somehow renders imperialism softer, more caring, as if the supposed 'naturalness' of motherhood removes the expropriation of children from the realm of economic and political exploitation. Leslie's solution to Gayle's question regarding what they should do about Nan's increasingly obvious unsuitability – 'I don't know. Be really good mothers to ours. Pray for Rosemary's baby' – is not intended as the 'message' of the film, but ultimately this is more or less the viewpoint it adopts as its naturalist bent causes it to depict contingent reality as fixed and unchangeable.

However, there are traces of hope to be found. Although the American women never question why their lack of children – and Skipper's loss of children – is more painful and significant than that felt by 'foreign' women who must surrender their children, the audience is perhaps brought closer to doing so, not only in the conversation between Eileen and Asunción, but also in the scene in which Asunción, cleaning Nan's room, peers out from between the shutters and over a wire fence into a school-yard, where a young girl, perhaps not much older than Esmerelda, stands alone while others play around her. This signifies both the childhood and the child Asunción lost, as well as her own sense of isolation in the world and the barriers which separate her from her daughter. But she is still able to reach out to Eileen, to share a moment of identification with her as, like all the other women, they struggle to make sense of their existence in a world whose workings are beyond their grasp. In their pain, and their ability to share it with each other, is the beginning of class-consciousness, the dawning of hope.

Silver City (2004)

When shooting a campaign advertisement at Arapaho Lake in the Colorado Rockies, Dickie Pilager, the son of Senator Pilager and gubernatorial shoo-in, casts a fishing line and hooks the corpse of an undocumented Mexican worker. Suspecting sabotage, his campaign manager, Chuck Raven, hires former journalist-turned-investigator Danny O'Brien to warn three potential perpetrators that they are being watched: right-wing radio talkshow host Cliff Castleton (Miguel Ferrer), who back in college should have been elected the national president of the American Students' League until Raven, with Senator Pilager's help, stole the election;[88] Casey Lyle (Ralph Waite), a former miner and Federal Health and Safety inspector who once got close to shutting down an illegally-polluting, large-scale tailings operation run by a company belonging to Wes Benteen (Kris Kristofferson), the Pilagers' millionaire friend and backer, but was set up and fired; and Dickie's sister, Maddy (Daryl Hannah), the rebellious 'black sheep' of the family. These leads take Danny nowhere, but in identifying the corpse as Lázaro Huerta (Donevon Martinez) he uncovers a web of corruption – so widespread and normalised as to constitute mere business-as-usual – involving the smuggling, supply and effectively indentured slavery of Mexican labourers. Huerta was working in one of Benteen's slaughterhouses with unsafe equipment and fell to his death. Vince Esparza (Luis Saguar), who organises the undocumented Mexican labourers for Benteen's and other companies, forced two such workers to help him cover up the death and dump the body in an abandoned mineshaft – the same one in which, years earlier, he disposed of the barrels of toxic waste from the tailings operation when framing Casey. Danny manages to connect these stories together, but only one person is interested in pursuing them – Mitch Paine (Tim Roth), his former editor who now runs an alternative news website. As the film ends, Danny, who has been fired by his agency, ensures that Huerta's body is returned to his family, and sends them his severance pay. He is tentatively reconciled with journalist Nora Allardyce, his former girlfriend, who has left corporate lobbyist Chandler Tyson and is out of a job herself as her newspaper has been bought up by one of Benteen's corporations, at least partly to stop her asking the would-be governor too many difficult questions. With soil safety standards lowered, the Silver City property development is able to go ahead on the old mining site. And as Governor Pilager, back at Arapaho Lake, delivers a television address, behind him, one by one, in their hundreds and thousands, dead fish rise slowly to the surface. They may not be chickens, but they have certainly come home to roost.

As *Silver City* was considered at some length in the opening chapter the treatment of it here will be relatively brief. Discussing the cycle of American conspiracy thrillers in the late 1960s and 1970s, Michael Ryan and Douglas Kellner (1990) identify a key dilemma the genre posed for liberal filmmakers. Building on a widespread distrust of government and large corporations fuelled by revelations concerning the Pentagon Papers, the Gulf of Tonkin incident, Watergate, the ITT scandal, the Church Committee hearings, and so on, filmmakers produced an array of popular films, including *The Parallax View* (1974), *The Conversation* (1974) and *Three Days of the Condor* (1975), which depicted such institutions as inherently corrupt or oppres-

Silver City: some day your shit's gonna catch up with you

sive. However, American liberalism's historical emphasis on the individual forestalled the possibility of suggesting necessary structural changes, even if the makers of such films had wished to advocate them. As recession and inflation worsened through the 1970s, this privileging of the individual and suspicion of powerful institutions was successfully transformed by the right into the 'need' to reduce federal social welfare expenditure and to liberate corporations from unnecessary regulation and constraint (that is, to institute anti-labour policies). *Silver City* offers a chilling example of this position when Benteen lectures Dickie on his vision of the future. Riding on horseback in the foothills of the Rockies, Benteen evokes an archetypal self-possessed American heroic individualism (to which *Limbo*'s Harmon King rather hopelessly aspires), not least because of the western masculinity Kristofferson always-already connotes, from *Pat Garret & Billy the Kid* (1973) and *Convoy* (1978) to *Blade* (1998) and his previous roles in Sayles' films. Of the mountains rising up before them, Benteen tells Dickie:

> I see a big sign that says 'No Americans Allowed' … You look at a map, they got half the West under lock and key … Bureau of Land Management, Forest Service, National Parks, the State … It's like a treasure chest waiting to be opened, only there's a five hundred pound bureaucrat sitting on it … The people got to be grabbed by the horns and dragged to what's good for 'em … You know what the big picture is, don't you, Dickie? … Privatisa- tion. The land was meant for the citizens, not them damn pencil pushers in Washington … Son, we got resources here you wouldn't believe, untapped resources. And you and your dad are the point men in the fight to liberate those resources for the American people. Aspen, Vail, that ain't shit compared to what I could build if they opened this up to somebody with some ideas, with some know-how … And the people won't get it done, not by a long sight. They get distracted worrying about some postcard idea of the Rockies, some black-footed ferret or endangered tumbleweed … How's that saddle feeling? … We'll make a cowboy out of you yet.

Beyond his contempt for 'the people', who he compares to livestock, beyond his quasi-Heideggerian perception of the land as in need of technological challenge so as to reveal its fully extractable nature and be set-in-order,[89] and beyond his claim that corporations and capital rather than governments and democracy represent the people, Benteen also performs a neat ideological sleight-of-hand: he treats environmental costs as side effects and reduces environmental concerns to ridiculous stereotypes; he describes expropriation as liberation (an issue already raised when Castleton agreed with a caller to his radio talkshow that a country invaded and occupied by the US should bear the costs of its own 'liberation') and regulation as constraint (as does Furman Temple in *Sunshine State*); he equates wilderness with emptiness (like the property developers, tour operators and loggers in *Limbo* and *Sunshine State*); he conflates the capitalist with the cowboy and the frontier with opening up new opportunities for profit (although in reality the western frontier was always about exploiting resources so as to maximise surplus-value, regardless of how it has been mythologised or the motives of individual settlers). The ease and effectiveness of his centripetal reduction of centrifugal heteroglossia, in which the meanings of terms are precisely inverted, is the symbolic equivalent of the material expropriation he proposes, an extension of the process Ryan and Kellner identify in the 1970s whereby the language of resistance to corrupt institutions was co-opted by corporations to promote deregulation of their activities.

For all the corruption *Silver City* depicts or suggests, it differs from most conspiracy thrillers by not actually containing a conspiracy as such. There are cover-ups, collusions and covert deals, but the intrigues behind the development of Silver City are only really discernible around the edges of the film's narrative and the only directly identifiable and attributable crime, the death of Lázaro Huerta, can be reduced, in the words of County Sheriff Joe Skaggs (James Gammon), to 'failure to report an accident and illegal burial' (or, as Raven puts it, 'murder by deregulation'). What Danny uncovers is business-as-usual, practices so normalised under late-capitalism and the aggressively pro-corporate agenda of the US state as to seem not only unexceptional but also, to many, unexceptionable. Ryan and Kellner criticise conspiracy thrillers for typically casting 'systemic wrongs' in 'excessively personalised' terms, pitting heroes against villains and substituting rogue elements for institutions or the systems within which they operate, while at the other extreme *The Parallax View* renders the corporation behind the assassinations as 'faceless businessman' and 'impersonal functionaries of a corporate society' (1990: 99). The former thrillers deny social totality in terms familiar from Hollywood narrative filmmaking, while the latter obscures it through over-abstraction. In its relative decentring of conspiracy – Danny resembles a Raymond Chandler protagonist, discovering things more or less by accident until the fabric out of which individual events emerged is woven back together, establishing their relationships to each other[90] – *Silver City* falls somewhere between the two extremes, attempting instead to capture the social totality within which this business-as-usual occurs. The information Danny uncovers does not point to some grand conspiracy played out by a cabal of secretive puppet masters, nor does everything connect in a seamless web: there are accidents and contingencies and actions whose outcomes could not have been anticipated; there are characters, such as two of the three people Danny is sent to warn off, whose stories do not really connect at all to his investigation; and the story which one might typically expect a film to tell – the ways in which Silver City has served to funnel campaign funds to the Pilagers – is peripheral to the narrative. Rather, the film concentrates on drawing out interconnections and interrelations, social and cultural as well as economic. Fredric Jameson argues that 'the social totality is always unrepresentable, even for the most numerically limited groups of people; but it can sometimes be mapped and allow a small-scale model to be constructed on which fundamental tendencies and the lines of flight can be more clearly read' (2005b: 14). When we first see Chandler, he is examining a scale-model of the proposed Silver City development; Danny lacks this god-like perspective, but his Raymond Chandleresque investigation, the fabric of *Silver City*, provides just such a map of the forces contending over the future of the Rockies and America more generally.[91]

The euphemisation which Benteen deploys is widespread: Dickie is not corrupt but 'user-friendly'; the 'Developers' Bill of Rights' is published as the 'Environmental Heritage Initiative'; maintaining "the cultural equilibrium' means, in Raven's words, 'no handouts for homos'; the social welfare system is 'Big Brother'; and, jokingly, 'anti-tobacco' positions are 'pro-oxygen'. Such intersections between language-worlds represent the pressure points between the social totality and capital's attempted colonisation of it, while also indicating that it has not yet triumphed, that diversity and difference persist. They are sites of conflict between monology and heteroglossia, and all they represent. They are nodes between the totally-commodified universe and material, social reality.

In the corporate machinations of Benteen and others we see not just an attempt to produce a hyperreality which will enable the maximal extraction of surplus-value to continue with as little resistance as possible but also the Information Age described by Manuel Castells. In his analysis, the global flows of capital-information have increasingly separated out from the local and lived materiality of labour (see 2000a), and the state has transformed from a political subject in itself to a political apparatus for itself, whose only legitimacy in the consolidating world market is derived from its commitment to economic growth and the goals of global capital rather than those of its population (see Castells 2000b: 284). The key to any resistance to late-capitalism in the information age, he argues, is 'a *networking, decentered form of organisation and intervention, characteristic of the new social movements*, mirroring, and counteracting, the networking logic of domination in the informational society' (2004: 427; emphasis in original).[92] Such a form enables heteroglossia to flourish in the disembodied space of cybercapital, but it also runs the risk of reducing material social totality to mere symbolic play, and of mappings of that totality to mere conspiracy theory.

Carl Freedman suggests that conspiracy theory might be 'considered as philosophically akin to commodity fetishism, since they both involve the instrumentalization of human beings' (2002: 154). Moreover, conspiracy theory supplants the production of material history with a graspable and desirable narrative- or image-commodity. Every narrativisation of social totality tends in this direction – whether it is Skaggs' delimitation of the results of Danny's investigations to a 'failure to report an accident and illegal burial, which begins and ends with Vince Esparza' because, whatever other motives he has, he knows that pursuing it any further would only result in the two undocumented workers forced to help Esparza dispose of the body being charged as 'accessories to wrongful death … possibly murder'; or the uncovering of connections between the Pilagers and Benteen, and their various shenanigans and machinations, documented on Mitch's website under the title 'The Pilager Dynasty – Greed Incorporated'. Freedman argues that the reason to be wary of invoking conspiracy in political discourse is that it tends 'to replace structural analysis with merely ethical finger-pointing', but that nonetheless 'given certain larger socio-economic determinants, consequential political conspiracies can and do occur' (ibid.). He continues:

> that in a late-capitalist state like modern America – intensely centralized and militarized but still governed according to bourgeois democratic forms – conspiracy is no voluntaristic aberration but a structural *necessity* for ruling-class politics. When actual political power is largely concentrated in a relatively compact network of corporate, military, and government bureaucracies – and yet when it is unfeasible to exercise this power in despotic ways that too openly flout popular sentiment or legislative and judicial sanctions – then the ruling elite may have only two choices. It can curtail the enforcement of its perceived interests out of prudence or out of (ethical) respect for the integrity of republican institutions; or it can adopt conspiratorial methods. (2002: 154–5; emphasis in original)

In the development state Castells describes as typical of the information age, collusion between the political and the corporate takes the form of ensuring the conditions for capital's reproduction, while, for example, the promotion of free-trade agreements and the granting of the bond market veto powers over federal taxation and public expenditure fosters the illusion that capitalism is neutral, a nature in which we live rather than a contingent economic system. Alternative media, like Mitch's website, through attempting to map and narrativise totality in the disembodied information space of cybercapital itself can at the very least challenge this hyperreality by drawing attention to its artefactual construction (although at the same time, capital-information's tendency to equivalise renders such media no more or less 'true' or 'untrue' than sightings of Elvis Presley and alien abductions). By decentring conspiracy, *Silver City*'s attempts to go beyond it to map its socio-economic determinants, to sidestep the allure of narrativisation in order to perceive the totality from which the narrative impulse would more commonly abstract and organise certain events into a story such as 'Greed Incorporated'. The principle of connectivity underlying the webpages about the Pilager dynasty – and Danny's method of thinking through the information he has uncovered by writing key names on his apartment wall and hypothesizing the connections between them – takes a much more material form in the film's potent metaphorisation of resistance as hydraulic pressure.

It is appropriate that Ralph Waite, who as Furman Temple in *Sunshine State* described the forces of capitalism as an irresistible undertow, should, as Casey Lyle, describe such pressure building up within the apparently unitary and solid mountain:

What you're looking at is honeycombed with hundreds, maybe thousands, of mineshafts. When you stop pumping the water out, over time those holes fill up, top to bottom, till there's nowhere else for it to go. A huge pressure builds up, looking for an outlet. In 1943, four miners broke a pick-hole in a wall to an adjacent area that hadn't been worked in twenty years. Water exploded out of that wall, drove those four fellas and their equipment back through the shaft they'd dug, out into the main tunnel that Newhouse had built to service the mine, blasted through an opening and blew the water clear across the river to the other side. For three days, water blasted out of that mountain, timber, tracks, loose rocks, half-ton ore cars, flying through the air like they were toys. You know, we think we can wound this planet. We think we can cut costs and stick the money in our pockets and just walk away with it. But some day the bill comes due.

It is this physical interconnectedness and water pressure which deposits Huerta's corpse in Arapaho Lake, as well as the toxic waste which kills the fish and ruptures the hyper-reality of Governor Pilager's television broadcast by intruding a material reality it would deny. In his screenplay for *Alligator*, Sayles achieved a similar effect by setting a giant alligator on the loose to eat its way up the economic system, from urban ghettos to a white millionaire patriarch's estate. In the monstrous normality of *Sunshine State*'s Florida, there is no possibility for the fantastic eruption of a repressed real because the real itself has become so thoroughly fantastic: the 'Man-Eating Alligator' displayed as an attraction is just an ordinary alligator, so torpid that the children watching it wonder if it is even alive – to which its owner replies, 'You paying anything to look at it him? Then don't complain.'[93] *Silver City* reworks the conclusion of *Piranha*, in which Paul deliberately floods the river with industrial pollution so as to destroy the genetically-engineered killer fish, but whose coda suggests that some have survived and will return. In *Silver City*, the dead fish which fill the screen deflate the soundtrack's rendition of 'America the Beautiful', but are nonetheless a hopeful image, of sorts, suggesting a similar kind of return: in Danny's earlier words to Raven, 'some day your shit's gonna catch up with you'.

This is, perhaps, in *Matewan*'s phrase, 'a cold comfort'. It certainly once more indicates some of the limitations of the naturalist methods of Sayles' films, even when used for allegorical or satirical purposes, and the political constraints of a left-liberal politics which can imagine no solution beyond reform. But as the opening chapter suggested, sometimes, in darker days, merely keeping alternative conceptualisations of 'reality' alive and in circulation is the most radical cultural goal tenable. Sayles' films have consistently done this, offering images of class-consciousness (in its broadest, 'two-sided' sense), of community and utopian homecoming. As Mitch says of his website, 'somebody has to plant the seed' and that is what Sayles' films do. Like Fiona Coneelly in *The Secret of Roan Inish*, and so many of his other characters, John Sayles tells us stories and perhaps even teaches us to speak. And he shows us over and again, from all the eggs the Secaucus Seven left unused to a Coloradan lake full of poisoned fish, that the story is never over, that along with consequences there is always also hope.

NOTES

1 For a critical treatment of the naturalist tradition in France, see Baguley (1990).

2 See Howard (1985), Michaels (1987), Kaplan (1988), Seltzer (1992), Civello (1994), Campbell (1997), den Tandt (1998), Zayani (1999), Dudley (2004), Fleissner (2004) and Link (2004).

3 *Silver City* and *Eight Men Out* are unusual, and rather different from each other, in their recourse to conspiracy narratives in order to trace the varieties of interconnection common to the worlds Sayles' films depict.

4 Stephen Crane wrote about his own attempts to write fiction set in Mexico: 'It might perhaps be said – if anyone dared – that the most worthless literature of the world has been that which has been written by the men of one nation concerning the men of another' (1970: 74). While this might seem a harsh judgement to pass on Sayles' films set in Latin America, it is nonetheless worth noting that the problem identified with them in chapters five and six might not be so much about their setting as with a broader problematic running through all of Sayles' films (derived from a naturalistic negotiation of the fiction of being an observer) which their setting merely makes more pronounced. An earlier group of films – *The Lady in Red*, written by Sayles but directed by Lewis Teague, *Matewan*, *Eight Men Out* and the never-filmed *Bob Merriman, the American Leader of the International Brigade*, written by Sayles but intended for Bille August to direct – offer a similar mapping of the US in the period about which Dos Passos wrote.

5 Such a pattern can repeatedly be discerned in American filmmaking: for instance, fallen woman films (for example, *Blonde Venus* (1932), *Baby Face* (1933)); film noirs (for example, *Phantom Lady* (1944), *Scarlet Street* (1945)); prison and mental institution dramas (for example, *I Am a Fugitive from a Chain Gang* (1932), *The Snake Pit* (1948), *The Wrong Man* (1956), *Shock Corridor* (1963)); dramas of working class life (for example, *Blue Collar* (1978), *Working Girls* (1986), *Kids* (1995)); comedies (for example, *Trading Places* (1983), *Bulworth* (1998)); ghetto melodramas (for example, *Colors* (1988), *Boyz N the Hood* (1991)); and documentaries (*Roger & Me* (1989), *Dark Days* (2000)).

6   While American naturalism has typically been considered a particularly masculinist form, this too has been challenged in recent years. See especially Fleissner (2004), whose re-reading of Norris's *McTeague* (1899) as a woman's marriage story radically reconceptualises one of the canonical naturalist texts.

7   Raymond Williams' complaint about positions similar to McCabe's is that 'the critics of this neo-realism contend that to re-create the apparently experienced world of the working class is a form of naturalization which renders it impossible either to explain that experience or to show that it could be otherwise: the diction of this drama, they say, is only a left version of the miming of working-class habits in advertising. The criticism has a lot of force: the trouble with it is that its alternative usually gets no further than one word, Brecht, and that powerful word is not even glossed – Brecht, as I've said, being the outstanding example of someone who didn't, with rare exceptions, solve the problem in his own work' (1981a: 269).

8   As Walter Benjamin noted, 'to supply a production apparatus without trying, within the limits of the possible, to change it, is a highly disputable activity even when the material supplied appears to be of a revolutionary nature. For we are confronted with the fact – of which there has been no shortage of proof in Germany over the last decade – that the bourgeois apparatus of production and publication is capable of assimilating, indeed of propagating, an astonishing amount of revolutionary themes without ever seriously putting into question its own continued existence or that of the class which owns it' (1973: 93–4). The Third Cinema advocated by Solanas and Getino not only more radically called for collective filmmaking arising directly from conjuncturally-specific struggle – bringing into question the assumptions about authorship underpinning First Cinema – but also recognised the overwhelming problem presented by the dominant circuits and institutions of distribution and exhibition.

9   On the relationship between late-nineteenth century American naturalism and the proliferation of utopian fiction in the decade after Edward Bellamy's *Looking Backwards, 2000–1887* (1888), see Link (2004: 68–99).

10   On how capitalism from its outset depended upon the removal of women from the sphere of labour and the exclusion of their domestic labour from the category of labour, see Federici (2004).

11   See Sayles' short stories 'Home for Wayfarers' (1979a: 3–23) and 'The Halfway Diner' (2004b: 15–38) for miniature evocations of this multiplicity of social being.

12   I am indebted to Turim & Turim-Nygren (2006: 154) for this translation.

13   Referring to Charles Laughton's eponymous performance in *Galileo*, Brecht wrote, 'At no moment must he go so far as to be wholly transformed into the character played. The verdict: "he didn't act Lear, he was Lear" would be an annihilating blow to him. He has to just show the character … his feelings must not at bottom be those of the character … This principle – that the actor appears on the stage in a double role, as Laughton and as Galileo; that the showman Laughton does not disappear in the Galileo whom he is showing … – comes to mean simply that the tangible, matter-of-fact process is no longer hidden behind a veil; that Laughton is actually there, standing on the stage and showing us what he imagines Galileo to have been.' (1964: 193–4). Given that Zane's self-conscious performance is of a self-conscious performer, it might even be described as meta-Brechtian.

14   On cynical reason, see Sloterdijk (1988).

15   As a naturalist, Sayles negotiates and struggles with this process of expropriation throughout his films and fiction – at what point does observation and imitation of the way people talk become putting words in their mouths? – and it is most pronounced in *Men with Guns*, his first foreign-language film. However, his thematic treatment of this process (see also *The Secret of Roan Inish*, *Lone Star* and *Casa de los Babys*) consistently demonstrate an awareness of his own position within it.

16   They do not share the frame again – and in the only subsequent scene in which they both appear, at Senator Pilager's party, the distance between them is physically exaggerated.

17   This is, of course, the central tension between observer and participant faced by the naturalist writer, and 'the aesthetic challenge of naturalism – namely how to maintain the distance of the scientific observer while avoiding the passive disengagement of the spectator' (Dudley 2004: 55). *Silver City* was, of course, intended to help prevent George W. Bush's re-election.

18   Appropriately enough, this echoes imagery in *Double Indemnity* (1944), co-scripted by Raymond Chandler .

19   In this context it is worth noting Louis J. Budd's argument that naturalism arose in the late nineteenth

century as the 'realistic temperament turned toward the disjuncture between optimistic rhetoric and what was actually happening' (1995: 33).

20 The box-office success of *She's Gotta Have It* (1986) enabled Lee to form relationships first with Columbia and then Universal, but since the end of the latter he has returned to 'more independently financed, lower-budget features, including *Girl 6* (1996) (with Fox Searchlight), *Get on the Bus* (1996), partly funded by a group of black investors, and the 16mm and DV production *Bamboozled* (2000)' (King 2005: 211). Soderbergh's hit *sex, lies, and videotape* (1989) was followed by 'the disappointing performance and reception of *Kafka* (1991) and the studio features *King of the Hill* (1993) and *The Underneath* (1995)' and then a 'return to low-budget basics with the zany *Schizopolis* and *Gray's Anatomy*, both produced on limited resources in 1996', before pursuing 'a career based on more assured movement between Hollywood and the independent sector' (2005: 262). This trajectory was undoubtedly stabilised by the formation with George Clooney in 1999 of the Section Eight production company (which lasted until 2007) under the auspices of Warner Bros.

21 This, too, is a point to contrast with Altman, whose films – such as *The Player* (1992) and *Short Cuts* – seem to be far more concerned with amnesia, disconnecting people not only from each other and the communities in which they live but also from history.

22 This excludes the costs of prints, marketing and advertising, which rose from $12 million in 1990 to $24.5 million in 1999.

23 This excludes average marketing and advertising costs of $34.5 million .

24 Woloch (2006) argues that Sayles' style, sometimes described as consisting of the lack of a specific style, is better understood in terms of self-effacement – a term which resonates strongly with the naturalists' 'attempt to redefine the author as intermediary between the characters and events of the text and the detached observation of an audience far removed' (Dudley 2004: 19).

25 It is easy to bemoan Hollywood's unwillingness to commit to making the kind of films Sayles makes, but any director-centred criticism must recognise that such conditions have determined, and not merely in a negative way, the films he has made. In some sense, his most important collaboration is with a system of film production with which he does not actively seek to collaborate.

26 Admittedly, though, Sayles did name a planet in *Battle Beyond the Stars* after Akira Kurosawa and a character in *Silver City* after Raymond Chandler.

27 *The Howling IV: The Original Nightmare* (1988) is a closer adaptation.

28 Such classic naturalist novels as Norris's *McTeague* and *Vandover and the Brute* (1914), the latter of which features a protagonist who suffers from lycanthropy, are concerned with the failure of such psychic mechanisms of repression. The concern with heredity and degeneracy evident in many naturalist fictions from the nineteenth and early twentieth centuries often vindicated Social Darwinist formulations in which the species (or white race) would evolve towards perfection while the individual was fated never to escape his past, typically succumbing to his inherited (and often non-white or proletarian) bestial nature.

29 This has obvious resonances with the interest of Sayles' own films in class and ethnicised difference, migrations and immigration.

30 It is not, then, surprising to find at the time of writing that Sayles is scripting *Jurassic Park IV*, currently scheduled for a 2009 release.

31 The copy of the screenplay I am working from is undated. Of the four different endings (see Osborne 1999: 36) Sayles wrote for the film, this version culminates with David hooking up gas tanks to a sprinkler system and setting fire to the alligator. As Sayles recalls 'I liked the idea of the alligator walking around on fire. They said no, because the [32-foot model of the] alligator was booked for personal appearances in a flatbed truck for publicity. We couldn't destroy it' (in Peary 1999: 62).

32 This characterisation is not entirely accurate: only the shooting of the deputy mayor is given no obvious motivation, and the narrative does not suffer from this omission.

33 In Sayles' films, this utopianism and its limitations are often figured through singers – J. T. in *Return of the Secaucus Seven*, Sheikh in *Baby It's You*, Malverne in *The Brother from Another Planet*, Bobby and Zip's band in *City of Hope*, Donna in *Limbo* and Steve in *Sunshine State* – and the various congregations of *Matewan* and the zydeco gig in *Passion Fish* bear a similar figurative weight. This tendency is most fully developed in *Honeydripper*, in which musical performance is envisaged as a means of liberatory

self-expression, which comes at a personal cost, and as an expression of community, which is hedged in by commodification and various forms of intolerance (for example, racist social structures, moral disapprobation). Tyrone Purvis (Danny Glover), a pianist and the owner of the Honeydripper roadhouse, struggles with his memory of killing a guitarist in self-defence when a young man; and with the commercial competition his juke joint, with its live performances and rhythm and blues face from a rival club's jukebox and the emergence of a whitened, mass-produced rock'n'roll. In a key speech, though, he imagines what it must have been like the first time a house slave was left alone in a room with a piano – an instrument unlike any of those transported from Africa but with which he instinctively knew he 'could do some damage'. Itinerant guitarist Sonny (Gary Clark, Jr), an ex-Army mechanic returned from the occupation of Japan, is certain that his home-made electric guitar will bring him success, if only he can avoid arrest for vagrancy and get a chance to play. In a typically Saylesian moment of utopian possibility, Sonny, hired by Tyrone to pretend to be no-show radio star Guitar Sam, lets rip, accompanied by a veteran saxophonist and harmonica player, a teenage drummer and Tyrone. The Honeydripper fills up with a crowd for whom Saturday night is their one time to kick loose from the constraints of labour, impoverishment and dull care. Tyrone's wife, Delilah (Lisa Gay Hamilton), who has been struggling to choose between her husband's way of life and the demands of a preacher that she break with it, turns away from the revivalist's altar call and returns to support him. Oedipal tensions are soothed as Sonny – who stands in for the guitarman Tyrone killed, and has started courting Tyrone's daughter, China Doll (Yaya DaCosta) – is accepted by Tyrone. Black and white creditors are paid off and depart. And two small boys sneak in to listen to this fabulous new version of the blues. This crowd-pleasing finale is followed by a morning after, full of hope as the blind guitarman who (like a father) has long haunted Tyrone, leaves town and the boys play at being electrified bluesmen. The utopian is thus reconfigured in the aftermath of the gig as a thread running through daily life and into a future which might yet arrive.

34 In slightly different ways, both Ryan and Bazin attribute to the 'real' (or at least the profilmic) a similar substantiality to that which Zola and other naturalists sought to observe, while also betraying some sense of the artful construction of the real by the director (if never reaching quite as far as the post-Barthesian orthodoxy that authors function within self-enclosed systems of representation – a position which has had a profound impact on the understanding of naturalism developed in and since the 1980s).

35 After the supposed success of the Peace Corps, established in 1961, President Kennedy instituted a domestic equivalent, VISTA (Volunteers in Service to America), in 1963 to work in underprivileged areas of the US.

36 One of the more curious aspects of the negative criticism of *Lianna* is the recurring desire for the film to have a happy ending, by which is normally implied one in which Lianna and Ruth stay together. It is as if, because we never see her, Jan is unimportant.

37 For a historicised critique of the category 'art cinema', see Wilinsky (2001), especially chapter one.

38 It was, of course, not as straightforward as this. When 20th Century Fox urged the second half of the story be dropped, Robinson and co-producer Griffin Dunne worked out a negative pickup deal with Paramount instead. Courtesy of studio backing, the budget leapt to $3 million, $300,000 of which was spent on the soundtrack. It also enabled Sayles to shoot in sequence and, for the first time, in 35mm. He delivered a first cut, edited by Sonya Polonsky, which ran for 140 minutes. Paramount, who wanted a 105-minute version, fired Sayles when he threatened to remove his name from the film if they recut it. The studio cut, edited by Jerry Greenberg, previewed indifferently so Sayles was re-hired to produce his own 105-minute version.

39 This is echoed in their later parting at the Florida airport: Jill is visible through a clear glass window on which we can see Sheik's reflection, but Sheik himself is not in the shot.

40 Springsteen's debut album was *Greetings from Asbury Park, N.J.* (1973). In 1985, Sayles directed Springsteen's videos for 'Born in the USA', 'I'm on Fire' and 'Glory Days'. Springsteen provided the end-credits song for *Limbo*.

41 See Pfeil (1995: 83) on the appearance of the early Springsteen and how dressing up to go out (and perform) further 'authenticated' Springsteen's working-class persona.

42 For a more detailed treatment of music in *Baby It's You*, see Garwood (2006: 145–59).

43 This sense of felt cultural difference recurs when they go to the cinema: Sheik wants to fool around, Jill wants to watch the film. 'You Jewish girls', he whines.

44 On *Star Trek*, see Bernardi (1998).

45. For example, *E.T.: The Extra-Terrestrial* (1982), which it openly spoofs, and *Blade Runner* (1982), whose premises it inverts, taking the viewpoint of the hunter rather than the hunted.

46 Paranoia about Latin-American immigration has often been paralleled by anxiety about the northward progress of foreign and potentially devastating species of insects, such as, currently, Africanised bees.

47 For an account of the sheer unlikeliness of such unconcern from a state organisation, particularly after 1994, see Nevins (2002). There are, of course, distinctions to be made between criminal law and treaty law, but the movie treats them as identical (both exist to be administered/enforced by a hierarchy of state agencies), while equating law-enforcement with justice. Kay's apparently liberal treatment of terrestrial illegal aliens, which is actually little more than an assertion of his position within the hierarchy, reinforces the otherwise unchallenged notion that extra-terrestrial illegal aliens pose some kind of 'genuine' threat. (Janus, of course, was two-faced.)

48 The casting of a black star inevitably renders generalisations about a film's racial politics more problematic. However, it is worth noting that Smith's star persona, from his early career as a pop hip-hop performer and his lead role in *The Fresh Prince of Bel-Air* (1990–96) through to starring roles in movies like *Bad Boys* (1995), *Enemy of the State* (1998), the depoliticised biopic *Ali* (2001), *I, Robot* (2004) and *The Pursuit of Happyness* (2006), has been predicated upon the desire to conform to the norms of a white bourgeois order. As Esther Leslie writes of Dumbo, once he 'discovers that his quirk – those freakish oversized ears – is actually his winning and bankable asset, he becomes a highly paid star … The circus … is turned into the sadistic arena where power parades its ability to buy off dissent, and injustice rules. There is no escape from the system, only conformity and the hope of triumphing within its terms' (2002: 201). For a critique of the supposed multiculturalism and ethnic egalitarianism of *Independence Day*, in which Smith also stars, see Mair (2002).

49 This sequence provides an interesting contrast to the one in which Lianna discovers that she lives in a world full of women.

50 In 1921 the temporary Quota Act limited 'the number of admissions of any particular nationality to three per cent of the group's population already in the United States as reflected by the 1910 census. This marked the first quantitative immigration restrictions in U.S. history' (Nevins 2002: 29). The 1924 'Johnson-Reed' Immigration Act, 'made the quotas permanent, but lowered the permitted percentage of immigrants to 2 per cent and used the census of 1890 as its base' (2002: 101), and 'also required immigrants for the first time to obtain visas from U.S. consular officials abroad before traveling to the United States' (2002: 29). The 1924 'legislation also included the Oriental Exclusion Act, which banned all Asian immigration except that from the Philippines. As opposed to the temporary Quota Act of 1921, economic arguments were secondary to ones of racial purity in 1924 ("alien indigestion" became "racial indigestion")' (2002: 101–2). In addition to creating 'fixed concepts of "race", which the legislation effectively conflated with the concept of the "nation"' (2002: 102), often regardless of the immigrants' self-identity or geographic origin, and to valorising both the classification of people by race and prejudices about which kinds of immigrants were capable of assimilation, the 1924 Act 'resulted in 85 per cent of the new immigrant quota [being] allocated to North-Western Europe' (ibid.).

51 Immigration 'came in three great tides, each stronger than the last. The first rose in the 1830s and 1840s to a high-water mark in 1854, when 427,833 new arrivals were recorded; the second, starting in the seventies, rose to a height of 788,992 in 1882; the third brought in an average of one million immigrants a year in the decade before the First World War' (Brogan 1990: 413–14). Brogan also notes that immigration 'rose from 216,397 in 1897 to 1,218,480 in 1914' (1990: 456). The effect of the 1924 Act was to end mass immigration: 'the annual average went down from 862,514 in the 1907–14 period to no more than 150,00 – all that was allowed … and discrimination against suspect nationalities was built into the system. Immigration from the so-called Asiatic Barred Zone – China, Japan, Indochina, Afghanistan, Arabia, the East Indies – was stopped almost entirely; and immigration from everywhere else but Northern and Western Europe was made exceedingly difficult' (1990: 512). Among the many tragic consequences of the implementation of this legislation was that of the 180,000 German Jews who might have entered the United States between 1933 and 1941, only 75,000 were given permission to do so (571).

52 Zerilli also notes that Bartholdi's original design for the Statue of Liberty included 'broken chains and Phyrigian cap' (2000: 326), traditional symbols of liberation from enslavement, but these were discarded so as not to provoke offence among potential financial backers from the Southern states.

53 For historial accounts of the Coalfield Wars, see Savage (1990) and Norwood (2002: 114–70); the latter provides a useful overview of the strikebreaking activities of the Baldwin-Felts Agency. Sayles offers an earlier fictional account in *Union Dues*. Although the Coalfield Wars are often described as the only occasion on which the US government has turned its airpower on its own civilian population, and although the '88th Squadron claimed in later years, when it became the 436th Bombardment Squadron, to be the only Air Corps unit ever to have participated in a civil disturbance' (Savage 1990: 146), their role was restricted to reconnaissance and they were not terribly effective: of the 21 planes sent to Charleston, only 14 arrived; three later crashed and one was stranded in a field. However, Logan County Sheriff Don Chafin did drop home-made bombs on miners' positions.

54 One of *Matewan*'s strengths over such comparable films as *Norma Rae* (1979) is its refusal to place a heterosexual romance at the centre of the narrative. Although Kenehan and Elma like and admire each other, they occupy the different worlds of melodrama and tragedy until it is too late.

55 When the miners' camp is attacked in the night, one of the casualties is the mandolin.

56 The ground for this betrayal is prepared not only by Bridey Mae's obvious yearning for something to come into and transform her life, captured by her watching the trains come and go, but also by the fact that she lives in isolation from the miners (itself largely a product of the social division of labour by gender under capital). As the film produces a sense of community through the shared playing of music, it is significant that she has a broken phonograph, which C.E. repairs.

57 On this terminology, see Scott (1990).

58 Despite his political sympathies, Sayles' departures from fact include the omission of some of the Baldwin-Felts agents' worst excesses, such as lacing with kerosene milk sent by charitable organisations to the miners' children, because 'What is true and what people will believe in a movie are two different things' (in G. Smith 1998: 127).

59 Something like this did actually happen, but at the end of the successful 1917 pennant run (see Asinof 1987: 22).

60 Again, this actually took place in 1917 (see Asinof 1987: 21–2).

61 Fullerton actually made an arrangement of this sort with Christy Mathewson, a journalist and former manager of the Reds (see Asinof 1987: 46–7).

62 Landis was the judge in the 1918 trial of 101 IWW members (165 were actually indicted) on five different charges of combination and conspiracy. After a five month trial, the jury, acting on Landis's instructions, took less than an hour to find all defendants guilty. Sentences ranged up to twenty years and individual fines up to $30,000; total fines amounted to $2,500,000 (see Renshaw 1968: 169–94). As Dos Passos expresses it in *Mid-Century* (1961), 'The crime our boys committed was to take the unpopular side in the struggle to keep America out of war. The statutes they were convicted on all infringed the Bill of Rights. Every good lawyer admitted that. Convictions were expected but the sentences knocked our breath out. How could a man live with himself after doing what Kenesaw Mountain Landis did to men's lives for just saying a few illegal words? He throve on it. His recompense was to be handed $25,000 a year as czar of organised baseball' (1963: 152–3).

63 This can be seen as an elaboration of the moving camera Sayles deployed in two scenes from *Return of the Secaucus Seven* discussed in chapter three. For a detailed treatment of such techniques, see Smith (2006).

64 This echoes the preoccupation of an earlier naturalism with not only the 'principle of production for the sake of production upon which capitalism thrives', which 'involves not only over-production (the priority of exchange-value over use-value) but also over-consumption (the pre-eminence of desire over need)', leading Mohamed Zayani to conclude that 'the driving impetus of the system is not production *per se* but the process of production, not consumption but the process of consumption' (1999: 121).

65 On these developments, see Aglietta (1979); Piore & Sable (1984); Marglin & Schor (1990); Armstrong, Glyn & Harrison (1991); Lee (1993); Davis (1999).

66 As Malcolm Bull argues, 'In the *Phenomenology*, there are repeated references to the splitting of self-consciousness into opposing extremes, and to the inescapable mirroring of one by the other. Both

metaphors suggest that we are dealing, not with the activities of separate human beings, but with component parts of the individual psyche … It is possible to conceive of the dialectic taking place internally between two self-consciousnesses, one of which masters the other and uses it as a medium through which it is conscious of material reality. But Hegel's account also employs several concepts such as recognition, fighting, and work – not to mention mastery and slavery themselves – that are extremely difficult to understand in anything other than interpersonal terms' (1998: 110–11).

67 A T-10 paraplegic is paralysed in the lower body, but will typically retain full use of hands and arms as well as full head and neck movement.

68 Du Bois, who was familiar with Hegel's work, argues that 'the Negro is … born with a veil, and gifted with second-sight in this American world – a world which yields him no true self-consciousness, but only lets him see himself through the revelation of the other world. It is a peculiar sensation, this double-consciousness, this sense of always looking at one's self through the eyes of others, of measuring one's soul by the tape of a world that looks on in amused contempt and pity. One ever feels his twoness – an American, a Negro; two souls, two thoughts, two unreconciled strivings; two warring ideals in one dark body, whose dogged strength alone keeps it from being torn asunder' (1965: 214–15).

69 *Honeydripper* articulates a very similar position: nostalgia for the blues is not enough, the energy of youth and electrification must also work their transformations on the mundane impoverishments of everyday life under capital. However, Dick Pope's cinematography at times seems to confuse the matter, as is evident in the title sequence's celebration of golden evening light falling on fields of cotton. On the one hand, it captures the end of the workday, respite from the poorly paid or corruptly indentured labour of picking the crop; on the other, it carries too much cultural baggage to escape connotations concerned with the white supremacist myth, frequently seen in classical Hollywood films, of a harmonious antebellum South, full of fields of cotton being picked by happy, childlike and (perhaps most problematically for *Honeydripper*) singing slaves. This stereotype is picked up during the scene in the jailhouse, in which the African-American men the county has rented out to landowners to pick the cotton, joke around and then join in when Sonny starts to sing 'Midnight Special'. As the scene comes to an end, its mood shifts, allowing Sonny, in long shot and surrounded by darkness, to sing a mournful solo version.

70 While a useful analytical model, this 'tipping-over' is of course a product of the fact that, as discussed in chapter two, modernism and postmodernism cannot effectively be distinguished on formal or stylistic grounds.

71 There remains a Todorovian hesitation (see Todorov 1975) in that the seals only ever appear as seals rather than, selkie-fashion, adopting human form.

72 On genre and varieties of verisimilitude, see Neale (2000: 31–9).

73 The absurdity of this reality can be seen in the derelict walls which scatter the landscape in the film, leading from nowhere to nowhere and enclosing nothing, which historically labourers were compelled to build in order to receive 'charity' – which by this very process is removed from the realm of charity and into that of wage-labour, however meaningless.

74 See also Barker (2001).

75 For example, Mexico's 1982 debt crisis forced agricultural diversification away from subsistence crops such as maize towards cash-crops like coffee, whose production is riskier because its profitability depends upon the stability of international markets. When coffee prices collapsed in 1989 – Mexico was not alone in being advised to pursue cash-crop policies, resulting in a glut on world markets – many Mexican farmers were left not only destitute but without a crop they could eat. See Collier with Quaratiello (1994) and Ceceña & Barreda (1998). Ironically, in the Chiapas region of Mexico, where parts of *Men with Guns* was shot, this was one factor in extending popular support for the EZLN (Ejército Zapatista de Liberación Nacional or Zapatistas), who led the 1994 uprising which delayed the shooting of *Men with Guns* until after *Lone Star*.

76 For a critique of Castells' tendency to succumb to capital's fantasy of transcendence, see Vint & Bould (2006).

77 In early naturalist fiction, such as Zola's *Rougon-Macquart* cycle of novels (1871–1893), even supposedly scientific notions of heredity and degeneracy function in this mystificatory manner. Norris's *Vandover and the Brute*, whose protagonist succumbs to lycanthropy during his long decline, bridges the gap

between the biological determinism evoked in the wolf imagery of Jack London's *The Sea-Wolf* (1904) and the more overtly fantastical 'beast within' of *The Howling* and other werewolf fiction. This imagery of wolves (and foxes) is picked up again in *Limbo*.

78 In this moment, Fuentes seems to offer a key with which to understand what Sayles attempts to do through his frequent use of familiar generic and narrative elements and stereotypical characters. However, just as Fuentes' success lasts only for a fleeting moment, so the cultural inertia of powerful stereotypes can sometimes prove problematic. This seems especially the case with *Honeydripper*, which tells a story of the black creation of rock'n'roll, but runs all kind of political risks by requiring its almost entirely black cast to just love singing and dancing. While the two most fully developed white characters are both also stereotypes, they are carefully allowed to demonstrate their departure from type. In her single scene, the mayor's wife, Amanda Winship (Mary Steenburgen), a fragile alcoholic and fading Southern belle, reveals her impoverished upbringing and the persistent class anxiety that has driven her to drink. Over a handful of scenes we are repeatedly set up to anticipate that the fat redneck Sheriff (Stacy Keach) will erupt into violence, casually beat or murder someone or rape Delilah – none of which he does, although a sense of the threat he poses remains. Although several of the black characters are rounded out in similar ways, one is left with a sense of a film which falls somewhat closer to one of the studio-produced all-black musicals (for example, *Cabin in the Sky* (1943), *Stormy Weather* (1943), *Carmen Jones* (1954), *Porgy and Bess* (1959)) than the independently-produced black cinema of Oscar Micheaux than it intends.

79 On Sayles' DVD commentary, he points out that this is fairly unexceptional practice when halibut fishing, but it nonetheless appears comical to the uninitiated, myself included.

80 Laskin provided the voice-over for the *faux*-promotional film, although it is not clear whether it is supposed to have been delivered by Albright.

81 This problematic equation of women with consumption can be traced back at least as far as Dreiser's *Sister Carrie*.

82 The film *is* set on the shore of an island simultaneously in, and off the coast of, the US.

83 Earlier, Nan told Skipper how her mother burned her wrist so as to teach her not to play with the stove – the wristband she wears to cover the scar is prominent throughout the scene.

84 The American Psychiatric Association (2000) does detail a version of bulimia in which instead of eating and purging, the sufferer balances calories consumed with calories expended and fasts when exercise is missed. Skipper's behaviour could be interpreted in this way.

85 One is immediately reminded of the voicelessness or struggling-into-voice of other socially-disempowered characters in Sayles' films – the Brother, Danny in *Matewan*, Nuala in *The Secret of Roan Inish*, Noelle in *Limbo*, Sonny in *Honeydripper*, and so on – as well as the problem of the effective silencing of non-Anglophones, even as they are given voice, by *Men with Guns*' predetermined subtitles.

86 A mirror version of this exchange takes place when Nan attempts to bully and bribe Ernesto into speeding up the adoption process. Noting in her file 'no entiende Español', he fakes a phone call in Spanish to appease her – while in fact checking for how long she has paid for her hotel room, thus determining whether it is time to stop delaying the adoption.

87 Ironically, the pregnant Celia is being taken by her mother to Miami, so as to have the baby out of sight, before returning with it to their own country to put it up for adoption by an American.

88 This back-story is based on the relationship between the Bush family and Karl Rove. In the 1972 campaign for the Presidency of the College Republicans, despite promising to investigate Rove's dirty tricks campaign, George Bush, Chairman of the National Republican Committee, ruled against Robert Edgeworth and in favour of Rove.

89 See Heidegger (1993).

90 The casting of Danny Huston nods intertextually to his father, John Huston, the director of *The Maltese Falcon* (1941), adapted from Dashiell Hammett's 1931 novel, who also played the monstrous capitalist patriarch and rapist of his own daughter, Noah Cross, in *Chinatown* – a conspiracy thriller, like *The Parallax View* and *Silver City*, in which water plays a significant part. Danny Huston bears a closer physical resemblance to, and shares mannerisms with, the perpetually out-of-his-depth Walter Neff (Fred MacMurray) in *Double Indemnity*, co-scripted by Raymond Chandler (after whom Billy Zane's character is named).

91 Fortunately, the romance narrative is sufficiently peripheral to minimise the problematic equation of the land with Nora as something to be competed over by Danny and Chandler, the representatives of these contending forces.

92 For a critique of this position, see Vint & Bould (2006).

93 It is perhaps significant that Sayles shot a scene of the alligator loose in a mall for *Sunshine State*, but cut it because it 'broke the tone' (Sayles 2004c: 164). One can only wonder whether this bored and unfantastical creature was too material for the hyperreal mallspace – not so much the fantastic rupturing the real as, uncomfortably, vice versa.

FILMOGRAPHY

Return of the Secaucus Seven (1980)
Production Company: Salsipuedes Production
Producers: William Aydelott, Jeffrey Nelson
Director: John Sayles
Screenplay: John Sayles
Cinematography: Austin De Besche
Editor: John Sayles
Original Music: Mason Daring, Timothy Jackson, Bill Staines, Guy Van Dusen
Main Cast: Bruce MacDonald (Mike Donnelly), Maggie Renzi (Katie Sipriano), Adam LeFevre (J. T.), Maggie Cousineau (Frances Carlson), Gordon Clapp (Chip Hollister), Jean Passanante (Irene Rosenblum), Karen Trott (Maura Tolliver), Mark Arnott (Jeff Andrews), David Strathairn (Ron Desjardins), John Sayles (Howie), Marisa Smith (Carol), Amy Schewel (Lacey Summers), Carolyn Brooks (Meg)

Lianna (1983)
Production Company: Winwood Productions
Producers: Jeffrey Nelson, Maggie Renzi
Director: John Sayles
Screenplay: John Sayles
Cinematography: Austin De Besche
Editor: John Sayles
Original Music: Mason Daring
Main Cast: Linda Griffiths (Lianna), Jane Hallaren (Ruth), John DeVries (Dick), Jo Henderson (Sandy), Jessica Wight MacDonald (Theda), Jesse Solomon (Spencer), John Sayles (Jerry), Stephen Mendillo (Bob), Betsy Julia Robinson (Cindy), Nancy Mette (Kim), Maggie Renzi (Sheila)

Baby It's You (1983)
Production Company: Double Play
Producers: Griffin Dunne, Amy Robinson
Associate Producer: Robert F. Colesberry
Director: John Sayles
Story: Amy Robinson
Screenplay: John Sayles
Cinematography: Michael Ballhaus
Editor: Sonya Polonsky
Main Cast: Rosanna Arquette (Jill Rosen), Vincent Spano (Albert 'Sheik' Capadilupo), Joanna Merlin (Mrs Rosen), Jack Davidson (Dr Rosen), Nick Ferrari (Mr Capadilupo), Dolores Messina (Mrs Capadilupo)

The Brother from Another Planet (1984)
Production Company: A-Train Films
Producers: Peggy Rajski, Maggie Renzi
Director: John Sayles
Screenplay: John Sayles
Cinematography: Ernest R. Dickerson
Editor: John Sayles
Original Music: Martin Brody, Mason Daring
Main Cast: Joe Morton (The Brother), Daryl Edwards (Fly), Steve James (Odell), Dee Dee Bridgewater (Malverne Davis), Sidney Sheriff Jr (Virgil), Bill Cobbs (Walter), Maggie Renzi (Noreen), Carl Gordon (Mr Price), John Sayles (Man in Black), David Strathairn (Man in Black)

Matewan (1987)
Production Companies: Cinecom Entertainment Group, Film Gallery, Goldcrest Films International, Red Dog Films
Producers: Peggy Rajski, Maggie Renzi
Associate Producers: Ira Deutchman, James Glenn Dudelson, Ned Kendall
Executive Producers: Mark Balsam, Amir Jacob Malin, Jerry Silva
Director: John Sayles
Screenplay: John Sayles
Cinematography: Haskell Wexler
Editor: Sonya Polonsky
Original Music: Mason Daring
Main Cast: Chris Cooper (Joe Kenehan), James Earl Jones ('Few Clothes' Johnson), Mary McDonnell (Elma Radnor), Will Oldham (Danny Radnor), David Strathairn (Police Chief Sid Hatfield), Ken Jenkins (Sephus Purcell), Gordon Clapp (Griggs), Kevin Tighe (Hickey), Bob Gunton (C.E. Lively), Nancy Mette (Bridey Mae), Jace Alexander (Hillard Elkins), Jo Henderson (Mrs Elkins), Joe Grifasi (Fausto), John Sayles (Hardshell Baptist)

Eight Men Out (1988)
Production Company: Orion Pictures Corporation
Producers: Sarah Pillsbury, Midge Sanford
Co-Producer: Peggy Rajski
Executive Producers: Barbara Boyle, Jerry Offsay
Director: John Sayles
Screenplay: John Sayles
Based on the book *Eight Men Out: The Black Sox and the 1919 World Series* by Eliot Asinof
Cinematography: Robert Richardson
Editor: John Tintori
Original Music: Mason Daring

Main Cast: John Cusack (George 'Buck' Weaver), Clifton James (Charles 'Commie' Comiskey), Michael Lerner (Arnold Rothstein), Christopher Lloyd ('Sleepy' Bill Burns), John Mahoney (William 'Kid' Gleason), Charlie Sheen (Oscar 'Hap' Felsch), David Strathairn (Eddie Cicotte), D. B. Sweeney (Joseph 'Shoeless Joe' Jackson), Michael Rooker (Arnold 'Chick' Gandil), Don Harvey (Charles 'Swede' Risberg), James Read (Claude 'Lefty' Williams), Perry Lang (Fred McMullin), Gordon Clapp (Ray Schalk), Jace Alexander (Dickie Kerr), Bill Irwin (Eddie Collins), Richard Edson (Billy Maharg), Kevin Tighe (Joseph 'Sport' Sullivan), Michael Mantell (Abe Attell), John Sayles (Ring Lardner), Eliot Asinof (John Heydler), Clyde Bassett (Ban Johnson)

City of Hope (1991)
Production Companies: Esperanza Films Inc., The Samuel Goldwyn Company
Producers: Sarah Green, Maggie Renzi
Executive Producers: John Sloss, Harold Webb
Director: John Sayles
Screenplay: John Sayles
Cinematography: Robert Richardson
Editor: John Sayles
Original Music: Mason Daring
Main Cast: Vincent Spano (Nick Rinaldi), Stephen Mendillo (Yoyo), Chris Cooper (Riggs), Tony Lo Bianco (Joe Rinaldi), Joe Morton (Wynn), Jace Alexander (Bobby), Todd Graff (Zip), Scott Tiler (Vinnie), John Sayles (Carl), Frankie Faison (Levonne), Gloria Foster (Jeanette), Tom Wright (Malik), Angela Bassett (Reesha), David Strathairn (Asteroid), Maggie Renzi (Connie), Marianne Leone (Joann), S. J. Lang (Bauer), Anthony John Denison (Rizzo), Kevin Tighe (O'Brien), Barbara Williams (Angie), Joe Grifasi (Pauly Rinaldi), Gina Gershon (Laurie), Miriam Colon (Mrs Ramirez), Jude Ciccolella (Paddy), Jaime Tirelli (Fuentes), Bill Raymond (Les)

Passion Fish (1992)
Production Company: Atchafalaya
Producers: Sarah Green, Maggie Renzi
Director: John Sayles
Screenplay: John Sayles
Cinematography: Roger Deakin
Editor: John Sayles
Original Music: Mason Daring
Main Cast: Mary McDonnell (May-Alice Culhane), Alfre Woodard (Chantelle), Lenore Banks (Nurse Quick), Vondie Curtis-Hall (Sugar LeDoux), Will Mahoney (Max), David Strathairn (Rennie), Leo Burmester (Reeves)

The Secret of Roan Inish (1994)
Production Companies: Jones Entertainment Group, Skerry Productions
Producers: Sarah Green, Maggie Renzi
Associate Producer: R. Paul Miller
Executive Producers: Glenn R. Jones, Peter Newman, John Sloss
Director: John Sayles
Screenplay: John Sayles
Based on the book *The Secret of Ron Mor Skerry* by Rosalie K. Fry
Cinematography: Haskell Wexler
Editor: John Sayles
Original Music: Mason Daring
Main Cast: Jeni Courtney (Fiona), Dave Duffy (Jim), Mick Lally (Hugh), Eileen Colgan (Tess), Richard Sheridan (Eamon), Fergal McElherron (Sean Michael), John Lynch (Tadhg), Frankie McCafferty (Tim), Gerald Rooney (Liam), Susan Lynch (Selkie), Suzanne Gallagher (Selkie's daughter), Cillian Byrne (Jamie), Linda Greer (Brigid)

Lone Star (1996)
Production Companies: Columbia Pictures Corporation, Castle Rock Entertainment, Rio Dulce
Producers: R. Paul Miller, Maggie Renzi
Associate Producer: Jan Foster
Executive Producer: John Sloss
Director: John Sayles
Screenplay: John Sayles
Cinematography: Stuart Dryburgh
Editor: John Sayles
Original Music: Mason Daring
Main Cast: Stephen Mendillo (Sgt Cliff), Stephen J. Lang (Sgt Mikey), Chris Cooper (Sheriff Sam Deeds), Elizabeth Peña (Pilar Cruz), Clifton James (Mayor Hollis Pogue), Toby Frank (Fenton), Miriam Colon (Mercedes Cruz), Kris Kristofferson (Sheriff Charlie Wade), Jeff Monahan (Young Hollis), Matthew McConaughey (Buddy Deeds), Joe Morton (Colonel Delmore Payne), Ron Canada (Otis Payne)

Men With Guns/Hombres armados (1997)
Production Companies: Anarchists' Convention Films, Clear Blue Sky Productions, Independent Film Channel, Lexington Road Productions
Producers: R. Paul Miller, Maggie Renzi
Co-Producer: Bertha Navarro
Executive Producer: Jody Patton
Director: John Sayles
Screenplay: John Sayles
Cinematography: Slawomir Idziak
Editor: John Sayles
Original Music: Mason Daring
Main Cast: Federico Luppi (Dr Fuentes), Damián Delgado (Domingo), Dan Rivera González (Conejo), Alejandro Springhall (Carlos), Tania Cruz (Graciela), Damián Alcázar (Padre Portillo), Mandy Patinkin (Andrew), Kathryn Grody (Harriet), Rafael de Quevedo (General), Carmen Madrid (Angela), Esteban Soberanes (Raúl)

Limbo (1999)
Production Company: Green/Renzi
Producer: Maggie Renzi
Associate Producer: Sarah Connors
Director: John Sayles
Screenplay: John Sayles
Cinematography: Haskell Wexler
Editor: John Sayles
Original Music: Mason Daring
Main Cast: Mary Elizabeth Mastrantonio (Donna De Angelo), David Strathairn ('Jumpin' Joe Gastineau), Vanessa Martinez (Noelle De Angelo), Kris Kristofferson ('Smilin' Jack Johannson), Casey Siemaszko (Bobby Gastineau)

Sunshine State (2002)
Production Company: Anarchists' Convention Films
Producer: Maggie Renzi
Associate Producer: Nancy Schafer
Director: John Sayles
Screenplay: John Sayles
Cinematography: Patrick Cady
Editor: John Sayles
Original Music: Mason Daring

Main Cast: Alex Lewis (Terrell), Alan King (Murray Silver), James McDaniel (Reggie Perry), Angela Bassett (Desiree Perry), Edie Falco (Marly Temple), Cullen Douglas (Jefferson Cash), Clifton James (Buster Bidwell), Eliot Asinof (Silent Sam), Timothy Hutton (Jack Meadows), Miguel Ferrer (Lester), Gordon Clapp (Earl Pinkney), Mary Steenburgen (Francine Pinkney), Marc Blucas (Scotty Duvall), Ralph Waite (Furman Temple), Jane Alexander (Delia Temple)

Casa de los Babys (2003)
Production Companies: IFC Films, Springall Pictures, Blue Magic Pictures
Producers: Alejandro Springall, Lemore Syran
Associate Producer: Melissa Marr
Executive Producers: Caroline Kaplan, Jonathan Sehring
Director: John Sayles
Screenplay: John Sayles
Based on the short story 'Casa de los Babys' by John Sayles
Cinematography: Mauricio Rubinstein
Editor: John Sayles
Original Music: Mason Daring
Main Cast: Angelina Peláez (Doña Mercedes), Vanessa Martínez (Asunción), Rita Moreno (Señora Muñoz), Daryl Hannah (Skipper), Lili Taylor (Leslie), Mary Steenburgen (Gayle), Marcia Gay Harden (Nan), Maggie Gyllenhaal (Jennifer), Susan Lynch (Eileen), Martha Higareda (Celia), Tony Marcin (Celia's mother)

Silver City (2004)
Production Company: Anarchists' Convention Films
Producer: Maggie Renzi
Co-Producer: Robert Lansing Parker
Associate Producers: Suzanne Ceresko, Sam Tedesco
Director: John Sayles
Screenplay: John Sayles
Cinematography: Haskell Wexler
Editor: John Sayles
Original Music: Mason Daring
Main Cast: Chris Cooper (Dickie Pilager), Richard Dreyfuss (Chuck Raven), Donevon Martinez (Lazaro Huerta), James Gammon (Sheriff Joe Skaggs), Danny Huston (Danny O'Brien), David Clennon (Mort Seymour), Mary Kay Place (Grace Seymour), Tim Roth (Mitch Paine), Maria Bello (Nora Allardyce), Miguel Ferrer (Cliff Castleton), Billy Zane (Chandler Tyson), Michael Murphy (Senator Judson Pilager), Ralph Waite (Casey Lyle), Kris Kristofferson (Wes Benteen), Daryl Hannah (Maddy Pilager)

Honeydripper (2007)
Production Companies: Anarchists' Convention Films/Honeydripper Films
Producer: Maggie Renzi
Associate Producers: Ira Deutchman, Susan Kirr, Mark Wynns
Director: John Sayles
Screenplay: John Sayles
Based on the short story 'Keeping Time' by John Sayles
Cinematography: Dick Pope
Editor: John Sayles
Original Music: Mason Daring
Main Cast: Danny Glover (Tyrone Purvis), Lisa Gay Hamilton (Delilah), Yaya DaCosta (China Doll), Charles S. Dutton (Maceo), Vondie Curtis-Hall (Slick), Gary Clark Jr (Sonny), Mable John (Bertha Mae), Stacy Keach (Sheriff), Mary Steenburgen (Amanda Winship), Albert Hall (Reverend Cutlip), Absolom Adams (Lonnie), Arthur Lee Williams (Metalmouth Sims), John Sayles (Zeke)

BIBLIOGRAPHY

Aglietta, Michel (1979) *A Theory of Capitalist Regulation: The U.S. Experience*, trans. David Fernbach. London: New Left Books.

Althusser, Louis (1971 [1970]) 'Ideology and Ideological State Apparatuses (Notes Towards an Investigation)', in *Lenin and Philosophy and Other Essays*. London: New Left Books, 121–73.

American Psychiatric Association (2000) *Diagnostic and Statistical Manual of Mental Disorders*, fourth edition. Washington: American Psychiatric Association.

Anderson, Terry H. (1995) *The Movement and the Sixties: Protest in America from Greensboro to Wounded Knee*. Oxford: Oxford University Press.

Armstrong, Philip, Andrew Glyn and John Harrison (1991) *Capitalism Since 1945*. Oxford: Blackwell.

Asinof, Eliot (1987) *Eight Men Out: The Black Sox and the 1919 World Series*. New York: Owl Books.

Badiou, Alain (2002) *Ethics: An Essay on the Understanding of Evil*, trans. Peter Hallward. London: Verso.

＿＿ (2006) *Being and Event*, trans. Oliver Feltham. London: Continuum.

Baguley, David (1990) *Naturalist Fiction: The Entropic Vision*. Cambridge: Cambridge University Press.

Bakhtin, M. M. (1981) 'Discourse in the Novel', in *The Dialogic Imagination: Four Essays*, ed. Michael Holquist, trans. Caryl Emerson and Michael Holquist. Austin: University of Texas Press, 259–422.

Barker, Jason (2001) *Alain Badiou: A Critical Introduction*. London: Pluto.

Baron, David (1999) 'Sayles Talk', in Diane Carson (ed.) *John Sayles Interviews*. Jackson: University of Mississippi Press, 133–5.

Baudrillard, Jean (1983) *Simulations*, trans. Paul Foss, Paul Patton and Philip Beitchman. New York: Semiotext(e).

Baudry, Jean-Louis (1985 [1970]) 'Ideological Effects of the Basic Cinematographic Apparatus', in Bill Nichols (ed.) *Movies and Methods, Volume II*. Berkeley: University of California Press, 531–42.

Bazin, André (1972) *What is Cinema? Volume II*, ed. and trans. Hugh Gray. Berkeley: University of California Press.

Benjamin, Walter (1973) *Understanding Brecht*, trans. Anna Bostock. London: NLB.

Berman, Marshall (1983) *All That Is Solid Melts Into Air: The Experience of Modernity*. London: Verso.

Bernardi, Daniel (1998) *Star Trek and History: Race-ing Toward a White Future*. New Brunswick: Rutgers University Press.

Biskind, Peter (1998) *Easy Riders, Raging Bulls: How the Sex'n'Drugs'n'Rock'n'Roll Generation Saved Hollywood*. London: Bloomsbury.

Bloch, Ernst (1986) *The Principle of Hope,* trans. Neville Plaice, Stephen Plaice and Paul Knight. Oxford: Basil Blackwell.

Bloom, Harold (1973) *The Anxiety of Influence: A Theory of Poetry*. Oxford: Oxford University Press.

Booth, Wayne C. (1961) *The Rhetoric of Fiction*. Chicago: University of Chicago Press.

Bordo, Susan (1989) 'Reading the Slender Body', in Mary Jacobus, Evelyn Fox Keller and Sally Shuttleworth (eds) *Body/Politics: Women and the Discourse of Science*. London: Routledge, 83–112.

Bottomore, Tom (ed.) (2001) *A Dictionary of Marxist Thought*, second edition. Oxford: Blackwell.

Bould, Mark (2002) 'The Dreadful Credibility of Absurd Things: A Tendency in Fantasy Theory', *Historical Materialism*, 10, 4, 51–88.

____ (2003) 'Apocalypse Here and Now: Making Sense of *The Texas Chain Saw Massacre*', in Gary D. Rhodes (ed.) *Horror at the Drive-In: Essays in Popular Americana*. Jefferson: McFarland, 97–112.

Brandner, Gary (1978) *The Howling*. London: Hamlyn.

Brecht, Bertolt (1964) *Brecht on Theatre*, trans. John Willett. London: Methuen.

____ (1980a [1938]) 'On the Formalist Character of the Theory of Realism', in Theodor Adorno, Walter Benjamin, Ernst Bloch, Bertolt Brecht and Georg Lukács *Aesthetics and Politics*, ed. Ronald Taylor, trans. Anya Bostock, Stuart Hood, Rodney Livingstone, Francis McDonagh and Harry Zohn. London: Verso, 70–6.

____ (1980b [1938]) 'Remarks on an Essay', in Theodor Adorno, Walter Benjamin, Ernst Bloch, Bertolt Brecht and Georg Lukács *Aesthetics and Politics*, ed. Ronald Taylor, trans. Anya Bostock, Stuart Hood, Rodney Livingstone, Francis McDonagh and Harry Zohn. London: Verso, 76–9.

____ (1980c [1938]) 'Popularity and Realism', in Theodor Adorno, Walter Benjamin, Ernst Bloch, Bertolt Brecht and Georg Lukács *Aesthetics and Politics*, ed. Ronald Taylor, trans. Anya Bostock, Stuart Hood, Rodney Livingstone, Francis McDonagh and Harry Zohn. London: Verso, 79–85.

Britton, Andrew (1992) '*Detour*', in Ian Cameron (ed.) *The Movie Book of Film Noir*. London: Studio Vista, 174–83.

Brogan, Hugh (1990) *The Penguin History of the United States of America*. London: Penguin.

Budd, Louis J. (1995) 'The American Background', in Donald Pizer (ed.) *The Cambridge Companion to American Realism and Naturalism: Howells to London*. Cambridge: Cambridge University Press, 21–46.

Buford, Bill (1983) 'Editorial', *Granta 8. Dirty Realism: New Writings from America*. Cambridge: Granta Publications, 4–5.

Bukatman, Scott (1998) 'Zooming Out: The End of Offscreen Space', in Jon Lewis (ed.) *The New American Cinema*. Durham: Duke University Press, 248–72.

Bull, Malcolm (1998) 'Slavery and the Multiple Self', *New Left Review*, 231, 94–131.

Campbell, Donna M. (1997) *Resisting Regionalism: Gender and Naturalism in American Fiction, 1885–1915*. Athens: Ohio University Press.

Carson, Diane (ed.) (1999) *John Sayles Interviews*. Jackson: University of Mississippi Press.

Carson, Diane and Heidi Kenaga (eds) (2006) *Sayles Talk: Essays on Independent Filmmaker John Sayles*. Detroit: Wayne State University Press.

Castells, Manuel (2000a) *The Information Age: Economy, Society and Culture, Volume I: The Rise of the Network Society*, second edition. Oxford: Blackwell.

____ (2000b) *The Information Age: Economy, Society and Culture, Volume III: End of Millennium*, second edition. Oxford: Blackwell.

____ (2004) *The Information Age: Economy, Society and Culture, Volume II: The Power of Identity*, second edition. Oxford: Blackwell.

Cavell, Stanley (1976 [1967]) 'A Matter of Meaning It', *Must We Mean What We Say?: A Book of Essays*. Cambridge: Cambridge University Press, 213–37.

Ceceña, Ana Esther and Andrés Barreda (1998) 'Chiapas and the Global Restructuring of Capital', in John Holloway and Eloína Peláez (eds) *Zapatista!: Reinventing Revolution in Mexico*. London: Pluto Press, 39–63.

Chute, David (1999 [1981]) 'John Sayles: Designated Writer', in Diane Carson (ed.) *John Sayles Interviews*. Jackson: University of Mississippi Press, 3–14.

Civello, Paul (1994) *American Literary Naturalism and its Twentieth-Century Transformations: Frank Norris, Ernest Hemingway, Don DeLillo*. Athens: University of Georgia Press.

Collier, George A. with Elizabeth Lowery Quaratiello (1994) *Basta! Land and the Zapatista Rebellion in Chiapas*. Oakland: The Institute for Food and Development Policy.

Comolli, Jean-Luc and Jean Narboni (1999 [1969]) 'Cinema/Ideology/Criticism', in Leo Braudy and Marshall Cohen (eds) *Film Theory and Criticism: Introductory Readings*, fifth edition. Oxford: Oxford University Press, 752–59.

Crane, Stephen (1970) 'Above All Things', in *Stephen Crane in the West and Mexico*, ed. Joseph Katz. Kent: Kent State University Press, 74–7.

Creed, Barbara (1993) *The Monstrous Feminine: Film, Feminism, Psychoanalysis*. London: Routledge.

Crowdus, Gary and Leonard Quart (1999 [1991]) 'Where the Hope Is: An Interview with John Sayles', in Diane Carson (ed.) *John Sayles Interviews*. Jackson: University of Mississippi Press, 145–55.

Csicsery-Ronay, Jr, Istvan (2002) 'Dis-Imagined Communities: Science Fiction and the Future of Nations', in Veronica Hollinger and Joan Gordon (eds) *Edging into the Future: Science Fiction and Contemporary Cultural Transformation*. Philadelphia: University of Pennsylvania Press, 217–37.

Daniel, Jamie Owen (1997) 'Reclaiming the "Terrain of Fantasy": Speculations on Ernst Bloch, Memory, and the Resurgence of Nationalism', in Jamie Owen Daniel and Tom Moylan (eds) *Not Yet: Reconsidering Ernst Bloch*. London: Verso, 53–62.

Davis, Mike (1999) *Prisoners of the American Dream: Politics and Economics in the History of the U.S. Working Class*. London: Verso.

Debord, Guy (1983) *Society of the Spectacle*. Detroit: Black & Red.

den Tandt, Christophe (1998) *The Urban Sublime in American Literary Naturalism*. Urbana: University of Illinois Press.

Dos Passos, John (1963) *Mid-Century*. London: Mayflower-Dell.

____ (1966) *U.S.A.* Harmondsworth: Penguin.

____ (1969) *Manhattan Transfer*. London: Sphere.

Du Bois, W. E. B. (1965) *The Souls of Black Folks*, in *Three Negro Classics*. New York: Avon, 207–389.

Dudley, John (2004) *A Man's Game: Masculinity and the Anti-Aesthetics of American Literary Naturalism*. Tuscaloosa: University of Alabama Press.

Dyer, Richard (1985 [1977]) 'Entertainment and Utopia', in Bill Nichols (ed.) *Movies and Methods, Volume II*. Berkeley: University of California Press, 220–32.

Ebert, Roger (1999 [1993]) 'A Filmmaker with "Passion"', in Diane Carson (ed.) *John Sayles Interviews*. Jackson: University of Mississippi Press, 160–3.

Engels, Friedrich (1975 [1844]) 'The Condition of the Working-Class in England', in Karl Marx and Friedrich Engels *Collected Works, Volume 4: 1844–1845*. London: Lawrence & Wishart, 295–583.

____ (1990 [1892]) 'Introduction to the English Edition of *Socialism: Utopian and Scientific*', in Karl Marx and Friedrich Engels *Collected Works, Volume 27, Engels 1890–1895*. London: Lawrence & Wishart, 278–302.

____ (2001 [1890]) 'Engels to Joseph Bloch [21–2 September 1890]', in Karl Marx and Friedrich Engels *Collected Works, Volume 49, Engels 1890–1892*. London: Lawrence & Wishart, 33–7.

Failler, Angela (2006) 'Appetizing Loss: Anorexia as an Experiment in Living', *Eating Disorders*, 14, 99–107.

Federici, Silvia (2004) *Caliban and the Witch: Women, the Body and Primitive Accumulation*. New York: Autonomedia.

Felleman, Susan (2006) 'Oedipus Edits (*Lone Star*)', in Diane Carson and Heidi Kenaga (eds) *Sayles Talk: New Perspectives on Independent Filmmaker John Sayles*. Detroit: Wayne State University Press, 158–73.

Fiske, John (1989) *Understanding Popular Culture*. London: Routledge.

Fleissner, Jennifer L. (2004) *Women, Compulsion, Modernity: The Moment of American Naturalism*. Chicago: University of Chicago Press.

Foner, Eric (1996) 'A Conversation Between Eric Foner and John Sayles', in M. C. Crane (ed.) *Past Imperfect: History According to the Movies*. London: Cassell, 11–28.

Freedman, Carl (2000) *Critical Theory and Science Fiction*. Hanover: Wesleyan University Press.

____ (2002) *The Incomplete Projects: Marxism, Modernity, and the Politics of Culture*. Middletown: Wesleyan University Press.

Freud, Sigmund (1955 [1919]) 'The Uncanny', in *The Standard Edition of the Complete Psychological Works of Sigmund Freud*, ed. and trans. James Strachey. London: The Hogarth Press and The Institute of Psycho-Analysis, 217–56.

Fry, Rosalie K. (1959) *Secret of the Ron Mor Skerry*. New York: E. P. Dutton.

Gaines, Jane (1990) 'Women and Representation: Can We Enjoy Alternative Pleasure?', in Patricia Erens (ed.) *Issues in Feminist Film Criticism*. Bloomington: Indiana University Press, 75–92.

Garnett, Rhys (1990) 'Dracula and The Beetle: Imperial and Sexual Guilt and Fear in Late Victorian Fantasy', in Rhys Garnett and R. J. Ellis (eds) *Science Fiction: Roots and Branches*. Basingstoke: Macmillan, 30–54.

Garwood, Ian (2006) 'The Pop Song in Film', in John Gibbs and Douglas Pye (eds) *Close-Up 01*. London: Wallflower Press, 89–170.

Geoghegan, Vincent (1997) 'Remembering the Future', in Jamie Owen Daniel and Tom Moylan (eds) *Not Yet: Reconsidering Ernst Bloch*. London: Verso, 15–32.

Geras, Norman (1971) 'Essence and Appearance: Aspects of Fetishism in Marx's Capital', *New Left Review* 65, 69–85.

Gledhill, Christine (1987) 'The Melodramatic Field: An Investigation', in Christine Gledhill (ed.) *Home Is Where the Heart Is: Studies in Melodrama and the Woman's Film*. London: British Film Institute, 5–39.

Gramsci, Antonio (1971) *Selections from the Prison Notebooks of Antonio Gramsci*, ed. and trans. Quintin Hoare and Geoffrey Nowell-Smith. London: Lawrence and Wishart.

Gunning, Tom (1994) *D. W. Griffiths and the Origins of American Narrative Film: The Early Years at Biograph*. Urbana: University of Illinois Press.

Hegel, G. W. F. (1977) *Phenomenology of Spirit*, trans. A.V. Miller. Oxford: Oxford University Press.

Heidegger, Martin (1993 [1954]) 'The Question Concerning Technology', in *Basic Writings from Being and Time (1927) to The Task of Thinking (1964)*, revised and expanded edition, ed. David Farrell Krell. London: Routledge, 307–41.

Higham, John (1975) *Send These To Me: Jews and Other Immigrants in Urban America*. Baltimore: Johns Hopkins University Press.

Hillier, Jim (1993) *The New Hollywood*. London: Studio Vista.

Howard, June (1985) *Form and History in American Literary Naturalism*. Chapel Hill: University of North Carolina Press.

Jameson, Fredric (1990) *Late Marxism: Adorno, or The Persistence of the Dialectic*. London: Verso.

____ (1991) *Postmodernism, or, The Cultural Logic of Late Capitalism*. London: Verso.

____ (1994) *The Seeds of Time*. New York: Columbia University Press.

____ (1998 [1989]) 'The Antinomies of Postmodernism', in *The Cultural Turn: Selected Writings on the Postmodern, 1983–1998*. London: Verso, 50–72.

____ (1999) 'Marx's Purloined Letter', in Michael Spriker (ed.) *Ghostly Demarcations: A Symposium on Jacques Derrida's Spectres of Marx*. London: Verso, 26–67.

____ (2005a) 'Introduction: Utopia Now', in *Archaeologies of the Future: The Desire Called Utopia and Other Science Fictions*. London: Verso, xi–xvi.

____ (2005b [1982]) 'Progress versus Utopia, or, Can We Imagine the Future?', in *Archaeologies of the Future: The Desire Called Utopia and Other Science Fictions*. London: Verso, 281–95.

Kaes, Anton (1989) *From Hitler to Heimat: The Return of History as Film*. Cambridge: Harvard University Press.

Kaplan, Amy (1988) *The Social Construction of American Realism*. Chicago: University of Chicago Press.

King, Geoff (2005) *American Independent Cinema*. London: I. B. Tauris.

Klevan, Andrew (2000) *Disclosure of the Everyday: Undramatic Achievement in Narrative Film*. Trowbridge: Flicks Books.

Larrain, Jorge (2001) 'Base and superstructure', in Tom Bottomore (ed.) *A Dictionary of Marxist Thought*, second edition. Oxford: Blackwell, 45–8.

Latour, Bruno (1993) *We Have Never Been Modern*, trans. Catherine Porter. Cambridge: Harvard University Press.

_____ (1999) *Pandora's Hope: Essays on the Reality of Science Studies*. Cambridge: Harvard University Press.

Lebowitz, Michael A. (2003) *Beyond Capital: Marx's Political Economy of the Working Class*, second edition. Basingstoke: Palgrave.

Lee, Martyn J. (1993) *Consumer Culture Reborn: Cultural Politics of Consumption*. London: Routledge.

Lehan, Richard (1995) 'The European Background', in Donald Pizer (ed.) *The Cambridge Companion to American Realism and Naturalism: Howells to London*. Cambridge: Cambridge University Press, 47–73.

Lenin, V. I. (1961 [1933]) 'Conspectus of Hegel's Book *The Science of Logic*', in *Collected Works, Volume 38: Philosophical Notebooks*. Moscow: Foreign Languages Publishing House, 86–237.

Leslie, Esther (2002) *Hollywood Flatlands: Animation, Critical Theory and the Avant-Garde*. London: Verso.

Levitas, Ruth (1990) *The Concept of Utopia*. Syracuse: Syracuse University Press.

Link, Eric Carl (2004) *The Vast and Terrible Drama: American Literary Naturalism in the Late Nineteenth Century*. Tuscaloosa: University of Alabama Press.

Lukács, Georg (1971) *History and Class Consciousness: Studies in Marxist Dialectics*, trans. Rodney Livingstone. London: Merlin Press.

_____ (1978a [1954]) 'Art and Objective Truth', in *Writer and Critic and other Essays*, ed. and trans. Arthur Kahn. London: Merlin Press, 25–60.

_____ (1978b [1936]) 'Narrate or Describe?', in *Writer and Critic and other Essays*, ed. and trans. Arthur Kahn. London: Merlin Press, 110–48.

McCabe, Colin (1985 [1974]) 'Realism and Cinema: Notes on Some Brechtian Theses', *Tracking the Signifier. Theoretical Essays: Film, Linguistics, Literature*. Minneapolis: University of Minnesota Press, 33–57.

McClintock, Anne (1995) *Imperial Leather: Race, Gender, and Sexuality in the Colonial Contest*. London: Routledge.

McHale, Brian (1989) *Postmodernist Fiction*. London: Routledge.

McNally, David (2001) *Bodies of Meaning: Studies on Language, Labor, and Liberation*. New York: SUNY Press.

Mair, Jan (2002) 'Rewriting the "American Dream": Postmodernism and Otherness in *Independence Day*', in Ziauddin Sardar and Sean Cubitt (eds) *Aliens R Us: The Other in Science Fiction Cinema*. London: Pluto, 34–50.

Marglin, Stephen A. and Juliet B. Schor (eds) (1990) *The Golden Age of Capitalism*. Oxford: Clarendon.

Marx, Karl (1975 [1844]) 'Economic and Philosophic Manuscripts of 1844', in Karl Marx and Friedrich Engels *Collected Works, Volume 3: 1843–44*. London: Lawrence & Wishart, 229–346.

_____ (1976) *Capital, Volume 1*, trans. Ben Fowkes. Harmondsworth: Penguin.

_____ (1979 [1852]) 'The Eighteenth Brumaire of Louis Bonaparte', in Karl Marx and Friedrich Engels *Collected Works, Volume 11: 1851–1853*. London: Lawrence & Wishart, 99–197.

_____ (1986 [1857–58]) 'Economic Manuscripts of 1857–1858', in Karl Marx and Friedrich Engels *Collected Works, Volume 28: 1857–1861*. London: Lawrence & Wishart.

_____ (1987 [1859]) 'Preface to *A Contribution to the Critique of Political Economy*', in Karl Marx and Friedrich Engels *Collected Works, Volume 29, 1857–1861*. London: Lawrence & Wishart, 261–65.

_____ (1989) 'Theories of Surplus-Value', in Karl Marx and Friedrich Engels *Collected Works, Volume 31: 1861–1863*. London: Lawrence & Wishart.

_____ (1996 [1863]) 'Capital, Volume One', in Karl Marx and Friedrich Engels *Collected Works, Volume 35*. London: Lawrence & Wishart.

Marx, Karl and Friedrich Engels (1976a [1845–46]) 'The German Ideology', in Karl Marx and Friedrich Engels *Collected Works, Volume 5: 1845–1847*. London: Lawrence & Wishart, 19–539.

_____ (1976b [1848]) 'Manifesto of the Communist Party', in Karl Marx and Friedrich Engels *Collected Works, Volume 6: 1845–1848*. London: Lawrence & Wishart, 477–519.

Mellen, Joan (1978) *Big Bad Wolves: Masculinity in the American Film*. London: Elm Tree.

Merck, Mandy (1986) '"*Lianna*" and the Lesbians of Art Cinema', in Charlotte Brunsdon (ed.) *Films for Women*. London: British Film Institute, 166–175.

Merritt, Greg (2000) *Celluloid Mavericks: A History of American Independent Film*. New York: Thunder's Mouth Press.

Michaels, Walter Benn (1987) *The Gold Standard and the Logic of Naturalism*. Berkeley: University of California Press.

Miéville, China (2002) 'Editorial Introduction', *Historical Materialism: Research in Critical Marxist Theory*, 10, 4, 39–49.

Molyneaux, Gerry (2000) *John Sayles: An Unauthorized Biography of the Pioneering Indie Filmmaker*. Los Angeles: Renaissance Books.

MPAA (1999) 'US Economic Review'. Online. Available at http://www.mpaa.org/useconomicreview/ 1999Economic/index.htm (accessed 28 September 2008).

_____ (2006) '2006 U.S. Theatrical Market Statistics'. Online. Available at http://www.mpaa.org/2006-US-Theatrical-Market-Statistics-Report.pdf (accessed 28 September 2008).

Mulvey, Laura (1975) 'Visual Pleasure and Narrative Cinema', *Screen*, 16, 3, 6–18.

_____ (1996) 'The Carapace that Failed: Ousmane Sembène's *Xala*', in *Fetishism and Curiosity*. London: British Film Institute, 118–36.

Neale, Steve (2000) *Genre and Hollywood*. London: Routledge.

Neff, Gina (2002) 'Reel to Real History: A Conversation with John Sayles and Howard Zinn', *Radical Society*, 29, 2, 25–38.

Nevins, Joseph (2002) *Operation Gatekeeper: The Rise of the 'Illegal Alien' and the Making of the U.S.-Mexico Boundary*. New York: Routledge.

Norris, Frank (1994a) *The Octopus*. London: Penguin.

_____ (1994b) *The Pit*. London: Penguin.

Norwood, Stephen H. (2002) *Strikebreaking & Intimidation: Mercenaries and Masculinity in Twentieth-Century America*. Chapel Hill: University of North Carolina Press.

Nye, David E. (1994) *American Technological Sublime*. Cambridge: MIT Press.

Osborne, David (1999 [1982]) 'John Sayles: From Hoboken to Hollywood – And Back', in Diane Carson (ed.) *John Sayles Interviews*. Jackson: University of Mississippi Press, 27–36.

Patton, Cindy (1995) 'What is a Nice Lesbian Like You Doing in a Film Like This?', in Tamsin Wilton (ed.) *Immortal Invisible: Lesbians and the Moving Image*. London: Routledge, 20–33.

Peary, Gerald (1999 [1984]) 'John Sayles: From Hoboken to Harlem, Via Outer Space', in Diane Carson (ed.) *John Sayles Interviews*. Jackson: University of Mississippi Press, 56–66.

Perkins, V. F. (1990a) *Film as Film: Understanding and Judging Movies*. London: Penguin.

_____ (1990b) 'Film Authorship: The Premature Burial', *CineAction!*, 21/22, 57–64.

Pfeil, Fred (1995) 'Rock Incorporated: Plugging into Axl and Bruce', in *White Guys: Studies in Postmodern Domination and Difference*. London: Verso, 71–104.

Piore, Michael J. and Charles F. Sable (1984) *The Second Industrial Divide: Possibilities for Prosperity*. New York: Basic Books.

Pizer, Donald (1995) 'Introduction: The Problem of Definition', in *The Cambridge Companion to American Realism and Naturalism: Howells to London*. Cambridge: Cambridge University Press, 1–18.

Renshaw, Patrick (1968) *The Wobblies: The Story of Syndicalism in the United States*. New York: Anchor.

Ricks, Christopher (1998) 'Literature and the Matter of Fact', in *Essays in Appreciation*. Oxford: Oxford University Press, 280–310.

Rieser, Klaus (2006) 'Men in Context: Gender in *Matewan* and *Men With Guns*', in Diane Carson and Heidi Kenaga (eds) *Sayles Talk: New Perspectives on Independent Filmmaker John Sayles*. Detroit: Wayne State University Press, 174–193.

Russo, Vito (1987) *The Celluloid Closet: Homosexuality and the Movies*, revised edition. New York: Harper & Row.

Ryan, Jack (1998) *John Sayles, Filmmaker: A Critical Study of the Independent Writer-Director; With a Filmography and a Bibliography*. Jefferson: McFarland.

Ryan, Michael and Douglas Kellner (1990) *Camera Politica: The Politics and Ideology of Contemporary Hollywood Film*. Bloomington: Indiana University Press.

Sardar, Ziauddin (2002) 'Introduction', in Ziauddin Sardar and Sean Cubitt (eds) *Aliens R Us: The Other in Science Fiction Cinema*. London: Pluto Press, 1–17.

Savage, Lon (1990) *Thunder in the Mountains: The West Virginia Mine War, 1920–21*. Pittsburgh: University of Pittsburgh Press.

Sayles, John (1978a) *Piranha*. Unpublished screenplay dated 1 March.

_____ (1978b) *Union Dues*. London: André Deutsch.

_____ (1979a) 'Home for Wayfarers', in *The Anarchists' Convention*. Boston: Little, Brown, 3–23.

_____ (1979b) 'At the Anarchists' Convention', in *The Anarchists' Convention*. Boston: Little, Brown, 24–34.

_____ (1987a) *Thinking in Pictures: The Making of the Movie 'Matewan'*. Boston: Houghton Mifflin.

_____ (1987b) *Pride of the Bimbos*. New York: Charles Scribner's Sons.

_____ (1992) *Los Gusanos*. London: Penguin.

_____ (1996) 'The Big Picture: John Sayles', *Mother Jones*. Online. Available at: http://www.motherjones.com/mother_jones/MJ96/sayles.html (accessed 3 August 2001).

_____ (1998a) 'Introduction', in *Men with Guns & Lone Star*. London: Faber and Faber, vii–x.

_____ (1998b) *Men with Guns & Lone Star*. London: Faber and Faber.

_____ (2004a) *Dillinger in Hollywood: New and Selected Short Stories*. New York: Nation Books.

_____ (2004b) 'The Halfway Diner', in *Dillinger in Hollywood: New and Selected Short Stories*. New York: Nation Books, 15–38.

_____ (2004c) *Silver City and Other Screenplays*. New York: Nation Books.

Schaefer, Dennis and Larry Salvato (1984) 'Haskell Wexler', in *Masters of Light: Conversations with Contemporary Cinematographers*. Berkeley: University of California Press, 247–66.

Schlesinger, Tom (1999 [1981]) 'Putting People Together: An Interview with John Sayles', in Diane Carson (ed.) *John Sayles Interviews*. Jackson: University of Mississippi Press, 15–26.

Scott, James C. (1990) *Domination and the Arts of Resistance: Hidden Transcripts*. New Haven: Yale University Press.

Seltzer, Mark (1992) *Bodies and Machines*. New York: Routledge.

Shapiro, Alan N. (2004) *Star Trek: Technologies of Disappearance*. Berlin: Avinus Verlag.

Shapiro, Mary J. (1986) *Gateway to Liberty: The Story of the Statue of Liberty and Ellis Island*. New York: Vintage.

Sloterdijk, Peter (1988) *Critique of Cynical Reason*, trans. Michael Eldred. London: Verso.

Smith, Gavin (ed.) (1998) *Sayles on Sayles*. London: Faber and Faber.

Smith, Greg M. (2006) 'Passersby and Politics: *City of Hope* and the Multiple Protagonist Film', in Diane Carson and Heidi Kenaga (eds) *Sayles Talk: New Perspectives on Independent Filmmaker John Sayles*. Detroit: Wayne State University Press, 117–33.

Smith, James (1973) *Melodrama*. London: Methuen.

Smith, Murray (1998) 'Theses on the Philosophy of Hollywood History', in Steve Neale and Murray Smith (eds) *Contemporary Hollywood Cinema*. London: Routledge, 3–20.

Solanas, Fernando and Octavio Getino (2000 [1969]) 'Towards a Third Cinema', in Robert Stam and Toby Miller (eds) *Film and Theory: An Anthology*. Oxford: Blackwell, 265–86.

Stacey, Jackie (1995) '"If You Don't Play, You Can't Win": *Desert Hearts* and the Lesbian Romance Film', in Tamsin Wilton (ed.) *Immortal Invisible: Lesbians and the Moving Image*. London: Routledge, 92–114.

Straayer, Chris (1984) '*Personal Best*: Lesbian/Feminist Audience', *Jump Cut*, 29, 40–4.

_____ (1996) *Deviant Eyes, Deviant Bodies: Sexual Re-Orientation in Film and Video*. New York: Columbia University Press.

Tichi, Cecelia (1987) *Shifting Gears: Technology, Literature, Culture in Modernist America*. Chapel Hill: University of North Carolina Press.

Todorov, Tzvetan (1975) *The Fantastic: A Structural Approach to a Literary Genre*, trans. Richard Howard. Ithaca: Cornell University Press.

Turim, Maureen and Mika Turim-Nygren (2006) 'Of Spectral Mothers and Lost Children: War, Folklore, and Psychoanalysis in *The Secret of Roan Inish*', in Diane Carson and Heidi Kenaga (eds) *Sayles Talk: New Perspectives on Independent Filmmaker John Sayles*. Detroit: Wayne State University Press, 134–57.

Turner, Bryan S. (1992) *Regulating Bodies: Essays in Medical Sociology*. London: Routledge.

Vint, Sherryl and Mark Bould (2006) 'All That Melts Into Air is Solid: Rematerialising Capital in *Cube* and *Videodrome*', *Socialism and Democracy*, 42, 217–43.

Walker, Michael (1982) 'Melodrama and the American Cinema', *Movie*, 29/30, 2–38.

Walsh, Martin (1981) 'Draft Outline: The Brechtian Aspect of Radical Cinema', in *The Brechtian Aspect of Radical Cinema: Essays by Martin Walsh*, ed. Keith M. Griffiths. London: British Film Institute, 129–31.

Wayne, Mike (2002) 'A Violent Peace: Robert Guédiguian's *La Ville est tranquille*', *Historical Materialism: Research in Critical Marxist Theory*, 10, 2, 219–27.

____ (2003) *Marxism and Media Studies: Key Concepts and Contemporary Trends*. London: Pluto.

Wegner, Phillip E. (2002) *Imaginary Communities: Utopia, the Nation, and the Spatial Histories of Modernity*. Berkeley: University of California Press.

Wilinsky, Barbara (2001) *Sure Seaters: The Emergence of Art House Cinema*. Minneapolis: University of Minnesota Press.

Williams, Linda (1987 [1984]) '"Something Else Besides a Mother": *Stella Dallas* and the Maternal Melodrama', in Christine Gledhill (ed.) *Home Is Where the Heart Is: Studies in Melodrama and the Woman's Film*. London: British Film Institute, 299–325.

____ (1998) 'Melodrama Revised' in Nick Browne (ed.) *Refiguring American Film Genres: Theory and History*. Berkeley: University of California Press, 42–88.

Williams, Raymond (1973) *The Country and the City*. London: Chatto & Windus.

____ (1981a) 'The English Novel From Dickens to Lawrence', in *Politics and Letters: Interviews with New Left Review*. London: Verso, 243–70.

____ (1981b) 'The Welsh Trilogy: The Volunteers', in *Politics and Letters: Interviews with New Left Review*. London: Verso, 271–302.

Williams, Robert R. (1997) *Hegel's Ethics of Recognition*. Berkeley: University of California Press.

Wollen, Peter (1985 [1972]) 'Godard and Counter Cinema: *Vent d'Est*', in Bill Nichols (ed.) *Movies and Methods, Volume II*. Berkeley: University of California Press, 500–9.

Woloch, Alex (2006) 'Breakups and Reunions: Late Realism in Early Sayles', in Diane Carson and Heidi Kenaga (eds) *Sayles Talk: New Perspectives on Independent Filmmaker John Sayles*. Detroit: Wayne State University Press, 51–78.

Wood, Robin (1991) *Hitchcock's Film Revisited*. London: Faber and Faber.

____ (2003 [1979]) 'The American Nightmare: Horror in the 70s', in *Hollywood from Vietnam to Reagan … and Beyond*. New York: Columbia University Press, 63–84.

Wyatt, Justin (1998) 'The Formation of the "Major Independents": Miramax, New Line and the New Hollywood', in Steve Neale and Murray Smith (eds) *Contemporary Hollywood Cinema*. London: Routledge, 74–90.

Zayani, Mohamed (1999) *Reading the Symptom: Frank Norris, Theodore Dreiser, and the Dynamics of Capitalism*. New York: Peter Lang.

Zerilli, Linda (2000) 'Democracy and National Fantasy: Reflections on the Statue of Liberty', in Jodi Dean (ed.) *Cultural Studies and Political Theory*. Ithaca: Cornell University Press, 167–88.

Zipes, Jack (1983) *Fairy Tales and the Art of Subversion*. London: Heinemann.

____ (1997) 'Traces of Hope: The Non-synchronicity of Ernst Bloch', in Jamie Owen Daniel and Tom Moylan (eds) *Not Yet: Reconsidering Ernst Bloch*. London: Verso, 1–12.

Žižek, Slavoj (1997) 'Multiculturalism, Or, the Cultural Logic of Multinational Capitalism', *New Left Review* 225, 28–51.

INDEX

Ackerman, Forrest J. 32
Alcázar, Damián 142
Alexander, Jace 87, 97, 105
Alexander, Jane 161
Alexander, John 75
Algren, Nelson 5
Alice, Mary 160
Allen, Phillip R. 48
Alligator 1, 30, 34–42, 117, 180
Althusser, Louis 35, 85
Altman, Robert 4, 6, 109
Anderson, John 99
Anderson, Terry H. 39
Aranha, Ray 107
Armendáriz, Pedro 167
Arnott, Mark 51
Arquette, Rosanna 66
Asinof, Eliot 26, 97–8, 105, 163
'At the Anarchists' Convention' 50

Baby It's You 23, 50, 66–74
Badiou, Alain 132
Bakhtin, Mikhail 2, 14–15, 17–18, 20, 82–5, 134, 141, 148, 154, 168, 172

Balaski, Belinda 32
Balzac, Honoré de 3, 8, 30
Baran, Edward 80
Barton, Charles 32
Bassett, Angela 106, 160
Bassett, Clyde 98
Baudrillard, Jean 153, 162–3
Baudry, Jean-Louis 8
Bazin, André 52
Bello, Maria 2
Bellow, Saul 5
Berman, Marshall 58, 93
Bichir, Bruno 167
Biskind, Peter 24
Bloch, Ernst 121, 131–2
Bloom, Harold 133
Blucas, Mark 160
Booth, Wayne 29
Bordo, Susan 170
Borrego, Jesse 134
Brandner, Gary 32, 34
Brecht, Bertolt 2–3, 8–9, 11, 16, 132, 157
Brooks, Elisabeth 32
Brother from Another Planet, The 2, 26, 50, 74–5, 77–8, 162, 172
Brown, Leslie 38

Budd, Louis 5
Buford, Bill 7
Bukatman, Scott 22
Bull, Malcolm 115
Burmester, Leo 151
Byrne, Cillian 123

Cameron, James 23–4
Canada, Ron 133
Carradine, John 31
Casa de los Babys 4, 7, 23, 49, 159, 167–74
Casseus, Gabriel 133
Castells, Manuel 144–5, 178–9
Castillo, Gonzalo 139
Cavell, Stanley 26–7
Chandler, Raymond 177–8
Chaney, Jr., Lon 31, 34
Chopin, Kate 5
Chute, David 46
Ciccolella, Jude 106
City of Hope 2–4, 7, 11, 27, 86, 105–114, 121, 142
Clair, René 12
Clapp, Gordon 51, 87, 98, 160
Clark, Jr, Gary 184
Clemmons, Clarence 71
Clennon, David 2

Cobbs, Bill 160
Cobo, Luis 134
Colgan, Eileen 14, 123
Colon, Miriam 106, 133
Comolli, Jean-Luc 8, 12
Conrad, Joseph 147
Conrad, Robert 48
Cooper, Chris 2, 87, 105, 122
Corman, Roger 1, 23, 30–1,
    36, 42
Courtney, Jeni 14, 123
Cousineau, Maggie 51
Craig, John D. 99
Crane, Stephen 4–5, 42
Creed, Barbara 39
Crosby, Bing 70
Cruz, Tania 142
Csicsery-Ronay, Jr, Istvan
    75–7, 82
Cuellar, Jr, Gilbert R. 133
Curtis, Liane 66, 79
Curtis-Hall, Vondie 121
Cusack, John 44, 98

DaCosta, Yaya 184
Daley, Mayor Richard J. 39
Daniel, Jamie Owen 131
Dante, Joe 23, 31–2, 34
Daring, Mason 146
Davidson, Jack 67
Davis, Angela 82
Davis, Mike 96
Davis, Rebecca Harding 5
de Anda, Ignacio 167
Debord, Guy 162, 164
Delgado, Damián 142
DeLillo, Don 5, 106–7,
    109–10
De Niro, Robert 16
Denison, Anthony John 106
den Tandt, Christophe 10
de Saussure, Ferdinand 14, 144
Desmond, Jim 100
De Vries, John 60
Dillman, Bradford 36
Dos Passos, John 5–6, 46,
    108–10, 142
Douglas, Cullen 163
Dreiser, Theodore 4, 5, 10,
    121
Dreyfuss, Richard 2
Du Bois, W.E.B. 118
Duffy, Dave 128
Dugan, Dennis 31–2

Dyer, Richard 44

Edson, Richard 97, 165
Edwards, Daryl 106
Eight Men Out 4, 8, 11, 26, 42,
    44, 86, 90, 93, 97–105, 108,
    112–13, 121
Engels, Friedrich 12, 47, 93,
    96, 113–14

Failler, Angela 156
Faison, Frankie 105
Falco, Edie 160
Farrell, James T. 5
Faulkner, William 5
Fauset, Jessie 5
Felleman, Susan 133
Ferrari, Nick 68
Ferrer, Miguel 165, 175
Fields, Chip 48
Fisher, Terence 132
Fiske, John 41
Fleissner, Jennifer L. 49
Fletcher, Louise 48
Ford, John 26
Forster, Robert 38, 48
Foster, Gloria 107
Francis, Freddie 32
Frazier, Randy 80
Freedman, Carl 11, 43–4, 121,
    178–9
Freeman, Mary E. Wilkins 5
Freud, Sigmund 28, 33, 131,
    133

Gabler, Mel 136
Gabler, Norma 136
Gaines, Jane 61–2
Gammon, James 177
Garnett, Rhys 76
Garrett, Brad 97
Gershon, Gina 106
Getino, Octavio 8–9, 149
Gibson, William 5
Gilman, Charlotte Perkins 5
Gist, Rod 48
Gledhill, Christine 88
Glover, Danny 184
Godard, Jean-Luc 9, 11, 132
González, Dan Rivera 142
Gordon, Carl 80
Graff, Tod 105
Gramsci, Antonio 35, 40–1
Greyeyes, Michael 166

Grifasi, Joe 87, 106
Griffiths, Linda 60
Grimké, Angelina Weld 5
Grody, Kathryn 146, 150
Gunning, Tom 29
Gunton, Bob 87
Gusanos, Los 7, 15
Gyllenhall, Maggie 167

Halleran, Jane 60
Hamilton, Lisa Gay 184
Hamilton, Richard 75
Hannah, Daryl 167, 175
Harden, Marcia Gay 167, 169
Harvey, Don 98
Hedren, Tippi 36
Hegel, G.W.F. 2, 14, 86,
    114–15, 117, 157
Heidegger, Martin 176
Heineman, Laurie 47
Hemingway, Ernest 5
Henderson, Jo 60, 87
Hernandez, Mary Jane R. 135
Higareda, Martha 167
Hillier, Jim 21, 36
Hobbs, Peter 48
Hogan, Robert 45
Holmes, Oliver Wendell 5
Honeydripper 1, 4, 7, 183–4,
    187–8
Howells, William Dean 5,
    10, 121
Howling, The 1, 30–5
Huston, Danny 2
Hutton, Timothy 160

Ingersoll, James 39
Irwin, Bill 98
Iván, Guillermo 171

James, Clifton 44, 97, 133, 163
James, Henry 89
Jameson, Fredric 7, 22, 43,
    145, 178
Jenkins, Ken 89
Johnson, James Weldon 5
Johnson, Robin 72
Jones, James 5
Jones, James Earl 87
Jones, Tommy Lee 75
Jovet, Serafin 106

Kaes, Anton 131
Kaplan, Amy 10

Keach, Stacy 188
Kellner, Douglas 175, 177
Kennedy, William 5
Kenton, Erle 32
King, Alan 163
King, Geoff 23
Klevan, Andrew 24
Korine, Harmony 4
Kristofferson, Kris 133, 150, 175–6
Kyles, Dwania 80

Lady in Red, The 1, 30, 42–9, 93, 97
Lagarrigue, Jean 82
Laine, Frankie 71
Lally, Mick 14, 123
Landers, Lew 32
Lane, Fredric 75
Lang, Fritz 12
Lang, Perry 165
Lang, S.J. 106
Larsen, Nella 5
Laskin, Michael 99, 153
Latour, Bruno 141, 143, 154
Lebowitz, Michael A. 12
Lee, Spike 22
Lefevre, Adam 51
Lenin, Vladimir Ilyich 103
Leone, Marianne 106
Lerner, Michael 44, 98
Lester, Eleese 135
Levitas, Ruth 44
Lewis, Alex 160
Lewis, Jerry 73
Lianna 2, 13, 50, 60–6, 72, 118
Lilly, J.K. Kent 88
Limbo 7, 23–4, 26, 44, 49, 122, 150–8, 162, 176–7
Linklater, Richard 4
Little Anthony and the Imperials 79
Lloyd, Christopher 48, 97
Loach, Ken 11
Lo Bianco, Tony 105
London, Jack 4–5
Lone Star 2, 4, 7, 26–7, 49, 122, 133–42, 147, 162
López, Iguandili 147
Lukács, Georg 2–3, 6–9, 30, 45–6, 103–4, 139
Lucas, George 21–2, 16
Luppi, Federico 142

Luxemburg, Rosa 103
Lynch, John 126
Lynch, Susan 129, 159

McCabe, Colin 8–9, 12
McCarthy, Kevin 31, 36
McCleery, Gary 72
McClintock, Anne 82
McConaughey, Matthew 133
McDaniel, James 160
McDonald, Bruce 11, 51
McDonnell, Mary 87, 114
McDormand, Frances 49, 140
McElherron, Fergal 14, 126
McHale, Brian 124, 156
McInturff, Dawn 154
McLeod, Don 32
McMurray, Sam 70
McNally, David 144
Macaluso, Dee 134
MacDonald, Jessica Wight 60
Macnee, Patrick 31–2
Mahoney, John 98
Mailer, Norman 5
Mantell, Michael 88, 98, 106
Marcin, Tony 168
Marcuse, Herbert 33, 35
Marsh, Richard 76
Martin, Dean 73
Martin, Pamela Sue 42, 46
Martinez, Corina 136
Martinez, Donevon 175
Martinez, Vanessa 49, 150
Martínez, Vanessa 159
Marx, Karl 2, 4, 7, 12–14, 25, 33, 35, 86, 91, 93, 95–6, 104, 112, 144, 162
Mastrantonio, Mary Elizabeth 150
Matewan 4, 8, 11, 24, 26–9, 42, 86–97, 102–4, 108, 113–14, 121, 166, 180
Mendillo, Stephen 66, 99, 105
Men with Guns/Hombres armados 7, 26, 122, 142–51, 154, 156, 164, 166
Menzies, Heather 36
Merck, Mandy 62–3, 65
Merlin, Joanna 68
Merritt, Greg 22–3
Messina, Dolores 68
Mette, Nancy 57, 87, 116
Michaels, Walter Benn 10
Miéville, China 130, 162

Miller, Dick 31, 47
Molina, Jacinto 32
Molyneaux, Gerry 46
Monahan, Jeff 133
Morton, Joe 74, 105, 133
Mostel, Josh 89, 106
Muellerleile, Marianne 116
Mulvey, Laura 8, 61, 65
Murphy, Philip 105

Narboni, Jean 8, 12
Neff, Gina 136
Neill, Roy William 32
Nelson, Alice Dunbar 5
Newfield, Sam 32
Nicholson, Jack 16
Norris, Frank 5–6, 10

Oates, Joyce Carol 5
Oldham, Will 28, 87
Ouspenskaya, Maria 34

Parsons, Nancy Anne 48
Passanante, Jean 51
Passion Fish 2, 7, 26, 44, 86, 112–21
Patinkin, Mandy 146
Patton, Cindy 60, 62
Peláez, Angelina 169
Peña, Elizabeth 122
Perella, Marco 134
Perkins, V.F. 25, 27
Petry, Ann 5
Pfeil, Fred 71
Phillips, Don 135
Picardo, Robert 32
Pickens, Slim 31
Piranha 1, 30–1, 34–42, 180
Pizer, Donald 5
Place, Mary Kay 2
Plana, Tony 140
Platt, Margie 39
Pope, Dick 187
Pride of the Bimbos 50
Proust, Marcel 22
Pulitzer, Joseph 81

Ramírez, Nandi Luna 147
Ramos, Hermínio 154
Raymond, Bill 106
Raymond, William Joseph 73
Read, James 97
Reagan, Ronald 8, 11, 71, 87, 136

Renzi, Maggie 51, 84, 87, 99, 106, 116, 149
Renzi, Marta 63
Return of the Secaucus Seven 2, 11, 23, 26, 50–60, 147, 159, 167, 180
Reyes, Richard 140
Richman, Roger 36
Ricks, Christopher 94
Riker, Robin 38
Robinson, Amy 67
Robinson, Eddie 133
Rodgers, Jimmie 71
Rooker, Michael 97
Rooney, Gerald 129
Ross, Diana 80
Roth, Tim 175
Russo, Vito 60
Ruth, George 'Babe' 26–7
Ryan, Jack 28, 52
Ryan, Michael 175, 177

Saguar, Luis 175
Sam the Sham and the Pharaohs 69
Sardar, Ziauddin 76
Saroyan, William 73
Sarris, Andrew 25
Schewel, Amy 51
Scott, Sir Walter 30
Secret of Roan Inish, The 14, 23–4, 44, 122–33, 142–3, 147, 166–7, 180
Sembène, Ousmane 11
Shapiro, Alan N. 83–5, 145, 148–9
Sheen, Charlie 98
Sheridan, Richard 123
Sheriff, Jr, Sidney 78
Siemaskzo, Casey 150
Silva, Henry 40
Silver City 2, 4, 7, 16, 20–1, 23–4, 27, 58, 159–60, 175–80
Simon and Garfunkel 71
Sinatra, Frank 67, 70–1, 73–4

Sinclair, Upton 5
Sirk, Douglas 89
Smith, James 92
Smith, Will 77
Smollett, JoJo 106
Soderbergh, Steven 22
Solanas, Fernando 8–9, 149
Sonnenfeld, Barry 74
Spano, Vincent 66, 105
Spector, Phil 70
Spielberg, Steven 21–2
Springsteen, Bruce 70–1, 106
Squire, Jane 36
Stacey, Jackie 61
Steele, Barbara 31, 36
Steenburgen, Mary 160, 167, 188
Steinbeck, John 5
Stevens, Fisher 78
Stoker, Bram 76
Stone, Christopher 32
Stone, Danton 99
Stone, Robert 5
Straayer, Chris 61–2, 66
Strathairn, David 26, 44, 51, 87, 97, 106, 121, 150
Strathairn, Tay 97
Styron, William 5
Sunshine State 7, 38, 159–67, 177, 179–80
Supremes, The 70
Sweeney, D.B. 44, 98

Taggart, Rita 150
Taylor, Lili 47
Taylor, Terri 167
Teague, Lewis 34, 42
Terkel, Studs 44, 97
Tichi, Cecelia 108
Tierney, Lawrence 107
Tighe, Kevin 28, 87, 98, 106
Tirelli, Jaime 84, 106
Tobey, Kenneth 31
Todorov, Tzvetan 129
Townsend, Jr, Edward Jay 106
Trott, Karen 51

Tubman, Harriet 79
Turner, Bryan S. 156

Union Dues 7, 15, 27, 51

Velvet Underground, The 71
Vives, Juan Carlos 167

Waggner, George 32
Waite, Ralph 161, 175, 179
Walker, Michael 89, 91–2
Wallace, Dee 32
Warren, Jerry 32
Wayne, Mike 6, 166
Wegner, Philip E. 132
Wells, H.G. 76
Welles, Orson 39, 110
Wexler, Haskell 24, 42
Wharton, Edith 5, 10
Williams, Barbara 106
Williams, Dee 31
Williams, Linda 89–90
Williams, Raymond 7, 143, 145, 153
Williams, Robert R. 115
Wilson, Chandra 140
Withrow, Glenn 48
Wollen, Peter 8, 25, 29
Wood, Robin 26–7, 32–5, 42
Woodard, Alfre 114
Worth, Thomas 82
Wright, Richard 5
Wright, Tom 106, 160
Wyatt, Justin 22

Young, Buck 49

Zane, Billy 2, 9, 15–16, 21
Zayani, Mohamed 10, 49
Zerilli, Linda 81–2
Zipes, Jack 131
Žižek, Slavoj 13, 138
Zola, Émile 5, 30, 45–6, 169
Zorich, Louis 106